FOUNDATION GNVQ CORE SKILLS

Communication

Desmond W Evans

LONGMAN

Addison Wesley Longman Limited
Edinburgh Gate, Harlow
Essex CM20 2JE, England
and Associated Companies throughout the world

First published 1996

British Library Cataloguing in Publication Data
A catalogue entry for this title is available from the British Library.

ISBN 0–582–29297–2

Set by 30 in 10/12pt Palatino
Printed in Great Britain by Henry Ling Ltd.,
at the Dorset Press, Dorchester, Dorset

FOUNDATION GNVQ CORE SKILLS

Communication

ALSO AVAILABLE IN THE SERIES

Advanced GNVQ: Core Skills:
COMMUNICATION
Desmond W. Evans
ISBN 0 582 28872X

Intermediate GNVQ: Core Skills:
COMMUNICATION
Desmond W. Evans
ISBN 0 582 29303 0

Both texts:

- comprehensively meet the needs of all students following the new GNVQ Core Skills 1995 specification
- follow the sequence of elements and performance criteria for easy reference and student self-directed study
- give detailed explanations of current principles and practices, and provide students with detailed guidance on how to develop communication expertise and practical skills
- contain a wide range of skills-building activities, discussion topics and self-review questions (with answers)
- include portfolio-building activities at the end of each chapter

OTHER TEXTS FROM ADDISON WESLEY LONGMAN

Foundation GNVQ Information Technology
Jenny Lawson
ISBN 0 582 29775 3

This brand new textbook covers the three mandatory units of the Foundation level GNVQ in Information Technology. It includes all the underpinning knowledge required by students at this level, and this is supplemented by numerous activities and exercises to reinforce understanding.

Foundation GNVQ Leisure & Tourism
Carole Jones & Margaret Radcliffe
ISBN 0 582 29339 1

This lively and easy-to-read text has been written specifically to provide a one-stop source covering all three mandatory units at this level. It follows the GNVQ structure and each element is broken down into the individual range categories, making the text easy to follow. Practical activities are included throughout, providing ample opportunity for students to test their knowledge and comprehension.

For further information about these and other titles, or to order a copy, please contact:

Addison Wesley Longman Customer Information Centre
PO BOX 88
Harlow
Essex
CM19 5SR

Telephone: 01279 623928
Fax: 01279 414130

Contents

Preface

To the student

As you read this, you are almost certainly about to begin your Foundation GNVQ studies in your selected sector of industry, commerce or public service. And by opting to follow a GNVQ path as part of your programme of studies, you have chosen to acquire some highly practical knowledge and skills which will be of direct use to you – whether you decide to move on to further GNVQ studies, or to proceed directly into the world of work.

Let me first assure you that you have, indeed, made a very good choice in deciding to pursue a GNVQ course of study. I have been closely involved in the creation and development of GNVQ study routes since they were first devised – as an educational manager, teacher, author and designer of GNVQ programmes. I am able to assure you, from my first-hand experience, that your GNVQ course will enable you to acquire both knowledge and skills directly relevant to the employment sector for which they are designed.

For example, you will find that your GNVQ studies intermix key knowledge and facts, with practical skills and know-how of, say, using a computer as a working tool, selling to customers, caring for an elderly person or booking a foreign holiday. Not only will you learn the essentials which underpin your course, but you will also get out and about, to interview people in many kinds of posts in various types of organisation.

As your studies proceed you will build up a portfolio of work (called activities) which demonstrates that you have mastered the various parts of your course which make up the whole. You will be able to show your portfolio to employers or to teachers, so as to prove to them the extent of your mastery of your GNVQ studies. And you will also take a series of external tests to back up your portfolio of evidence.

Unlike many other kinds of study, a GNVQ course enables you to select some of its parts yourself (as options or additional studies), and to take charge of and be responsible for your own studies (not forgetting the support your teachers will provide). It also includes a set of core or key skills – communication, information technology, application of number (as well as working with others and improving your own learning and performance skills). Moreover, you can progress to Intermediate and Advanced GNVQ levels of study in a structured and well-linked way.

For these reasons, a GNVQ course of study is challenging, exciting and refreshingly different! There is, however, an important but. But it depends to a very great deal on you. On the extent of your commitment to your studies to your studies and your willingness to work hard. On you being prepared to enter into the spirit of role-play or simulations and to take an active part in group work. Much also depends on your ability to work hard on your own, without your teacher's constant supervision. Yet all these buts form a precious part of your personal development, which will enable you to succeed in your chosen career path.

The proverb states: *You're only young once!* And indeed, it's true. So get on with it, enjoy your GNVQ studies – *for they will be enjoyable* – and make the most of your study opportunities, for today's working world is demanding – but not too demanding for a good GNVQ student!

Good luck and best wishes for your success!

Desmond W Evans
July 1996

Introduction

By the time you start to read this introduction, you will have decided to start out on a GNVQ Foundation course of study. All GNVQ courses have been designed to help you prepare for a working career in a particular field, such as business, leisure and tourism, health and social care, manufacturing and so on.

Each GNVQ study programme forms a step, like three rungs in a step-ladder:

And no matter what your subject of study, each step in the ladder has been carefully designed to lead on to the next in terms of increasing the breadth and depth of the knowledge and skills you acquire. In this way, you could progress in some three or four years from acquiring a basic and essential set of skills enabling you to start out on a first job (Foundation level) to a level from which you could progress either to a professional post (say as a trainee manager) or to a university degree course (Advanced level). So, it is well worth the effort of working hard – right from the start of your Foundation course – to acquire the key knowledge and skills which will prove so important when you decide upon the kind of work you wish to do during your career.

How Is My Course Structured?

At Foundation level, each course of study is made up of:

- three units which must be studied (called **mandatory** or compulsory **units**)

plus:

- any three **option units** (which you can choose from a set on offer where you study)

plus:

- three skills which lie at the heart of all jobs today (therefore called **core skills**):

Communication **Application of number** **Information technology**

How do I show that I have acquired new knowledge and skills?

Some courses of study expect students to take examinations, say two or three hours long after one or two years of study. So the students have to memorise a great deal of information only to be tested on a small part of it. GNVQ courses work differently. At regular intervals during your studies, your teachers will prepare you to carry out activities which have been carefully designed to check your grasp of a particular section of your studies (which forms part of your mandatory or option units and your core skills subjects). Very often these activities will involve you in finding out about real organisations which work within your chosen GNVQ study area.

Each activity you undertake is assessed so as to make sure that you have fully understood the topics it tests, that you can talk and write about it fluently, and produce clear and accurate graphic illustrations.

To help you understand exactly the areas in which you will be assessed, each mandatory, option and core skills unit is broken down as follows:

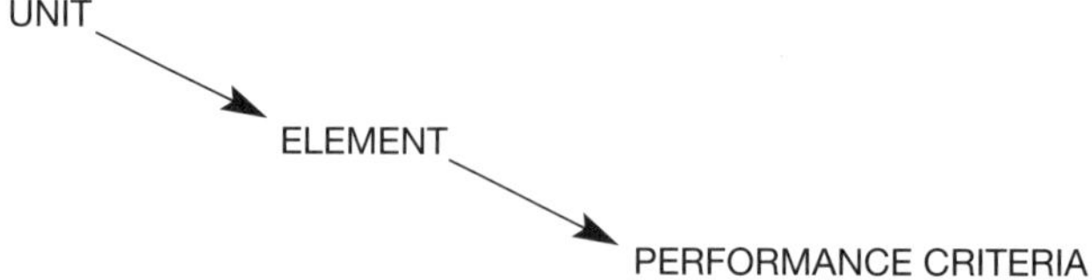

A unit is one of the large building blocks which make up your study programme. Each unit is divided into several elements (like chapters in a book), and each element is divided again into performance criteria (like paragraphs in a chapter). The term *performance criteria* simply means: clear and simple explanations of the specific piece of knowledge or particular skill you have to acquire.

Thus an individual activity which you have to carry out will enable your teachers to assess your knowledge and skills for just some of the performance criteria (PCs) which make up the whole of your course.

Example of an Element in the Foundation Business Award

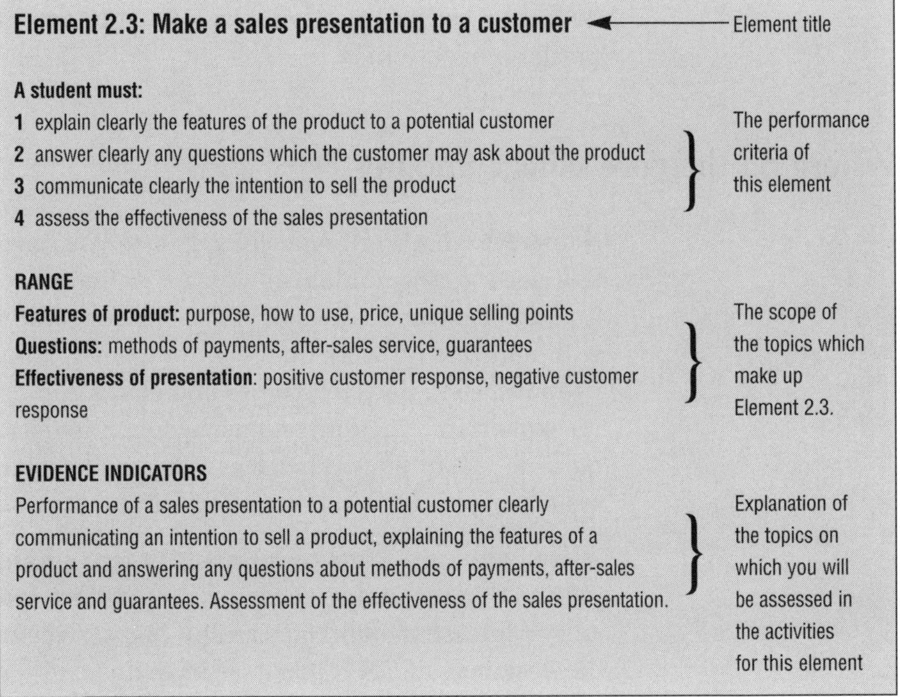

Element 2.3: Make a sales presentation to a customer ← Element title

A student must:

1 explain clearly the features of the product to a potential customer
2 answer clearly any questions which the customer may ask about the product
3 communicate clearly the intention to sell the product
4 assess the effectiveness of the sales presentation

} The performance criteria of this element

RANGE

Features of product: purpose, how to use, price, unique selling points
Questions: methods of payments, after-sales service, guarantees
Effectiveness of presentation: positive customer response, negative customer response

} The scope of the topics which make up Element 2.3.

EVIDENCE INDICATORS

Performance of a sales presentation to a potential customer clearly communicating an intention to sell a product, explaining the features of a product and answering any questions about methods of payments, after-sales service and guarantees. Assessment of the effectiveness of the sales presentation.

} Explanation of the topics on which you will be assessed in the activities for this element

In undertaking each activity, you will also be involved in producing a kind of report which enables your teachers to follow the steps you took to:

- plan your activity
- find out and handle information
- make sure that your plan is working and that you are keeping to self-imposed deadlines
- look back on how you undertook the activity in order to consider whether/how you might have done better or differently.

Each completed activity is assessed by your teacher and, if you have worked particularly well, your teacher may decide that the activity is worth a merit or distinction grade. Such grades are held over until the end of your course (this is why they are called interim grades), until you have completed the whole course. They are all then carefully considered (using a formula which your teacher will explain) so as to see whether you have earned a merit or distinction overall.

In this way, at regular and manageable intervals, you build up a set of activities which clearly show the knowledge and skills you have acquired – just like an artist who paints pictures which become a collection called a portfolio. Indeed, your activities are also called a portfolio of activities.

Where do the core skills come in?

No matter what work-related study area you have chosen to follow, you will need to be confident and expert in the skills of: speaking and writing (to customers, colleagues or your managers); estimating and calculating with numbers (to work out quantities, areas, volumes, percentages, fractions, etc.); devising graphs and charts and using graphic illustrations (to explain information) and using computer-based and telecommunication equipment (such as PCs, photocopiers, scanners, telephone systems, fax equipment, manufacturing software, etc.).

Indeed, the core skills of communication, application of number and information technology have become so important in all employees' jobs in industry, commerce and public service organisations today that the designers of GNVQ courses have decided – quite rightly – that all students pursuing GNVQs at each of the three levels should become expert in them.

So, a parallel set of units has been designed (in the same way as the mandatory and option units) to enable you to build upon your existing skills. And they are assessed within your course activities for the most part. As you develop your grasp of mandatory and option unit topics, so you improve your core skills expertise.

A word from the author

Once you get into the swing of your GNVQ studies, you will soon find the design of the course easy to follow and that the steps you take to submit your activities for assessment become routine.

At the outset of your studies, it is really important to get your motivation right. Your success in them very much depends on you, and the pains you take! The quality of the work you submit for assessment relies to a large degree on how much effort you put into researching information and setting it down clearly. And it is precisely because you take on a great deal of responsibility yourself for the work you produce that you will find your GNVQ much more challenging and rewarding than some other types of study.

Moreover, today the United Kingdom really does need its citizens and workforce to be highly educated and expert in their chosen work fields. We are faced with economic competition from abroad which has never been harder to beat. Nevertheless, I have a great deal of faith in the ability of your GNVQ studies – with the help of your teachers and your own hard work – to provide you with an excellent springboard to launch you into your world of work or further study, so that you can help UK Limited take on and see off the competition – from no matter where!

I wish you both good luck and all success in your GNVQ studies.

Desmond W Evans

NCVQ programme specification for core skill communication at foundation level

Communication (level 1)

Element 1.1: Take part in discussions with known individuals on routine matters

PERFORMANCE CRITERIA

1 own contributions are clear and appropriate to the subject matter

2 own contributions are made in a tone and manner suited to the audience

3 contributions from others are listened to attentively

4 own understanding of points made by others is actively checked and confirmed

RANGE

Subject matters: routine matters (e.g. responding to day-to-day enquires; discussing routine tasks)
Mode: face to face
Audience: people familiar with the subject matter and in frequent contact with the individual (e.g. supervisors, colleagues, peers, tutors)

Element 1.2: Prepare written materials in pre-set formats

PERFORMANCE CRITERIA

1 documents are complete and accurate

2 documents are legible

3 grammar and punctuation follow standard conventions, and words used routinely are spelled correctly

RANGE

Subject matters: routine matters (e.g. day-to-day work processes; breakdown of equipment; minor incidents)
Formats: pre-set format (e.g. record and report cards, memos)
Conventions: use of full stop, comma, capital letters, sentences
Audience: people familiar with the subject matter and in frequent contact with the individual (e.g. supervisors, colleagues, peers, tutors)

Element 1.3: Use images to illustrate points made in writing and in discussions with known individuals on routine matters

PERFORMANCE CRITERIA

1 images selected are relevant to the point(s) made
2 images are used at appropriate times/places

RANGE

Subject matters: routine matters (e.g. day-to-day work processes; breakdown of equipment; minor incidents)
Images: selected from those readily available in the context (e.g. sketches, diagrams, still photographs, charts)
Audience: people familiar with the subject matter and in frequent contact with the individual (e.g. supervisors, colleagues, peers, tutors)

Element 1.4: Read and respond to written material and images in pre-set formats

PERFORMANCE CRITERIA

1 main points are accurately identified
2 the meaning of unfamiliar words, phrases and images is accurately identified using the sources provided

RANGE

Subject matters: routine matters (e.g. day-to-day work processes; breakdown of equipment; minor incidents)
Formats: pre-set format (e.g. record and report cards, memos)
Images: used commonly in the context (e.g. sketches, diagrams, still photographs, charts)
Sources of clarification: provided for the individual; written (e.g. dictionaries, manuals), oral (e.g. supervisors, tutors, colleagues)

1 Take part in discussions

I hear what you say!

Anon

What Chapter 1 Covers

As its title makes clear, Chapter 1 is all about using the spoken word in discussions and other situations at work to enable people to carry out tasks and jobs they have been asked to do. By using the spoken word effectively, they help to achieve the goals which their work organisation has set itself.

A main aim of Chapter 1 is to help you to improve the oral skills you will need to carry out a job successfully in a workplace organisation. Thus a structure has been created for the chapter which takes you through a series of study and practice sections. These will both enable you to develop a knowledge of why people use the spoken word in certain ways at work, and help you to improve your own oral communication skills.

The main sections of Chapter 1

- How people relate and talk to each other at work
- The uses of the spoken word at work
- Developing spoken word skills
- Discussions and body language
- How to take notes in discussions
- How discussions and meetings are run
- The art of active listening
- The do's and don'ts of taking part in discussions
- Message taking and giving

In addition, Chapter 1 includes:

- Sets of discussion topics
- Key tips on good practice
- Opportunities to practise newly acquired skills
- Sets of case studies for discussion and analysis
- Activities for assessment and portfolio building

How people relate and talk to each other at work

The aims of organisations

To understand how people relate to one another and talk to each other at work, it is important, first, to think about why people work at all, and what the aims of the organisations are in which they work.

Basically, there are two kinds of work organisation. Firstly, there are those which have been set up to make a profit – by selling goods or services, like food in supermarkets, cars and motor-bikes, insurance or entertainment. Secondly, there are those which have been created to provide services to the public, like local councils, health authorities and charities.

The first type of organisation is often referred to as:

the private sector   business   commerce   industry

The second type of organisation is usually called:

the public sector   local government   government agencies

or in the case of charities:

the voluntary sector

Key organisational aims: profit-making and efficient public services

Remember, then, that the basic aim of the private sector is to make a profit, and that of the public sector is to provide services which are efficient and good value for money.

This being the case, all the employees working in a private sector organisation will need to pull together in order to achieve the profit-making aim. In a business which makes products, this will mean:

- buyers seeking to purchase good quality raw materials and parts as cheaply as possible
- factory managers and workers turning them into top quality products with a minimum of waste of time and materials
- the sales force selling them on to wholesalers or retailers at a satisfactory profit
- the marketing staff researching into changes in the market place and feeding information back to designers and researchers for new product ideas and improvements to existing products.

In a public sector local council, the aim to supply effective local services involves:

- councillors and council officers deciding what levels of local taxes to raise to help pay for services supplied
- managers in various departments – highways, housing, education, etc. – ensuring that budgets are not overspent
- departmental staff working to make sure that the laws which govern local government are upheld, say by inspecting health and safety in cafés and restaurants or investigating outbreaks of certain dangerous illnesses, or by caring for the local needy
- obtaining feedback from local inhabitants, so as to improve services continually.

Why people work

If organisations themselves have aims and goals, so indeed do their individual employees. Almost everyone today needs to work. Our civilisation has evolved a system in which the essential goods and services which we need to survive – housing, food, clothing, travel services, etc. – are paid for out of earnings from doing work, either as a single, self-employed worker, or as an employee within an organisation. Our social system also provides people with opportunities to earn more money than they need to buy essentials, so that some people are able also to afford foreign holidays, expensive cars, etc. Such extra earnings usually stem from individuals gaining promotion to a better paid job, or receiving more pay as a result of gaining specialist experience over the years.

The drive to get on at work

Thus most people at work respond to the chance of earning more money by gaining promotion or by receiving extra bonuses for doing their jobs well. This natural desire to get on affects directly how people relate to and talk to each other at work. For example, a junior employee's chances of promotion are likely to be greatly affected by how his or her line manager rates:

- the quality of work done
- the ability to get on with and work well with others (including the manager him/herself)
- the potential to develop in the future.

Since such a junior employee's prospects at work can depend so much on his or her immediate line manager or supervisor, the employee is likely to take pains to develop a good working relationship with the manager by being polite, courteous and cheerfully carrying out work instructions. Further, most employees work in groups or teams, often called sections or units, which make up departments. In order to carry out the dozens of tasks which make up an employee's daily routine, employees are constantly involved in helping each other out – by supplying information, lending a hand, passing on a message, etc. And so all employees need to be on good terms with their fellow workers, so as to get the job done and to make the working day a pleasant experience. Groups of co-workers very quickly let an individual know if he or she is 'out of order', say by lowering the level of co-operation for a while.

The customer is king (or queen)!

Another most important aspect which affects the ways in which people talk at work is, of course, the customer. Ensuring that an organisation's customers are kept happy and enjoy the process of buying a product or service lies at the heart of all private sector businesses. In an open market society like that in the UK, an unhappy customer can always take his or her business somewhere else. So all employees quickly realise how important it is to create the right approach when talking to a customer.

Structures and communications

Another important influence on the ways in which people relate and talk to each other at work is the shape or structure which an organisation builds as it grows. Almost all private and public sector organisations work on this basis:

- all employees occupy positions on a scale, from most junior to most senior
- it is the most senior who drive the organisation along, since they are given most authority, and are able to pass instructions down the various levels of the organisation for jobs to be done by less senior staff
- less senior staff are obliged (according to employment law) to carry out 'all reasonable requests' from the managers they report to; but they do not have to carry out illegal or possibly dangerous requests, or tasks which lie outside their given job roles

Small and large organisational structures

The following diagrams illustrate two typical structures, one of a small retail business possessing three branches (Figures 1.1 and 1.2) and the other of a national manufacturing company (Figure 1.3).

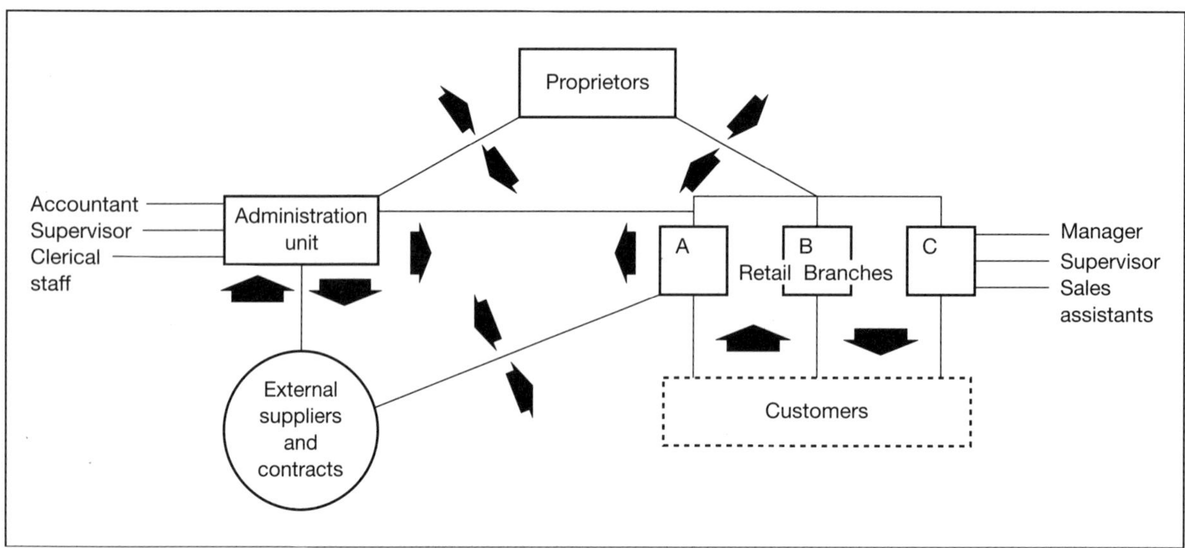

Figure 1.1 **Structure of a small retail business**

The structure of an organisation such as the small retailing business in Figure 1.1 might be: a husband and wife as proprietors, an administrative unit of an accountant/book-keeper, supervisor and two or three clerks, and three retail branches, each made up of a branch manager, supervisor and three sales assistants, totalling some twenty-two staff. In such an organisation, each employee is likely to have met all the others and to know a lot about the other staff with whom he or she works closely, in either a retail branch or the administrative unit. All staff are likely to see quite a lot of the proprietors as they monitor their business.

However, what is not entirely clear from the diagram is the fact that even a small business has within its structure what is known as a hierarchy. A hierarchy in an organisational sense is a term used to describe the relationships which employees have with others, depending on the level of authority at which they work. For example, if the retail business were examined in the shape of a stepped, Aztec pyramid, it would look like Figure 1.2:

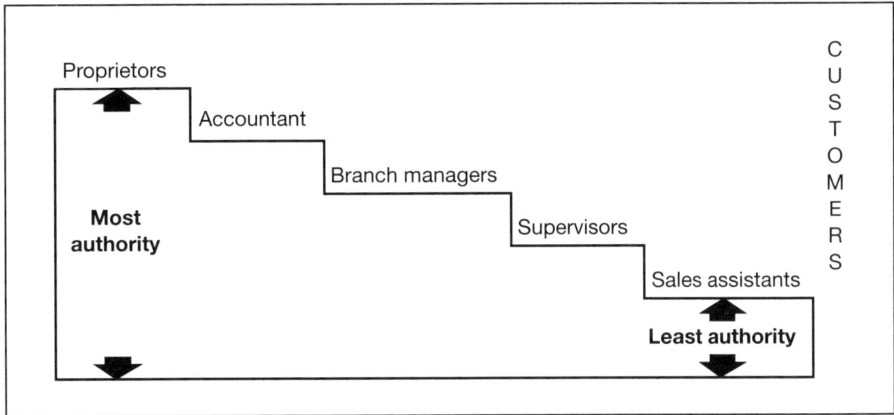

Figure 1.2 **The small retail business as a hierarchy**

As Figure 1.2 clearly indicates, the business's owners (since they have invested their money and taken the risk) enjoy most authority. However, as Figure 1.1 shows, they have in fact passed some of their authority to the firm's middle managers, the accountant and the three branch managers. This practice is called delegating and enables managers to carry out activities up to a certain level of authority without having constantly to refer to the boss for permission.

In turn, as the stepped hierarchy (Figure 1.2) illustrates, the four managers each have a supervisor, who is given a limited authority for such matters as, say, checking the work of the sales assistants. While undertaking important work selling directly to customers, the sales assistants are obliged to carry out the reasonable instructions of those staff to whom they report. In virtually all organisations which are shaped as hierarchies, managers are only given authority over staff within their own department or unit who report directly to them. And so, the branch manager of Branch A could not insist on a sales assistant or supervisor in Branch C carrying out an instruction. Branch A's manager would have to go through the manager of Branch C, and ask, rather than tell. By the same token, any one of the branch managers would be likely to take a dim view of the accountant interfering in a sales matter. He or she might justifiably complain to the proprietors that the accountant was exceeding his or her job role. Then the proprietors might have to intervene to calm ruffled feathers.

In hierarchies, then, employees must respond to reasonable instructions delivered down a line, say from branch manager, through supervisor to sales assistant. Such a process is called **line management** and is the most frequently used line of communication for both oral and written messages, which may flow **up or down the line**.

Where, you may well ask, do the business's customers fit into this communications structure? Normally, they will only relate to whoever is serving them – say an assistant or supervisor. However, if a complaint arises, a customer may wish to take it to the top, to a proprietor:

> Put me through to the owner, please !

Once the hierarchic structure of a business has grown beyond the sole proprietor phase, its owner has to rely heavily on the quality of those employees directly in *contact* with the customers. Similarly, as messages often have to pass between two or three levels of staff (from proprietor to sales assistant), there is more chance of them becoming garbled and misunderstood.

As Figure 1.3 illustrates, large organisations have more tiers or levels of authority. This means that the thousands of messages which travel up and down the organisation each day have to pass through more people, and thus are more likely to become lost or distorted in the process. Also, the places in which the employees work may be scattered across the UK, and staff may have to deal frequently with colleagues they never or seldom meet. For such reasons, employees who work in large organisations face more complex challenges and demands when it comes to communicating because:

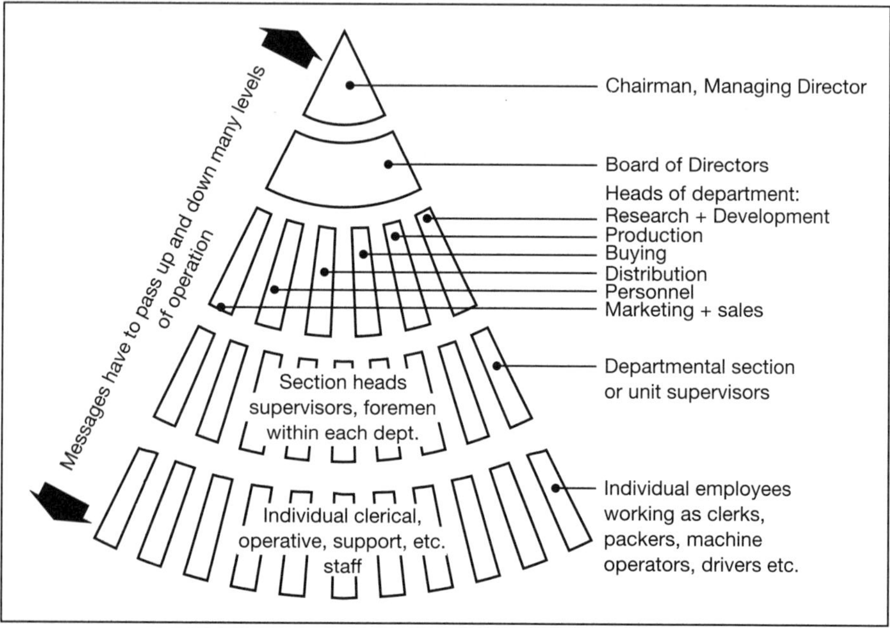

Figure 1.3 **Structure of a large manufacturing company**

- the organisation's employees occupy more layers or tiers in the hierarchy – instead of three or four, perhaps six or seven, which may lead to poor information sharing and exchanging
- large organisations tend to have detailed rules and regulations to manage their affairs, and do less business 'by word of mouth'; thus employees have to follow set procedures, cope with high levels of paperwork and have less opportunity to use their initiative
- key information is sometimes difficult to obtain; it may be stuck in a bottleneck and out of date by the time it becomes available
- information takes much longer to flow around the organisation, and may become stuck on the desk of an insecure employee who hoards it for the power it supplies
- employees may come to relate only to those few people with whom they work closely, and to regard other departments' personnel as rivals or odd-balls.

Employees and networks at work

In studying this section of Chapter 1, you will have noticed that the employees who work in large business organisations are obliged to develop and maintain good working relationships with all kinds of people inside and outside the organisation:

TYPICAL NETWORK OF RELATIONSHIPS OF A JUNIOR EMPLOYEE

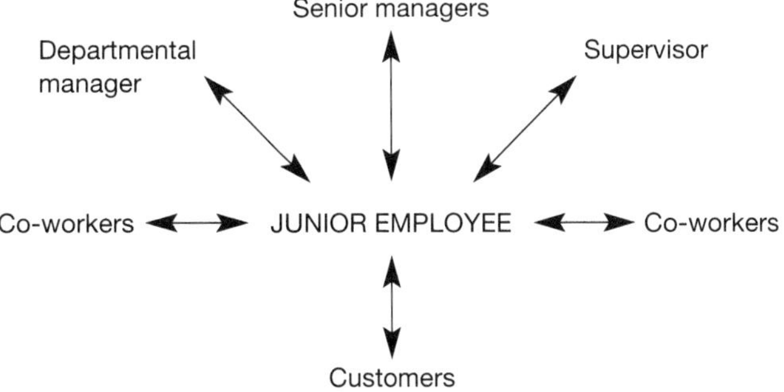

Maintaining such a network of relationships in the workplace is not easy. In terms of spoken word skills, the junior employee may have to listen to and show acceptance of a matter his or her line manager discusses, while knowing inwardly that the manager is too remote from the routine item being discussed and has got some key facts wrong.

In terms of relating to an immediate supervisor, the employee has the demanding job of having to work closely with him or her, and of carrying out instructions cheerfully, whatever the chemistry between them. Many junior staff are also in frequent contact with customers, and thus have to take especial care about how they serve them and generally meet their needs. And if this were not enough, the junior employee has to cope with being on the receiving end of work requests and instructions which he or she cannot delegate any further down the line!

WHAT DO YOU THINK?

1 Do you think that there are any differences in the ways in which people in a private sector business and people in a public sector organisation communicate?

2 What sort of oral communication problems do you see developing as an organisation grows from a one-person business into a national company?

3 'Without modern telecommunication systems (telephones, faxes, electronic mail, messaging bleepers, etc.), large organisations could not exist today.' True, or false?

4 'The trouble with society today is, simply, too many people! The average customer can never reach the person with the answer to his or her problem or needs. The average employee deals with so many people each day that he or she tends to switch off, adopting a take it or leave it attitude. So nobody wins.' Is this true in your experience? How can the skilful use of the spoken word help both customers and employees get more enjoyment from their buying and working experiences?

5 Is a junior employee likely to adopt a different spoken word approach when talking to a senior manager, a supervisor, a co-worker and a customer? Can you supply any good reasons why this might be the case?

6 Is it a good or a bad thing if an employee adopts a different speaking style with different people at work?

SUMMARY OF KEY POINTS

How people relate and talk to each other at work

The first section of Chapter 1 emphasised the key factors which affect how people interact with each other at work and why they adopt a range of approaches when talking to various people in their communication network:

- Organisations are created to achieve specific goals – either to make a profit or to provide an efficient public service. Therefore, all the people who work in them must pull together to enable these goals to be reached.
- The relationships between people at work are affected by a number of factors:
  - (a) almost all need to keep a job in order to survive, and holding a job down means getting on well with managers, co-workers and customers alike
  - (b) employees also want to get on and to build careers; they will need to earn more money to pay for rent or a mortgage, to start a family and to afford some luxuries as well as essentials; they must therefore make it their business to impress favourably those who can influence their progress up the ladder
  - (c) customers are given special treatment in organisations, since in the end they keep everyone in a job and pay their wages
  - (d) employees inevitably work within networks of other people, inside and outside the organisation; to enable its goals to be met, all employees must create and maintain good communications with the others in the network
- The ways in which employees talk to others – inside or outside the organisation – is directly affected by the kinds of relationships they have, such as senior manager – junior employee, co-worker – co-worker, employee – customer.
- Many employees use the spoken word as their main communications tool; for some, like sales assistants, travel agency staff or care workers, the spoken word may form as much as 80% of all their communications at work; this is why it is so important to develop effective spoken word skills.

SELF-CHECK REVIEW TEST

How people relate and talk to each other at work

1 List four types of organisation which are common in the world of work.

2 What is the key aim of an organisation in a) the private sector and b) the public sector?

3 List three factors which influence the way in which an employee relates to another at work.

4 Why is the customer king or queen at work?

5 What is meant by the term *hierarchy* in connection with organisational structures?

6 List three communication problems which tend to increase as an organisation grows.

7 List three other types of employee a junior employee will relate to in his or her network.

When you have completed the above questions, turn to page 297 to check the answers provided with your own. If need be, revise the appropriate section of Chapter 1 if you got an answer wrong.

STUDENT PAIR SKILLS-BUILDING ACTIVITIES

Checking out how people relate and talk to each other at work

This activity requires you to team up with another student in your class and then to plan and carry out the following activity and to report back on it to your class as a whole.

Task 1 Look back through the above section, and discuss with your co-student the main factors which affect the ways in which people relate to and talk to each other at work. Then make a list of what you see as the main factors.

Task 2 Your next task is to plan to interview a member of your family or a family friend. One of you should interview someone you know who works in a private sector organisation, and the other someone who works in a public sector organisation.

Before arranging the interviews, you both should devise a series of questions to ask. These questions should be the same for both interviewees. These are some suggestions for the sort of questions you might ask to help you start:

Q1 Can you explain your job role and describe the kinds of people you come into regular contact with?

Q2 In your opinion, do your colleagues at work adopt different ways of speaking to other employees who occupy different positions? If so, could you explain why you think they do?

Q3 How does your boss ask you to carry out an instruction? Can you give me some examples, please.

You should devise about six or seven questions which explore how, in your interviewees' experience, employees relate to their internal and external contacts at work and the ways in which they talk to each other in order to get the job done.

Task 3 Arrange a suitable time and place to conduct your interviews (separately). Note down briefly the answers you are given to your questions, and compare notes with your co-student.

Task 4 With your partner, decide which answers were the same and which different, and produce notes to enable you to report back to your class on what you found out.

Task 5 In a general class discussion, find out whether you made any generally common discoveries about the ways in which people relate and talk to each other at work, or whether it depended on what sort of work the interviewees did in what sort of organisation. With your teacher's help, make brief notes of the discussion for your folder.

The uses of the spoken word at work

So far Chapter 1 has referred in general terms to people talking to each other at work *to get the job done*, or *to achieve the organisation's goals*. This section now turns our attention to the detailed uses to which the spoken word is put at work. Once these uses have been understood and absorbed, you will have a clear idea of the skills and techniques you will need to make a similar use of the spoken word in your own full- or part-time work. The following checklist illustrates some of the major uses of the spoken word in both private and public sector organisations.

CHECKLIST

Major uses of the spoken word at work

The spoken word is used:

- **to pass instructions to staff**, so that they are able to carry out tasks within their job roles (e.g. to set up a credit purchasing account for a new customer, or to prepare a bed for an incoming patient)
- **to ask for explanations or further information in order to carry out a task effectively** (e.g. to check out the settings for a lathe or drilling machine before starting to manufacture a new batch of parts)
- **to provide feedback on events or activities** to help managers review work which has been carried out (e.g. how have customers reacted to a new perfume)
- **to sell to customers**; selling is the life-blood of private sector organisations – sell or die! – and so a great deal of time and effort is spent on developing spoken word selling skills among sales representatives and sales assistants
- **to make decisions and to solve problems**; today, most organisations devote a great deal of time, in meetings and discussions, to consulting various managers and their staff about proposed actions and policies; effective organisations listen to their employees at all levels since they are the best informed about matters directly relating to their work
- **to trouble-shoot**; wherever people interact, sooner or later the fur will fly! Thus managers sometimes have to resolve a personality clash among their staff, or to put right a customer's complaint, say about faulty goods or what was taken to be rudeness from a sales person.
- **to persuade**; everyday, millions of people in the UK need to be persuaded to do something, whether to buy, to pay an overdue bill, or to take some action; similarly, employees sometimes need to be motivated, say to accept a pay offer.

As the above checklist illustrates, the spoken word at work is used in a host of different situations.

What makes someone's spoken words effective at work?

As we have already come to realise, the spoken word is used a great deal at work. But what makes its use effective? Clearly, an employee's status and power position will help to ensure his or her words are

CHECKLIST

Effective features of the spoken word

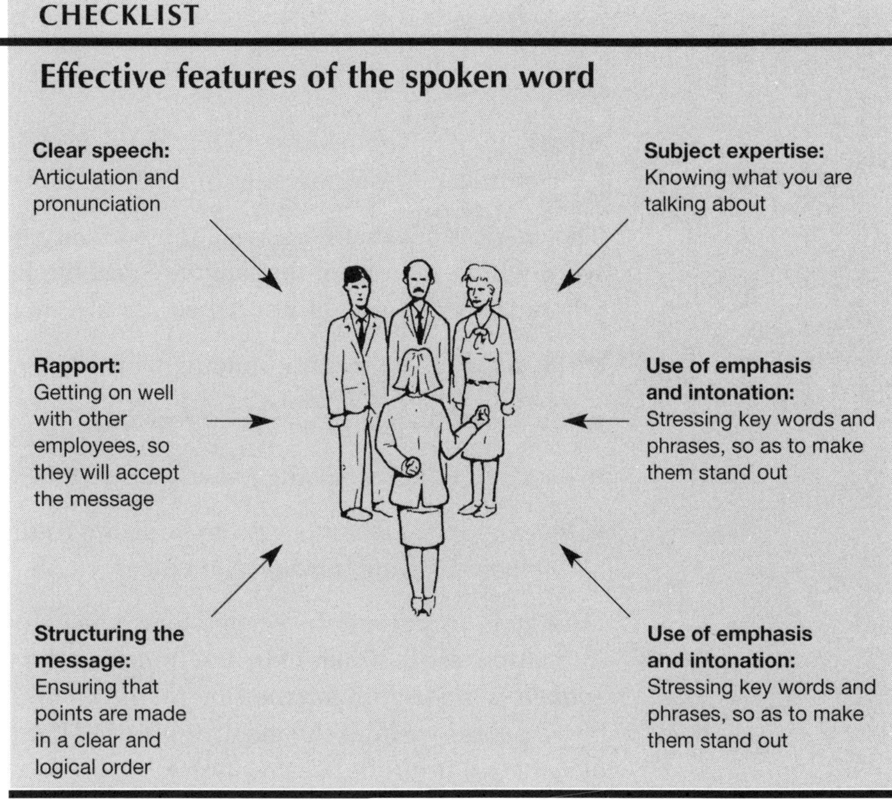

listened to carefully. Yet there are other, often more important aspects which users of the spoken word need to develop in order to get their oral messages across.

Clear speech:
Articulation and pronunciation
Subject expertise:
Knowing what you are talking about
Rapport:
Getting on well with other employees, so they will accept the message
Use of emphasis and intonation:
Stressing key words and phrases, so as to make them stand out
Structuring the message:
Ensuring that points are made in a clear and logical order
Use of emphasis and intonation:
Stressing key words and phrases, so as to make them stand out

Putting all the above features together while using the spoken word is a tall order. In fact it is rather like learning to drive. At first, a learner driver's entire concentration may be on getting the clutch pedal and hand shift gear movements together; only later can this be managed automatically, while the driver concentrates on estimating the road speeds of other vehicles and measures the likelihood of a particular pedestrian crossing in front of the car. In other words, as with so many skills, practice makes perfect, and advanced skills are built around basic ones as progress is made.

This section, therefore, will enable you to focus first on the essential skills you need to develop further. These are the skills of speaking clearly and with interest.

The skills of speaking clearly

As we become adult, virtually all of us come to speak automatically. We use the words regularly which form part of our active and working vocabularies. But we seldom stop to consider

a) whether we are speaking them clearly enough for others to understand

or

b) whether we are making them sound sufficiently interesting to capture and hold the attention of our audience.

The chances are that we have adopted many features of the spoken word which stem from the language and the English in common use where we were brought up. All across the UK, variations occur in:

- the accent used in pronouncing words
- the use of dialect or slang expressions
- habits of either stressing heavily or clipping off parts of words
- the way in which clusters of words are intoned – the patterns of rising and falling tones of the voice.

Here it is important to accept that a person's accent or patterns of intonation are neither here nor there *as long as the message being spoken is clearly understood by the listener(s).* Indeed, English would be far poorer without the musical lilt of a Highland Scot or the soft burr of someone from the West Country.

What does matter, however, in communicating the spoken word effectively is the breakdowns which occur as a result of:

- the use of local, dialect or slang words which others from outside the district will not understand:

  I was on me way to buy a whistle and flute when I saw the Ol Bill sortin' out a geezer who was Brahms and Liszt!

  (I was on my way to buy a suit when I saw the police attending to a man who was drunk.)

  He took the *snicket* (narrow alley) as a shortcut. They couldn't move for hordes of *grockles* (holiday-makers). She won't cut it right, she's *cack-handed!* (left-handed).

- speaking lazily, running words together or slurring them:

  Gissand, gotisedstuckinit!

  Yewgoghabejokin!

  Eyentpullinimeyt!

  Sizzownfoghtfergettinstukinafirsplace!

  Fanxfernuffin!

- speaking flatly, without giving sentences any appeal by using emphasis or intonation:

  D'you fan-cy go-ing to the dis-co to-night?

  Don't re-ally know. I might. It de-pends.

  Oh, what on?

  Whe-ther Dar-ren phones me or not

  Oh.

  Such conversations quickly become dull and boring, since neither speaker is bothering to add any stress to key syllables or to raise the voice at suitable intervals:

  ↗
  Do you **fan**cy going to the **dis**co tonight?

  Don't **really know**. I **might**. It de-**pends**.

  ↗
  Oh, what **on**?

  Whether Darren **phones** me or **not**.

  Key: bold = emphasised words or syllables, ↗ = a rising lift to the voice

  Interest can be added to even the simplest of conversations if emphasis and intonation are used to stress key words and phrases.

- using an unsuitable register (scale of softness or strength, formality or familiarity, formal or colloquial words, etc.) in which to set a message:

  Oi you! Yes, you! Get off your backside and start unloading that lorry. Now!

  (Supervisor instructing a work-hand to unload some incoming goods)

  I say! So sorry to bother you. You've left the door open. Would you mind awfully if I asked you to close it, I wouldn't normally bother but there's a terrible draught ...

  The work-hand who is the subject of such a rude and aggressive instruction as the one above would be justified in talking to his or her grievance officer if spoken to in such terms, while the commuter who makes a request in such a soft and uncertain manner is so half-hearted as to encourage the offender not to bother. Thus speaking effectively also involves using a suitable style in which to deliver the words.

WHAT DO YOU THINK?

1 What do *you* think are the spoken word skills used by someone at work who speaks effectively? Can you provide any examples – say of people you know in your study centre or where you may work part-time?

2 What features of the way some people talk irritate you most? Why?

3 Are you put off by people who 'put on airs and graces' by adopting what they consider to be a 'posh accent'? If so, why?

4 Is it possible for people – perhaps unconsciously – to develop ugly patterns of speech? If so, do you think the way such people speak might have a negative affect on their prospects at work?

5 Some people believe it wrong to 'bow and scrape' to bosses by talking to them in a flattering and fawning way. Others maintain that people at work should 'pick and choose' their words carefully when speaking to certain other people – like senior managers or customers. What do you think is the best approach to using the spoken word effectively with a range of other people at work?

SELF-CHECK REVIEW TEST

The uses of spoken word at work

1 List five main uses of the spoken word at work.

2 Explain briefly three of the features of the effective spoken word.

3 Give three reasons why spoken word communication can break down.

4 Explain what is meant by the term *register* in connection with the spoken word.

5 Explain briefly what is meant by the terms *emphasis* and *intonation* to describe the use of the spoken word.

When you have completed the above questions, turn to page 298 to check the answers provided with your own. If need be, revise the appropriate section of Chapter 1 if you got an answer wrong.

INDIVIDUAL AND STUDENT PAIR SKILLS-BUILDING ACTIVITIES

Task 1 **Practice in clear and interesting speaking**

Study the following sentences carefully, and then record your spoken word versions of them for you to play back in order to hear how you sound to others.

1 I love sunny beaches, a warm, safe sea, and clear, blue skies!

2 She was removing the wrapping-paper, before unpacking the bottles, when she heard someone knocking at the window.

3 'He's had his second helping already, and I haven't even had a first one yet!'

4 The habit of betting on the lottery is getting more and more popular, and people are putting millions of pounds on each week!

5 They were all overweight, but keen to lose it as soon as they could, by training regularly and keeping to a strict diet.

Play your recordings back and listen carefully to your own words. Check carefully how you pronounce the vowel sounds. Are they full and round, or distorted? Are your consonants strong and complete, or half-swallowed – bo*tt*le or bo*gh*le? Are you sounding your *h's* or dropping them? *He's had his*, or *'Es 'ad 'is*? Are you sounding final *g's* and *t's* or not – *helping* or *helpin'*, *strict* or *stric'?*

Play your recording back to your teacher or a friend and listen to the friendly and constructive responses they give you. Then try recording the sentences again to listen to your changes.

Task 2 In a similar way, first study one of the following passages and decide on which syllables emphasis should be placed in order to make the message sound interesting to a listener. Then plan how you will let your voice rise and fall also to provide emphasis and interest. Practise speaking the passage first and then record it.

1 I've just had the most marvellous piece of luck! I was browsing through the sales goods of Western's January sale, when I came across them, hidden in a pile of returned clothes, on one of those tables they jumble everything upon.

A pair of Westwood slacks for 20% off the normal retail price! And when I tried them on, they fitted like a glove. And, believe it or not, they were a caramel colour, which is one of my favourites!

2 I wanted it the moment I saw it! The petrol tank had one of those leather covers on it, and was sloped down, so you could really hug the frame. Instead of chrome handle-bars, forks and wheels, the finish was in a matt gun-metal, which I think is far more stylish. The bodywork is finished in white, green and blue, with flashes that make the bike look really streamlined! And it was shaft-driven, which I think is much safer. Fantastic bike, shame about the price!

3 I was very sorry to learn about Sharon's accident. I gather someone collided with her Fiesta when she was waiting to make a right turn. Mum told me she was in intensive care for over a week. How is she now? I do hope she's over the worst and well on the way to recovering. It must have been a nasty shock for you both. Please give her my very best wishes, and tell her we can't wait to visit, as soon as we're allowed.

Arrange to play back your version of the passage you chose to your class. Class members should listen carefully, and then decide whose recording sounded most interesting and appropriate, given the situation of the passage.

Task 3 In student pairs, carry out the following activity.

Each student should, during the course of a week, make three or four audio recordings of a radio programme in which either a single presenter (such as a news presenter) or several people (such as a quiz panel) are engaged in using the spoken word. Each recording must not exceed 2 minutes in length, and should seek to capture an interesting point in the programme.

When some six to eight recordings have been collected, the student pair should listen to them and pick out the two they believe provide the best examples of:

- a person or people **speaking clearly** in terms of the ways in which words are spoken and ideas strung together
- a person or people **speaking interestingly** in terms of the ways in which they use emphasis, intonation, pauses, etc. to make their words appealing and attention-holding.

With the help of your teacher, arrange to play back either one or both of your recordings to your class. Then, together, explain to your class what features of the recording(s) prompted you to select it as a good example of clarity and interest in the use of the spoken word.

SUMMARY OF KEY POINTS

Uses of the spoken word at work

People in the workplace use the spoken word to help them achieve many of the objectives of the organisation they work for.

- The spoken word is frequently used: to pass on instructions, to ask for explanations, to provide feedback, to sell, to aid decision making and problem solving, to persuade and to motivate employees.
- The main features of effective speaking are: clear speech, subject expertise, being on good terms with those spoken to, a logical structure for the message, the appropriate use of emphasis and intonation and the choice of a speaking style suited to the situation and the audience.
- Effective speakers avoid using slang or dialect words which others may not understand; they do not run words together into a slurred gabble, nor do they clip endings off words; they pronounce vowels and consonants fully and precisely.
- In order for a spoken word message to be accepted by those for whom it is intended, a suitable register has to be used; this means selecting a point on a scale – say from distant to friendly, or from demanding to suggesting – at which to pitch the message; getting the register wrong may result in the listener becoming angry or bored, or feeling put down, etc.

Developing spoken word skills

So far, Chapter 1 has examined the general aspects of the use of the spoken word at work, explaining how people tend to relate to each other and how and why they use the spoken word in the workplace. This section considers in detail the techniques you need to acquire in order to develop your own spoken word skills. In order to make progress in this important area, you will need to make the following commitments:

- to accept that you can improve upon your existing spoken word skills
- to admit that it takes time and personal effort to change speaking habits and outlooks, and to extend noticeably an active vocabulary

Provided that you do take on board (and keep to) the two above commitments, you will be surprised at how quickly your speaking skills will grow. It is all a matter of determination and stickability.

How to grow a larger and more expressive vocabulary

Imagine words were colours. Some people would be able to paint word pictures made up of a whole spectrum of colours – crimsons, flamingo pinks, jungle greens, ice blues and desert yellows, etc. They would also be able to paint such colours in either broad sweeps, dainty dots or stark lines. The overall effect would stay in the observer's mind's eye for a long time. While others would only manage to dab faint biscuit or drab grey patches on the canvas, which the eye barely notices and instantly forgets. The difference between two such 'word painters' lies in the range of colours they are able to employ, and their expertise in painting.

Exactly the same is true of those who truly paint in words. Words, just like colours, can conjure up pictures, and can communicate ideas just as strongly. However, a person who is a wordsmith as opposed to an artist needs to build up a palette of words – a working vocabulary – which is as large and as varied as the colours which a skilled artist can mix.

Full right up! No room for any more!

Three kinds of vocabulary

1 **Active vocabulary:** These are the words and expressions a person fully understands and regularly uses. Some people close their minds to acquiring new, active vocabulary once they think they possess enough.

2 **Passive vocabulary:** These are the words and expressions which a person comes across occasionally, but never bothers to look up, so that he or she has only a rough and hazy notion of what they mean. People do not use the words in their passive vocabulary themselves, and so remain unsure about them.

3 **Absent vocabulary:** These are the words and expressions which remain entirely alien and unfamiliar to a person, never used and completely unknown when met.

When it comes to building up a working vocabulary, most adults are incredibly lazy! Have you ever seen an adult on a train or bus pull out a dictionary to check up on the meaning of an unfamiliar word?

Perhaps it is a mixture of laziness and vanity that prevents people gaining a more expert and fluent word-base.

As the cartoons suggest, some people have to make do with the words they have collected so far in their lives, others find half-familiar words remain fuzzy and out-of-focus in their brains, if not on the page, while others find what are empty gaps in the printed matter they read, since the words which are absent vocabulary mean nothing to them. For people with large passive vocabularies and even larger absent ones, reading must seem like moving at regular intervals from a familiar home territory to the smoking craters, valleys and mountain ranges of an alien planet!

Of course, the knack of building up an extensive working vocabulary is to move words regularly from their absent and passive 'boxes' into your active 'word processor'. How is this done? Well, there are no easy short-cuts, but the following system has been proved over the years (by countless foreign language students) to work well.

The five stages in developing an active vocabulary

- **Stage 1** Obtain a strong lined notebook, about 10cm by 17cm. Divide each page vertically with a straight line. Give this notebook a suitable title e.g. WORD TOOLKIT or NEW WORD POWER TOOLS.
- **Stage 2** Obtain a handy, pocket English language dictionary (see below) which will fit snugly in your briefcase or book-bag. Make sure your dictionary includes for each entry details on how to pronounce words and what parts of speech they are, etc. (see Chapter 4 page 239). Keep both notebook and dictionary handy at all times.
- **Stage 3** Whenever – yes, really, *whenever* – you come across a word or expression you have either never met before, or have but do not really fully understand, *jot it down on the left-hand side of your notebook directly* (a process taking just a few seconds). If possible, ask your teacher what the word or phrase means, but at all events, at the first suitable moment (which may be during a private study period or at home) *look your entry up in your dictionary.*

- **Stage 4** Make sure you write down the word's meaning, its plural (if unusual), its part of speech, and its pronunciation if this is unfamiliar to you. All this detail is to be found in a good English language dictionary. The very act of making these twin entries in your notebook will help to imprint the word and its meaning into your long-term memory.
- **Stage 5** From time to time, browse through your notebook to refresh your mind and to engrave the new words and meanings in your memory. Also, seek to use your new words in both speech and in writing as soon as possible after you have collected them. In this way, you will embed them into your existing active vocabulary.

KEY POINT

The value of the notebook approach

It is tempting, to save time, merely to look an unfamiliar word up in a dictionary and to read the entry for it. You may remember the meaning for a time, but not nearly as well or as long as you would by using the notebook method. The notebook way may be more demanding, but then, as the Americans say about physical training: 'No gain without pain!'

The key features of a good English language dictionary

Today there are many different English language dictionaries for sale in bookshops and even supermarkets. Their quality varies, and the most expensive is not necessarily best value. Study the following section carefully to find out what features a good English dictionary possesses, and what to look for if you decide to buy one.

- **latest edition date**: English language dictionaries are time-consuming and expensive to produce; they tend therefore to be reprinted more often than published in a new edition. Take pains, therefore, to check the inside page and look, not for the latest reprint date, which changes little or nothing, but the latest new edition date, e.g. *12th edition March 1996*. The English language is constantly changing with new words being added and old ones falling out of use. Only a recently published dictionary provides up-to-date word-lists and current meanings and uses.
- **publishing house**: Some publishers, like Addison Wesley Longman, Oxford University Press and Collins are experienced and reputable. Choose a dictionary produced by long-standing experts.

- **entries**: Check carefully the range and type of entry for each word. Key entry features include:

  (a) *emphasis: on which syllable the main stress is placed (usually followed by this symbol: '); whether a syllable is long – or short ∪*

  (b) *tips on pronunciation: e.g. lingerie lā' nzherē (The Concise Oxford Dictionary)*

  (c) *part of speech: n = noun, v = verb, adj = adjective, etc*

  (d) *plural spellings acceptable: e.g. stadium pl stadia or stadiums*

  (e) *common uses of the word: e.g. cat ~ of nine tails: whip used to flog sailors in 18th cent; ~ nap: to doze or sleep for a short period (note: the symbol ~ is used to stand for the root word)*

  (f) *origin: some dictionaries supply details of where the entry originated, e.g. L = Latin, Gk = Greek, OHG = Old High German, etc.*

- **abbreviations**: Some dictionaries include lists of abbreviations in common current use, e.g. *TUC* Trades Union Congress, *RSVP* répondez s'il vous plaît, *E&OE* errors and omissions excepted, etc.

- **conversions**: Tables converting imperial/metric measures, distances, areas and volumes, e.g. 1 pint = 20 fluid ounces = 0.568 litres (The Concise Oxford Dictionary).

- **addenda**: Some dictionaries include a section of changes to words inserted just before going to print, under the heading Addenda – entries added.

Spelling dictionaries

Teachers are fond of saying to their students something like: *You'd spend a long time looking up pneumonia under n*! The point they love to make is that a standard English language dictionary is of little use if you do not know for sure how a given word is spelled. Thus the cry: 'Why don't you look it up in the dictionary' is both irritating and frustrating for someone (among the millions of UK citizens who share the problem today) who has difficulty with spelling.

Fortunately a most useful source of help is readily available for such people, though most remain unaware of it. 'It' is a spelling dictionary. Unlike its language counterpart, it lists entries phonetically, that is to say how the word sounds, rather than how it is written.

Example of phonetic spelling dictionary entries

new-moaniah:	pneumonia
fizzickle:	physical
konshuss:	conscious
airess:	heiress
higher - arckick:	hierarchic
dya-reeya:	diarrhoea

Various spelling dictionaries employ different phonetic systems, but all are simple and easy to use. If you find spelling a personal area of difficulty, then consult your study centre librarian and local bookseller and purchase a spelling dictionary. It could change your life, and your career prospects!

The English language thesaurus

You should also be aware of another type of reference text: the English language thesaurus. This is a text which contains a large number of lists of words and expressions which are similar and which build out from a root or core word. For example the word *bad* would be followed by similar words or expressions like:

bad: rotten, gone off, rancid, curdled; evil, wicked, tainted, demonic, nasty; gone mouldy, putrefied, decomposed; gone to the dogs, up to no good

Such a thesaurus also provides cross-references to other wordlists which take the user further away from the original root word in a set of related moves, say from *bad* to *nasty* to *unpleasant* to *disturbing* and thus to *worrying*. As you can see, an English language thesaurus is extremely handy when someone is stumped for another word or expression to replace an over-used one, and is an essential reference for the serious speaker or writer.

INDIVIDUAL AND SMALL GROUP SKILLS-BUILDING ACTIVITIES

Developing your active vocabulary

Task 1 Study the following sentences carefully, especially those words in italics. As you will see, the italicised words all tend to be over-used, and have therefore become dull and empty of meaning. Your task is to choose two or three alternatives for each of the words in italics which you think would fit into the sense and situation described in each sentence, so as to make them more interesting to read.

1 [Scene in a travel agent's shop] 'That's a *good* idea! Why not Spain? We've had some *good* times in Spain. The weather's always *good*, the food's not *bad*, and the wine's usually *good* too. Can you suggest any *good* tour operators?

2 [Scene on a factory floor] 'You'll have to *do* that one again. Finish is *poor*, and that joint's been *poorly done*, and the drawer's a *poor* fit. Altogether a *poor* job!'

3 [Scene in an office] 'Ah, that's *nice*, you've put the brochure together very *nicely*, Kerry! The cover's *nice* and you made a *nice* choice of lemon paper. Layout's extremely *nice*, Everyone should be able to read it *nicely*. And the illustrations catch the eye *nicely* where you have *put* them. Well done, Kerry, a *really nice job!*'

4 [Scene in a rest home] 'That's *OK*, Jack, delivery by lunch-time will be perfectly *OK*. Oh, and if it's *OK* by you, I'd like the fish to be boned and skinned, *OK*? Have you got any kippers? The last lot were really *OK* and went down *OK* with Mr Johnson and Mrs Wills. How many? I think four should be *OK*. *OK*, then, see you at twelve.'

5 [Scene in a computer technician's workshop] 'What do you think of the *new bit of kit?*' 'The anti-flicker screen's *not bad*, and the 120 Pentium processor's *nippy*. I think the modem's a *bit iffy* – too slow if you ask me. The six speed CD-Rom's *not bad*, though. *Not a lot* of RAM, only eight. All in all, I'd say it's *very fair*.' 'Oh, *you really like it*, then?'

When you have completed all five sentences, share your versions and alternatives with your class, and decide which words have the best effect in replacing the tired words in italics, which are called 'clichés'. If you come across any words new to you – yes, you've guessed, jot them down in your notebook!

Task 2 Look up the following words in your dictionary and check out how they are pronounced. Write them down phonetically in order to remember.

1 aghast **2** amphitheatre **3** asphyxiate **4** charade **5** début **6** forte
7 loquacious **8** occidental **9** pharmaceutical **10** schizophrenia
11 sleight **12** rouge **13** ratatouille **14** suave **15** soufflé **16** toupee
17 vermicelli **18** vivacious **19** wholly **20** xylophone

With the help of your teacher, take turns to be given one of the words to pronounce correctly. Make sure you put into your notebook those words which you did not know beforehand how to pronounce. Also make sure that you know how to interpret the pronunciation signs in your dictionary.

Task 3 Form small teams of three to four students. Use your dictionaries or thesauruses to find a set of ten words which are tricky either to pronounce or to spell (or both!). In team turns, ask each member of each team to spell and/or pronounce one of your selected words. If the challenge is to pronounce, then say the word; if the challenge is to spell, then write it on the board. Award one mark for each correct answer, with your teacher as referee and scorer. Build on your active vocabulary by noting down any new words you meet, and record their spelling and pronunciation clearly.

Task 4 Working on your own, find out what the following stand for (by using your dictionary):

1 an ampersand **2** AA **3** B Sc **4** circa **5** DDT **6** ea. **7** fig. **8** HB **9** i.e. **10** JP **11** Kt **12** Ltd **13** mm **14** NB **15** OAP **16** pp **17** SAE **18** trans. **19** UNO **20** vol.

Check your answers with your co-students, and bear in mind that some of the above have more than one meaning.

Task 5 Use your initiative to find out what the following prefixes and suffixes stand for (a prefix is an add-on at the start of a word, and a suffix an add-on at the end of a word):

Prefixes: ad- ambi- ante- anti- bi- circum- contra- duo- hetero- in- kilo- multi- non- poly- sub- super- tri- uni-

Suffixes: -ability -ant -arch -craft -dom -ette -graph -hood -ism -less -logue -monger -oid -ware

When you have found out what each of the above entries stands for, find two examples of words for each. Then share your collection with other students in your class, and decide whether prefixes and suffixes always convey the same meaning. Clue: what you discover may help you to guess the correct meanings of new words you meet!

Putting the words together

So far in this section of Chapter 1, we have concentrated on words as if they only came along singly. Of course, nothing could be further from the truth in terms of the spoken word in action at work. And so it is time to move on to an examination of the techniques of communicating ideas orally in clusters of words. These clusters tend to take the form of short or long sentences:

> I quite agree. I'm not sure. That's absolutely right! Sorry, could you repeat that?

You see,| if we decide to follow Sara's proposal,| it will mean completely refurnishing the whole restaurant,| whereas my idea is| to concentrate simply on the breakfast bar area!

Expressing thoughts and ideas well in sentences in the course of a discussion is a skill that it takes time to acquire. In this section you will find advice and guidance to enable you to develop just such a skill. The place to start is with the natural patterns in which ideas are created and delivered in spoken English.

Our language follows a very simple basic order of words:

The doer word	The action word	Added meaning words
The steward	served	free drinks
Three letters	arrived	in the same post
Love	makes	the world go round!

When speaking, most people tend to start their sentences with the doer word. As the above examples illustrate, doer words can be people, things or abstract ideas. Doer words are given the specialist label of **subject of the sentence**. All sentences contain at least one action word. As you already probably know, action words are called **verbs**, and when they are linked to subjects in sentences, they are called **finite verbs**. This label simply means that they have to agree with the subject, by being either singular or plural, and by being in a person – either first person: *I*, second person: *you* or third person: *he, she, it, they*.

Indeed, the simple test of whether a cluster of words is a grammatically correct sentence or not, is to check whether it has:

a) **a subject**

b) **a finite verb**, expressed in **a number** (singular or plural), **a person** (first, second or third) and **a tense** (present, past or future)

If it does, then it is a fully paid-up sentence! For a more detailed examination of this area, see Chapter 2 page 97.

The following examples illustrate further this commonly occurring structure of expressing ideas in sentences.

Subject word clusters →	Finite verb clusters →	Extension of meaning word clusters
The suggestion	has a lot of merit	–
(Excuse me,)* I	have to disagree	completely!
The decision	was made	after a heated discussion

(* This is in reality a short sentence tacked on to the main one – see Chapter 2)

If, when using the spoken word in a discussion, people always spoke in such short sentences, however, their fellow participants would quickly become bored, as the following passage illustrates:

> I like Sara's proposal. We could do a Mexican decor. It would make a change. Hang sombreros on the walls. Play guitar music. Get a cactus or two. What do you think?

While the above set of remarks succeed in getting the key points across using the simple sentence structure described above, they are neither very fluent nor persuasive. Consider the alternative version below:

> I *entirely support* Sara's proposal. We could *redecorate* in a *colourful* Mexican decor, **which** would make a *welcome* change. *Imagine* sombreros hanging on the walls, some *exotic* cacti and *soft* guitar music playing *in the background!* What do you think?

This version runs on more smoothly in four sentences than seven. Joining two or more ideas together into a single sentence makes for more interesting listening than having them doled out one at a time. Notice, too, how the choice of more imaginative and persuasive words makes the remarks more persuasive and effective: *entirely support* is much more emphatic than merely *like*; *redecorate* more accurate than *do*. Similarly, the use of *imagine, exotic, soft* and *in the background* encourage us to create a mental picture of the decor and atmosphere being proposed.

Of course, it is much easier to construct a succession of short sentences in the middle of a discussion than it is to express them in the form of the second example. And so you can see how important it is to have that developed active vocabulary at your finger-tips, for immediate use.

KEY POINT

Vary sentence length for interest and effect

Remember that short sentences have their place in a discussion, if you wish to emphasise a particular point: *I disagree completely. The solution must be to sell it. Kevin's entirely right! All I hear is claims, but no facts!* Such utterances are best made either as one-off statements, or as the final remark in a longer statement. But remember, too, that a series of such short sentences can become boring and switch listeners off. Try to vary your sentence length, so as to keep your listeners interested.

Constructing longer sentences

If you were observant, you will have noticed that, so far, no mention has been made of the word which is in bold type in the example about the decor above. If you check back, you will see that *which* connects two separate ideas together in a single sentence:

> We could redecorate in a Mexican decor. It would make a welcome change.

In fact, a number of such words exist in English to carry out this particular connection job:

> and but yet
>
> next then
>
> although though even though
>
> because as since
>
> whether if as if
>
> so that in order that with the result that
>
> when where why
>
> that which

Examples

> *Although* the cabinet had been shoddily finished, the craftsmen were able to restore it to a sales quality standard.
>
> Sara's proposal was accepted, *because* it had been so persuasively explained.
>
> *As* the steward was very busy, a colleague helped to serve the drinks.
>
> Kerry worked very hard at designing the brochure, *in order to* help the sales drive.

As the above examples illustrate, the connecting words, technically called **conjunctions**, can be used in two ways, either to introduce the first part of the sentence (called a **clause**) or to link it to a second part or clause. If you study the above examples, you will see that when the conjunction starts the sentence, a sense of expectation is created, because the listener has to wait to find out what the main part is. Experienced speakers in discussions use this technique to create an effect which emphasises what is said last:

> *Despite* all the difficulties this committee has experienced ... I am delighted to tell you that our proposals have been accepted!

Although Sara has argued persuasively for a complete redecoration ... I'm afraid she has ignored the immense costs involved.

In examining ways in which to construct longer sentences, keep also in mind that the conjunctions *and, but, next* and *then* all link together clauses which are of equal importance:

Sara's proposal is clear *and* it is also cost-effective.

Sara's proposal is interesting *but* it will require a great deal of funding.

The committee voted in favour of Sara's proposal *then* moved on to the next item of business.

Supporting and countering words

Just as conjunctions help a speaker to link ideas together in an interesting way, so other words are helpful in enabling a speaker either to support or to counter what someone else has just said:

Examples of supporting words

I agree with Asha. *Moreover,* I think the idea of opening seven days a week will increase profits, rather than add to costs.

Steve's right, chair. *Indeed,* the point he makes about the need to advertise more frequently is just what I had in mind.

Moving over to a system of contract cleaning will save money. *Furthermore,* it will release our maintenance staff to carry out more important jobs.

Other examples of supportive words and phrases used to start remarks include: *Absolutely ... Definitely ... That's right! Of course ...* Also, the insertion of these expressions early in a set of remarks serve the same purpose: *Lucy's hit the nail on the head ... Phil's perfectly correct to point out that ...*

As most discussions unfold, there emerge three types of people groupings: those in favour of, those against and those neutral about an idea or suggestion. By showing support for other speakers in the above ways, you can signal that you are moving towards either the pros or the antis, and this may help to sway the neutrals to your point of view.

Examples of countering words

There's some truth in what Ahmed says. *However,* I believe he's overlooked the problem of recruiting suitably qualified staff.

> Lisa's right about the lack of consultation. *Nevertheless*, the research carried out does show that unless the proposed changes are introduced, sales will suffer.
>
> Naomi says the camera never lies. *Even so*, I wouldn't want these pictures used to advertise our organisation. They're much too damaging.

Such words effectively state: *What has just been said may be true, up to a point, but what I'm about to say needs also to be taken into account.* Other ways of introducing a countering remark or statement include:

> I think Peter has got the wrong end of the stick ...
>
> What worries me about the last point is ...
>
> Jane is misguided in believing that ...
>
> While there's some truth in Tania's view ...
>
> On the other hand, what about ...
>
> Andy seems to have overlooked the fact that ...

The main point to remember when using such countering remarks in a meeting or discussion is that you should never descend into personal attacks, sarcasm or rudeness, etc. when disagreeing with other participants. People will take much more notice of what you have to say if you stay calm, reasonable and courteous when disagreeing.

STUDENT TRIO SKILLS-BUILDING ACTIVITIES

Developing speaking skills in discussions

Task 1 By arrangement with your teacher, form a trio group and then audio-record a 5–7 minute discussion of *one* of the following topics, after having taken about 10 minutes to prepare the points you will make.

1 Big money is ruining sport today.

2 My favourite foreign holiday would be ...

3 What I expect from working full-time.

4 Marriage? It's history, isn't it?

5 Fashion magazines, television and newspapers all promote images of women as being waif-like and incredibly good looking. As a result, some girls start dieting from the age of nine, and most spend large sums on cosmetics. Not only is this emphasis on being thin and good-looking daft, it is positively unhealthy – for both body and mind.

6 All young men care about is being regarded as macho, especially by young women!

Each trio should listen to two successive play-backs of the discussion:

- First, to review how they themselves performed, and to note what went well and what needed to be improved in terms of clarity of speech, appealing delivery, structure of points, fluency of expression, etc.
- Second, to carry out the same review of the performances of the other participants

At the end of this activity, the class as a whole should exchange views on experiences and reviews.

Task 2 First, form a group of six students in two groups of three. Then, in turn, each trio should carry out the following task. One group should engage in the discussion, while the other observes and makes notes (see below).

Select *one* of the following discussion topics:

1 Taking part in a team sport for at least two hours each week should be made compulsory in all schools and colleges for students in the 14–19 age range.

2 In reality, women are still at a disadvantage when it comes to entering and developing a worthwhile career.

3 No matter what jobs they do, all adults in full-time employment should have to pay into a compulsory personal pension scheme from the age of 18 in order to insure themselves against poverty and reliance on the state in old age.

4 The ways in which schools and colleges prepare teenagers for vocational careers need a complete rethink!

5 The organisation I would want to work for would have to possess these characteristics ...

In turn, each trio should spend some 5–10 minutes discussing their selected topic, after having devoted about 10 minutes to making notes of the points they wish to make. The observing trio should sit at a discreet distance, so as not to intrude into the discussion. Their role is to each select one speaker from the discussion trio, and to observe how they contribute to the discussion, noting down especially:

- the extent of their contributions, and how fluently they were made
- examples of effective vocabulary; linking, supporting and countering expressions
- the extent to which their points were actively listened to and taken note of

Each observing trio should feed back to the discussion trio *anonymously* on what they said, concentrating on giving constructive advice and analysis.

At the end of each trio's sessions of discussing and observing, the whole class should engage in a general discussion of some 10–15 minutes on what was learned from this activity about speaking and discussing without rehearsal (technical term: speaking **extempore**). Remember to keep your views anonymous, since the object is to develop as an individual and group, not to wound people's feelings!

WHAT DO YOU THINK?

1 How would *you* design a means of increasing a person's active vocabulary?

2 Why, in your opinion, are most people so lazy when it comes to consulting a dictionary? Does it matter?

3 'As long as the meaning remains clear in a document someone produces at work, the spelling doesn't matter a jot!' Do you agree?

4 What do you consider to be the speaking skills which make a person a strong and effective performer in discussions?

5 'When you're taking part in a really interesting discussion, you haven't got time to think about how you will say something, you're too busy thinking about what to say next!' True, or false? Is how you say something as important as what you say in a discussion, or not?

6 People seldom change their minds as a result of a discussion. The views they bring into a meeting are the ones they leave with. Do you agree? Can you recall how you were persuaded to change your mind in a recent discussion, or can you suggest how you would set about changing someone else's opinion during a discussion?

SUMMARY OF KEY POINTS

Developing spoken word skills

The following points about developing spoken word skills are particularly important to remember:

- Everyone possesses a three-part vocabulary, consisting of a) active words and phrases which are familiar and regularly used b) passive words and phrases which are more or less recognised when met, but not used actively and c) absent words and phrases, which are not recognised when met nor ever used. The challenge is to move as much vocabulary as possible from absent and passive to active.

- A key tool needed to enable anyone to develop their spoken word skills is a good English dictionary which provides helpful detail for each entry concerning pronunciation, part of speech, common usage, permitted plural spellings and origins, etc. Spelling dictionaries are particularly helpful if phonetically structured and thesauruses also help to enlarge an active vocabulary.
- Constructing interesting spoken word sentences requires an understanding of how English is constructed into sentences, typically by the sequence of: SUBJECT -> FINITE VERB -> EXTENSION. Also, to keep an audience's interest, sentences need to be varied – neither a series of short and simple ones, nor overly long ones, but a mixture of longer and shorter ones which makes use of connecting conjunctions.
- Joining ideas and sentences together is helped by the use of supporting and countering words like: *moreover, nevertheless, furthermore, however, even so.*

SELF-CHECK REVIEW TEST

Developing spoken word skills

1. Explain what is meant by a person's a) active, b) passive and c) absent vocabulary.
2. Outline briefly the steps to be taken in order to improve and extend one's active vocabulary.
3. List four features of a good English dictionary.
4. What is an English language thesaurus?
5. What is it about the structure of a spelling dictionary that helps someone who finds spelling difficult?
6. What are the grammatical terms for a) doer word and b) action word?
7. What features does a finite verb possess?
8. What two key features must a sentence possess for it to be grammatically correct?
9. List five different connecting words called conjunctions.
10. List two supporting and two countering words used to introduce ideas in sentences.

When you have completed the above questions, turn to page 298 to check the answers provided with your own. If need be, revise the appropriate section of Chapter 1 if you got an answer wrong.

Discussions and body language

Until now, we have studied the spoken word within the framework of discussions as if it worked completely alone as a medium of communication. In fact, the spoken word is used together with another form of communicating in order to send messages. This other form is called body language, or non-verbal (without words) communication (NVC).

From its earliest days, a new-born baby focuses on its mother's eyes and face in order to receive messages of love, security, presence and so on. As children grow up, they quickly come to recognise (and react to) body language signals – of anger, sadness, or worry, – which those around them show in their facial expressions. Moreover, they recognise gestures just as quickly, such as a beckoning finger, or a hand raised to threaten a smack. Equally, they pick up and respond to the signals which are sent by the ways in which people arrange their bodies, whether of a parent prepared to allow a child to snuggle up, or of a parent hunched busily over a desk, wanting no interruptions.

The three main features of body language

Continuing well into adult life and beyond, all human beings learn to send and to interpret body language signals which sometimes replace the spoken word, or reinforce it. As the following paragraphs explain, body language centres upon:

Facial expression

The human face is made up of dozens of muscles which make it possible for someone to adopt a wide range of expressions which signal:

anger, aggression, fear, worry, shock, irritation, frustration, embarrassment, self-consciousness, nervousness, rapture, happiness, contentment, amusement, disbelief, scepticism, disagreement, opposition, dislike, hatred, disgust, etc.

'So what went wrong? . . .'

'Good morning, may I help you?

CHECKLIST

Parts of the face used to construct body language signals

The main features of the human face which are used in various combinations are:

- the forehead, the skin of which can be wrinkled; the hairline raised upwards or the lower forehead knitted together in a frown
- the eyebrows, which can also be lifted or dropped
- the eyelids, which can be opened wide to show more eye, or closed into slits
- the eyes, which can be made to stare fixedly, or to roll, or to flash from side to side, or to look heavenwards or to the ground
- the nostrils which can be made to flare in the remnants of a primitive snarl or expression of utter fear
- the lips and surrounding muscles, which can form smiles, grimaces, curled lips, open-mouthed surprise, etc.
- the chin, which can be stuck out or tucked in
- the neck, which can cause the whole head to nod or to shake sideways, and to look right up or down, or sideways

When you stop to consider, the human head is a truly remarkable machine for communicating hundreds of responses – feelings, attitudes and inner thoughts – all through body language!

INDIVIDUAL SKILLS-BUILDING ACTIVITIES

Developing body language recognition skills

Task 1 Use the above checklist to help you draw up a series of brief explanations of how the human face would appear in order to signal three of the feelings or emotions listed at the start of this section (anger, aggression, fear, etc.). For example, a person expressing fear in his or her facial expression might have the forehead wrinkled upwards, eyebrows raised, eyes wide open, skin paled and mouth dropped wide open.

Task 2 To inject a little fun into the proceedings, take it in turns to mime a suitable facial expression for one of the emotions listed above (or another of your own choosing), and get your fellow students to guess what you are miming.

Gesture

'Here's the crucial point'

'Search me'

Gestures are signals given by either a finger, fingers, hand or hands and arm or arms – or a mix of all three. We are all familiar with the signal which turns both palms upwards and with a shrug of the shoulders signals, *Search me*! Gesturing as a social habit goes back a very long way in time. Experts believe that the handshake originated from two strangers meeting and needing to convince each other that neither concealed a weapon in his or her hand, such as a sharp flint. The following checklist illustrates some of the commonly occurring gestures and what they signal.

CHECKLIST

Common gesture signals

Gesture	Meaning
stabbing a finger at someone	aggression or hostility
patting down the air with both palms open	asking for calm or for people to quieten and settle down
folding arms across chest	opposition, disagreement
tapping fingers on table or desk	impatience, irritation
lacing fingers of both hands behind head	relaxed attitude, comfortable feeling
slapping someone's back	congratulating, showing full agreement
scratching chin or head	uncertainty, doubt
chopping downwards with side of open hand	emphasis, rejection, dislike

The above list illustrates only a few of the very many gestures people make to signal attitudes and feelings. Some, of course, are intended to be rude or offensive, like making a screwing motion with a forefinger into the side of the head to tell someone that they've *got a screw loose!*

GENERAL SKILLS-BUILDING ACTIVITY

Developing body language skills

Firstly, as an individual, think of some attitudes, emotions or views which people signal with a simultaneous mix of facial expression and gesture, e.g. violent disagreement – wagging a finger under someone's nose and staring hard at them with head and chin jutting forward.

In a general class group, mime your combined body language signal and let the class guess what it stands for. The student who guesses correctly takes the next turn.

Posture

'Hi, Joe, What'll it be?'

It helps to think of posture as the ways in which people arrange their bodies. We have all seen someone casually leaning against a bus stop with legs slightly bent and ankles crossed as a means of passing the waiting time in a relaxed and unstressed manner. We may also have seen wretchedly unfortunate people on televised war-zone newscasts sitting on the ground, their torsos hunched over their thighs, rocking backwards and forwards in terrible grief. Between these two extremes, human beings signal a wide range of feelings by the ways in which they arrange their bodies.

By and large, the more a person stretches out his or her body, the more secure and relaxed the person is feeling. Recall, for instance, how someone leans back on a chair, legs stretched right out, arms hanging down its sides and head thrown back – in an attitude of complete relaxation and security. Think also of the animal pictures you have seen, say of gorillas or polar bears playing with their young. Only when such animals feel completely secure in their surroundings will they roll over to display a vulnerable, soft underbelly. We humans are not much different!

In a similar way, the tighter a person holds limbs and torso together, the more anxious and stressed they are feeling. Sitting forward, hunched up in a chair outside a door, a person may be signalling anxiety or nervousness, say about being hauled over the coals by the head as a mischievous pupil, or as an interviewee waiting to be interviewed for a job.

CHECKLIST

Commonly occurring posture

Posture	Meaning
seated, leaning forward	either close attention and interest, or disagreement/firm opposition
seated, sprawling back	total comfort, perhaps boredom, feeling of being in control and unthreatened
seated, legs crossed and hands in lap	much like a car in neutral gear: relaxed, but ready to handle a situation
standing erect, at full stretch and leaning slightly forward, legs a little apart	a show of potential aggression, or of being ready to stand one's ground
standing, shoulders and head slumped down, arms hanging downwards	dejection, sorrow, upset

As the three lists of commonly occurring facial expression, gesture and posture signals reveal, people 'say' a very great deal through the use of body language. Moreover, their NVC signals may convey messages which conflict with or contradict the words they are actually speaking. For example, if someone breaks eye-contact with a group and looks away from them while saying for instance:

> I can positively assure you all here today that there will be no further action taken, if the culprit owns up to me by lunch-time ...

it is very possible that he or she is not actually telling the truth!

Body language can sometimes reveal inner thoughts and feelings at times when people are trying to communicate something very different. More often, however, NVC signals act to reinforce what is being said, or to signal a message in place of a silence. For example, someone listening passively to a speaker in a discussion while frowning and folding arms tightly is in all probability 'saying actively' *I don't go along with this argument at all!*

KEY POINT

Interpreting body language is not an exact science!

There is no doubt that it pays to develop an ability to recognise body language signals in others, and to remember to make them oneself as a speaker – say to smile at the start of a contribution in order to help build up rapport and to reassure others. Spotting the signals which others may send unconsciously during meetings and discussions and interpreting them correctly frequently supplies additional, helpful information about a person's views and responses.

However, be on your guard! Analysing body language is not an exact science. It is all too easy to misinterpret such signals, and become upset, say, because someone did not make eye-contact with you and smile, in either High Street or corridor. The simple answer might well be that he or she was wrapped up in personal thoughts and did not see you.

INDIVIDUAL AND GENERAL SKILLS-BUILDING ACTIVITIES

Developing skills in interpreting body language signals

Task 1 Over the course of a week, scour the newspapers, magazines and advertising mail, etc., you receive at home. Look for photographs of people who are displaying body language signals – facial expressions, gestures or postures. Check through the stories or captions for clues as to what sort of signal they are conveying and why. Then, after checking with the family that no one will mind, cut out the photograph, making sure that you remove any textual clues.

In your baseroom and with the help of your teacher, set up a display of selected photographs and number them. Then, as a class group, set down on paper a brief description of what body language message you think each photograph is communicating. Your teacher will decide on what are the correct answers (in liaison with each contributor).

Task 2 With the help of your teacher, a parent or a friend, seek to sit in as a silent observer at a local meeting, such as a church council, student association, youth club leaders' or sports club committee. Or, if this proves difficult to arrange, watch a televised documentary discussion programme, such as *Panorama, World In Action* or *Newsnight,* etc. Or again, you may decide to monitor the body language signals participants send during a particular lesson.

Your task is to make discreet notes of examples of the body language which participants use in the course of either making oral contributions, or responding to them.

When all class members have completed this research a general discussion should be held which explores what class students discovered and how body language signals appeared to influence the discussions' proceedings. Special attention should be given to those areas which several class members found to be common among different people and different types of discussion.

Task 3 The class should be divided into groups of about six students each. At all events, the total number of such groups should be an even number, so that groups can pair off.

Each paired group operates both as a discussion group and an observer group in turn. All groups must select one of the following discussion topics. Firstly, for 10 minutes, each student should individually prepare a personal approach, producing supportive notes. Then the group should discuss the topic for some 7–10 minutes.

Discussion topics

1 'You're only doing wrong if you get found out!' Are honesty and good morals dead and buried today? In this regard, what beliefs and behaviour should a new employee bring to a job these days?

2 'Computers are causing the loss of many more jobs than they are creating. Moreover, they are developing a nation of screen-hooked zombies, unable to kick their computer game habit. Get rid of them, that's what I say!'

3 Despite all the women's movements in the world, and the so-called evolution of the 'new man' as house-husband or job-sharing partner, women will never achieve equality with men at work, simply because the men are not prepared to share the status and power of the better paid jobs!

4 'In the middle of the nineteenth century, the leaders of the newly formed Trades Union Congress sought eight hours for work, eight hours for rest and sleep, and *eight hours for education and personal improvement.* If they saw how much trivial rubbish is broadcast and published today, and how little the bulk of the adult population cares about self-improvement, they would truly wonder whether their struggle to improve the lot of the ordinary worker was worth the costly efforts they made!'

The observer group should arrange to monitor discreetly the students taking part in the discussion in terms of the body language signals they send and respond to, and to check on which signals affected and influenced the discussions, and which appeared to be ignored, and why.

At the end of this activity, each group should feed back to the class in a suitably anonymous way on what they observed and noted. With help from your teacher, your class should produce a summary on the role of body language in discussions. From these discussions, a factsheet should be produced of the key points and distributed to each class member as a revision source.

WHAT DO YOU THINK?

1 Body language – a reality or a myth? What do you think?

2 'Reading other people's so-called body language is a dangerous occupation. Not only might you read it all wrong, but by making an inappropriate response, you may well deeply offend and upset a fellow employee?' Is this so? Or do you believe that a study of body language is as acceptable as, say, reading their writing carefully or listening to their words attentively?

3 While some people can tell dark lies without blushing, almost everyone finds it impossible to fake body language! What do you think?

4 Without extensive training as an actor, it is very difficult to employ body language while speaking to an audience. True, or false?

5 'The thing about body language is that we are all far more affected by it than we realise. Not only are the signals sent unconsciously by others, but we also respond to them without realising it.' Do you agree?

SUMMARY OF KEY POINTS

Discussions and body language

A study of body language is an important part of developing discussion skills, since it often reveals what a person is thinking or feeling but not saying.

- Body language signals are sent by means of facial expressions, gestures and postures.
- Sometimes body language or non-verbal communication signals are made up of a mix of the above two or three body elements.
- A person's face is particularly expressive, since it contains dozens of muscles which are used to create various sets of signals which humans are accustomed to recognising from babyhood onwards.
- Generally, the more stretched out a person's gestures and posture, the more relaxed he or she feels; the more tightly wound up (like a spring), the more anxious and stressed a person feels.
- Body language signals should be read in close conjunction with what a person is saying.

SELF-CHECK REVIEW TEST

Discussions and body language

1 Explain briefly what is meant by the term 'body language'.

2 Outline the three main ways in which body language signals are sent

3 Why does body language sometimes reveal what a person's spoken words do not?

4 Explain briefly what body language signals a speaker can use to help the delivery of a contribution to a discussion

5 By and large, what body language signals is someone sending who is:

a) stretched out in a chair
b) huddled on a bench?

When you have completed the above questions, turn to page 299 to check the answers provided with your own. If need be, revise the appropriate section of Chapter 1 if you got an answer wrong.

How to take notes in discussions

By now, in your educational or social life, you will certainly have already taken part in a number of discussions. Almost certainly, you will have noticed – especially in lively or heated discussions – how fast and furious the debate can become. Further, if the discussion is a lengthy one, you will also have come to realise how difficult it is to remember exactly what an early speaker said. When several people make a series of points quickly, it is as though each one were slapping down a personal playing-card on top of one just laid down. In this way, it is the most recently made point (or laid card) which is best recalled. And yet, a discussion point made early on may be just the one you wish to support and take further, or to counter and oppose.

Because of the fast-moving, hurly-burly of some discussions, it is important – if your own contributions are to be made effectively – that you develop the skill of taking down notes at speed for later reference at a meeting. The following section describes a practical approach to this important skill and provides opportunities for you to acquire practice in it.

Getting organised for note-taking

Before a meeting or discussion starts, you should take your place and set out your papers and note-making materials. A large firm-backed notepad, A4 in size, is recommended, since taking notes at speed requires plenty of writing space. Several pens or pencils are also needed, in case one dries up or breaks. A ruler is also sometimes useful.

An essential rule for effective note-taking is to ensure that you know the names of all taking part. Also, to assist you in identifying speakers quickly on your pad, you should give each participant a shorthand title:

CH = Chairperson (Sue Parker) JJ = Julie Jackson Pat = Patrick McCoy etc.

Next (and before the discussion or meeting starts), you should mark out your pad like the one in Figure 1.4:

As the example in Figure 1 illustrates, the notepad needs to indicate at its head the nature of the meeting and its date. There is no need to enter the names of all present unless you will be producing the minutes of the meeting (see Chapter 2, page 56), since these are your personal notes.

	NOTES OF STUDENT ASSOC MEETING 23.3.9		
	DISCUSSION TOPIC: IDEAS FOR CHARITY ACTIVITY		
	SPEAKER	MAIN POINTS	MY RESPONSE
	CH	£300 Max funds available Activity date: 8 May Deadline for chosen idea: 30.3.9–	? enough
	JJ	Suggested Pram Race: always popular	Done 2 years ago -diff then get prams
O	Pat	Sponsored Fancy Dress * Three-legged race – round town	? injuries Gd idea tho'

Figure 1.4 **Example of a discussion note-taking pad**

Under the heading, mark out three columns. Note that the first, entitled 'Speakers', needs only to be some 1.5 cms wide, since you will identify speakers with abbreviations. The widest column is the one for detailing the main points successive speakers make. The right-hand column needs to be wide enough to display your immediate responses to points made.

In the example shown above, the note-taker has jotted down, in a very compact way, the chairperson's three main opening points. There is a maximum of £300 in the Student Association's kitty to cover organisational expenses, such as advertising. The charity event will take place on 8 May 199-, and a final decision on the kind of activity has to be made no later than 30 March 199-. Using his experience, the note-taker jots down a quick response as to whether £300 will be enough. Julie Jackson starts off the discussion by proposing a pram race. The note-taker recalls this activity was mounted only two years ago, and that there were problems in obtaining enough prams. Pat McCoy counters with a suggestion for a sponsored three-legged, fancy dress race round the town. The note-taker thinks this could be a good idea, but raises the question of possible injuries to participants – again, perhaps recalling previous experience.

When the note-taker finds an opportunity to speak, he or she has a most useful prompt in the form of the outline notes taken. Referring to them with quick eye-flicks, the contribution may take this form:

> Chair, going back to your opening remarks, and thinking back to the costs of last year's charity event, I do wonder whether £300 is enough to generate a good response from the community. Also, though Julie's right in saying that pram races are always popular, we did mount one only two years ago. Moreover, I remember we had an awful problem in getting enough of those prams large enough to contain our masculine lumps! However, I do support Pat's idea of a sponsored race round the town. At lunch-time we should get lots of support. My only worry is about possible injuries if people get carried away, or start elbowing each other ...

The above example illustrates how the note-taker is able to pick out quickly the points to make from the notes, and to expand them in an extempore way. Did you notice that the note-taker was tactful in disagreeing with Julie's point, partly by agreeing about the popularity and also by adding some light-heartedness to the point about large prams and heavy male students? Also, by deliberately not referring to a *three-legged* sponsored race, the door is left open for an alternative type of race to be suggested, which might prove safer. Lastly, outline notes are made easier to read quickly if some use is made of symbols such as bold asterisks and wavy lines denoting key points which catch the eye.

CHARITY EVENT IDEAS

IS £300 ENOUGH FUNDING? NB COSTS FOR LAST YEAR

DID PRAM RACE ONLY 2 YRS AGO PROBS GETTING ENOUGH BIG PRAMS

SPONS. 3-LEGGED FANCY DRESS RACE ROUND TOWN-

- GOOD IDEA - ESPECIALLY IF RUN LUNCH-TIME
- BUT WHAT ABOUT INJURIES IN EXCITEMENT?

NB: SUPPORT PAT BUT OPT FOR SAFER TYPE OF RACE

Figure 1.5 **Example of handwritten discussion notes**

Sometimes, in long-winded discussions, it may prove possible to condense outline notes into an ordered set of points before speaking, as the example in Figure 1.5 illustrates. Notice the use of shortcut abbreviations (YRS, NB, SPONS, PROBS, etc.) and the use of underlining of key points. Note also that the notes are set down in capital letters for quick reading while speaking.

CHECKLIST

Useful abbreviations and symbols for use in outline notes

Abbreviations

EG	for example
NB	note particularly
IE	that is
ASAP	as soon as possible
EXCL	excluding
YR(LY)	year (yearly)
PA	per annum, per year (each year)

Symbols

*	of especial note/importance
@	approximately
✓	agree, yes, support etc.
X	disagree, no, oppose, etc.

+	and, plus, in addition
−	minus, from, less
?	I doubt, not sure, is this true? etc.
∴	therefore, and so, this means, etc.
=	this is the same as, equals, means, etc
( )	inside these brackets is a minor or sub point
←↑→↓	this leads to, results in, is linked to, etc.
<u>underlining</u>	used for emphasis

The key techniques for effective outline note-taking, then, are:

- Identify clearly (using an abbreviation) who said what point.
- Jot down only essential points in capital letters – sometimes as single words – to act as memory joggers, e.g. £300, ? INJURIES etc., or express a key point in a very short three or four word phrase, e.g. GD IDEA THO', and use abbreviations whenever possible, e.g. GD, THO', YR. But *never* use abbreviations you make up on the spot and will not recognise instantly!
- Make use of emphasising symbols like ✓ * ~ = to help make key words hit your eye
- Use linking symbols as a shorthand way of connecting two or more entries on your note sheet: → ↱ ↘
- If possible, and especially in connection with a discussion item important to you, try to make a quick copy of your main notes points (see Figure 1.5) in a logical sequence.
- When referring to your notes while speaking, be sure to keep eye contact with your audience, and flick your eyes only briefly to your notes.

KEY POINT

Feeding back is most important

At work, you may be involved in a discussion or meeting where something is discussed or where a decision is taken which is of interest to, or affects other colleagues in your department or unit. In such instances, it is important to write up a full and clear version of your notes as soon as possible afterwards. Your line manager will certainly welcome such timely support and your co-workers should also be grateful for being kept in the picture. But remember what is and what is not confidential information, and think carefully whether a written or oral briefing would be more appropriate for your manager.

WHAT DO YOU THINK?

1 What tips can you provide on taking effective notes quickly?

2 Can you suggest any alternative ways of setting out notes of discussions?

3 Can you think of any additional shorthand abbreviations or symbols which could be useful when taking notes?

4 Why is it important to keep eye contact with an audience when speaking from notes?

5 Can you suggest, with three points for each, why taking notes during discussions helps a person either to support or oppose other speakers more effectively?

SUMMARY OF KEY POINTS

How to take notes in discussions

The ability to take outline notes rapidly during discussions is most helpful, since they can be used as ready prompts when it is your turn to speak.

- Taking effective notes requires you to organise beforehand your notepad, pens and documents for rapid access and use.
- Also before the discussion starts, you should jot down the abbreviated versions you will use for all the participants in the discussion, and divide your notepad into three vertical sections as shown in Figure 1.4.
- Your outline notes should be made up quite simply of one to three word entries of key numbers, dates, facts, who was speaking, and your initial responses.
- If time allows, it is helpful to draw up a separate cue card of points in a sequence which you wish to make when it is your turn to speak (see Figure 1.5, and also Chapter 4, page 260).
- Also, it is helpful to use regularly a set of abbreviations and symbols which serve instead of longer expressions and thus save time (see pages 48 and 49).
- Use your outline notes as a ready prompt to refer to as you make your own contribution.

SELF-CHECK REVIEW TEST

How to take notes in discussions

1 Why is it helpful to create abbreviations for the names of the people taking part in a discussion?

2 Outline briefly how a notepad should be designed in order to make rapid outline notes.

3 How should a speaker use the outline notes produced during a discussion?

4 What do the following stand for: ie, pa, excl. ?

5 For what do these symbols stand when used in notes: @ ( ) ← ?

6 What symbols could you use to emphasise something you have written in your notes?

When you have completed the above questions, turn to page 300 to check the answers provided with your own. If need be, revise the appropriate section of Chapter 1 if you got an answer wrong.

How discussions and meetings are run

Discussions at work take place in a wide variety of situations:

- during meetings of boards of directors or trustees, which are run according to legal rules and follow formal procedures
- during meetings of organisational committees, which may be run according to established customs
- in departments, either as departmental or section meetings, which are more informally run, but where the 'pecking order' of staff has an influence on how discussions are conducted
- started spontaneously, as the result of a sudden crisis or problem occurring; such meetings are usually very informal with no pre-set procedures or rules
- brainstorming discussions which are deliberately kept flowing by barring objections, rejections or criticisms; these discussions are intended to promote the creation of new ideas for products and services or solutions to problems, etc.

As you can see from the above list, the ways in which discussions are held at work vary enormously. In the more formal ones, such as meetings of boards of directors or committees, some members carry out specific roles, such as chairperson or secretary, and such meetings have their discussions recorded in the form of circulated minutes (a written record of what decisions are made, and sometimes of who said what).

Figure 1.6 illustrates the range of meetings listed above.

It helps to understand the reasons why some meetings are formally held, with their business recorded, if the responsibilities of their main players are outlined:

- **Board of directors/trustees meetings**: The meetings of private and public limited companies, as well as charitable organisations, are controlled by Act of Parliament. As a result, directors and trustees are legally responsible for ensuring that their meetings are conducted according to legal rules, ensuring, for example, that all participants receive a notice of the meeting so many days ahead of it, and keeping an accurate record of proceedings in a bound book (to avoid pages being changed at a later date, etc.)

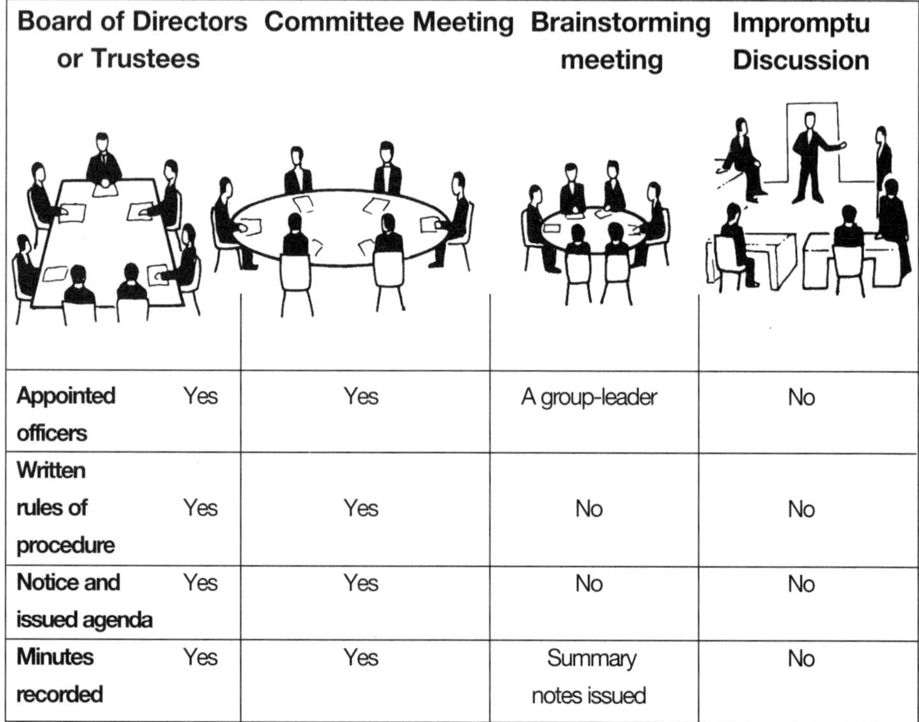

	Board of Directors or Trustees	Committee Meeting	Brainstorming meeting	Impromptu Discussion
Appointed officers	Yes	Yes	A group-leader	No
Written rules of procedure	Yes	Yes	No	No
Notice and issued agenda	Yes	Yes	No	No
Minutes recorded	Yes	Yes	Summary notes issued	No

Figure 1.6 **Range of meetings at work**

- **Committee meetings**: Committees are formed both in work and social or sports organisations to administer activities and to make decisions. Such committees outside the workplace tend to allocate the following roles to members either by election or appointment:

  Chairperson   Vice-Chair   Secretary   Treasurer

  Each of these officers undertakes a specific range of responsibilities (see Figure 1.7 on page 54) to enable the committee to work effectively. Also, the committees of social and sports clubs usually has a **written constitution** (a set of rules of procedure) which has to be kept to during committee meetings. Such a constitution may, for instance, indicate how many members have to be present for a meeting to start, and whether the chairperson can cast a second vote if the committee is deadlocked over a decision, etc.

- **Brainstorming meetings**: Many organisations encourage their employees to contribute ideas and suggestions for improvements and new products, etc. If brainstorming meetings are held, they deliberately have few if any procedures, other than requiring someone to lead the discussion and someone (outside the discussion group) to take notes. Normally, no one is permitted to contradict another, nor to 'put down' any suggestion. It is hoped that in a free and supportive atmosphere, every now and then, someone may hit upon a brilliant new idea.

- **Impromptu meetings**: Impromptu means *without prior warning or arrangement*. Often, a departmental head may pass a desk in the departmental office, and start a conversation with a member of staff which develops informally into a group discussion among surrounding staff. Such discussions are neither pre-planned nor anticipated. They usually occur as a result of some immediate and pressing problem or situation. Such meetings are conducted without any written rules or records being kept. The only thing that governs them is the sense among the group members of what may or may not be said, and if said, in what manner, according to the culture or usual ways in which people relate to each other in the organisation.

The documents which support meetings and discussions

To employ the spoken word effectively in meetings and discussions, it is important to be familiar with the documents which are produced to support them, and to know what their purposes are, as well as the courtesies which relate to them.

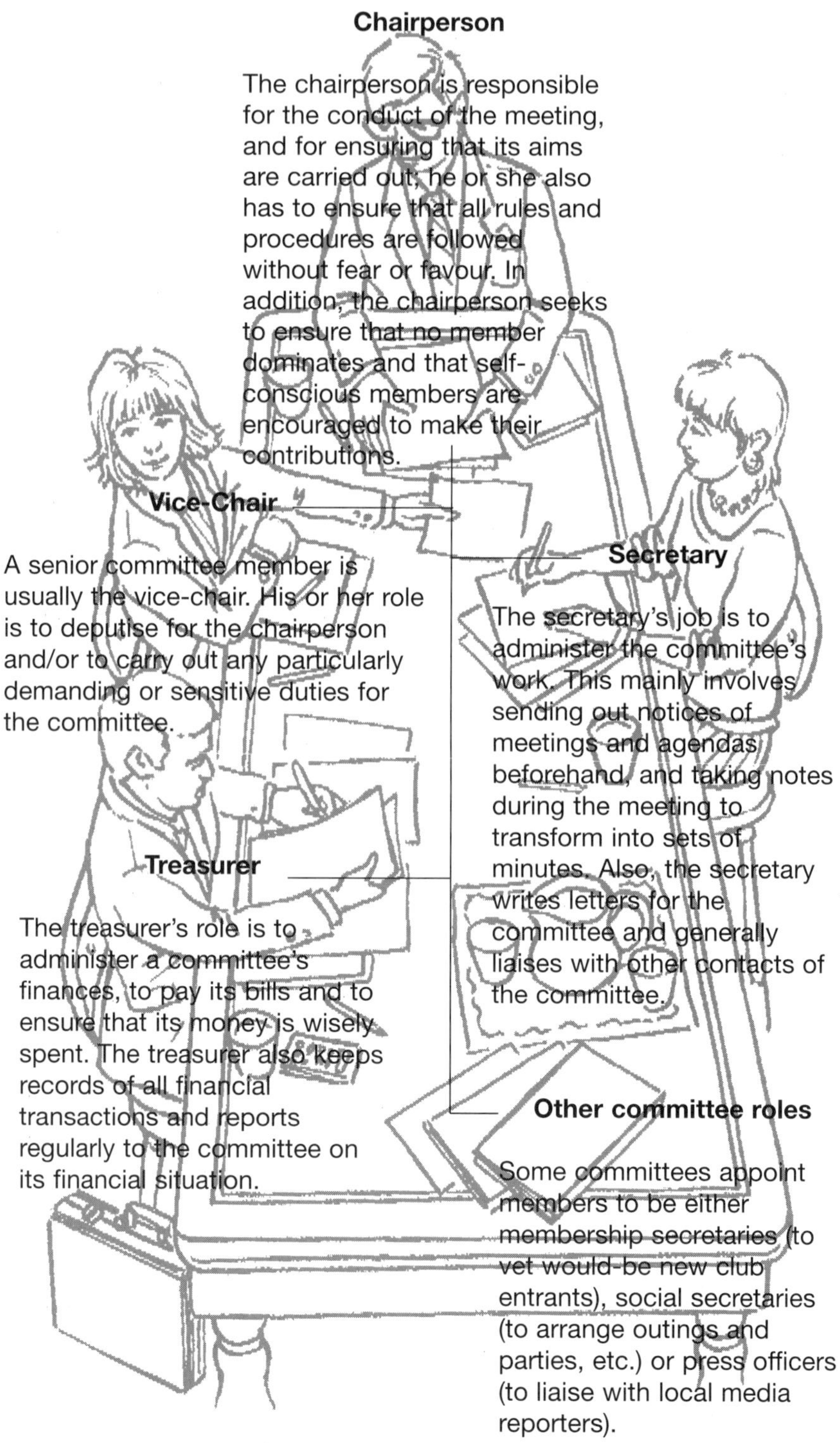

Chairperson
The chairperson is responsible for the conduct of the meeting, and for ensuring that its aims are carried out; he or she also has to ensure that all rules and procedures are followed without fear or favour. In addition, the chairperson seeks to ensure that no member dominates and that self-conscious members are encouraged to make their contributions.
Vice-Chair
A senior committee member is usually the vice-chair. His or her role is to deputise for the chairperson and/or to carry out any particularly demanding or sensitive duties for the committee.
Secretary
The secretary's job is to administer the committee's work. This mainly involves sending out notices of meetings and agendas beforehand, and taking notes during the meeting to transform into sets of minutes. Also, the secretary writes letters for the committee and generally liaises with other contacts of the committee.
Treasurer
The treasurer's role is to administer a committee's finances, to pay its bills and to ensure that its money is wisely spent. The treasurer also keeps records of all financial transactions and reports regularly to the committee on its financial situation.
Other committee roles
Some committees appoint members to be either membership secretaries (to vet would-be new club entrants), social secretaries (to arrange outings and parties, etc.) or press officers (to liaise with local media reporters).

Figure 1.7 **Roles and responsibilities of committee members**

The notice of meeting

This may take the form of a postcard, letter, A5/A4 schedule or email message, which is sent out to members to confirm the date, time and place of a meeting. Remember that if you are unable to attend a meeting because of a prior appointment or more pressing need, you must always send your apologies for absence to either the secretary or meeting caller. Sometimes a phone call is sufficient, sometimes a letter is the correct means.

The agenda

Agendas are simply checklists of the items which make up the business which the meeting will discuss. They usually keep to a traditional 'top and tail' set of entries, with the middle items being descriptions of the individual items for discussion, as in Figure 1.8.

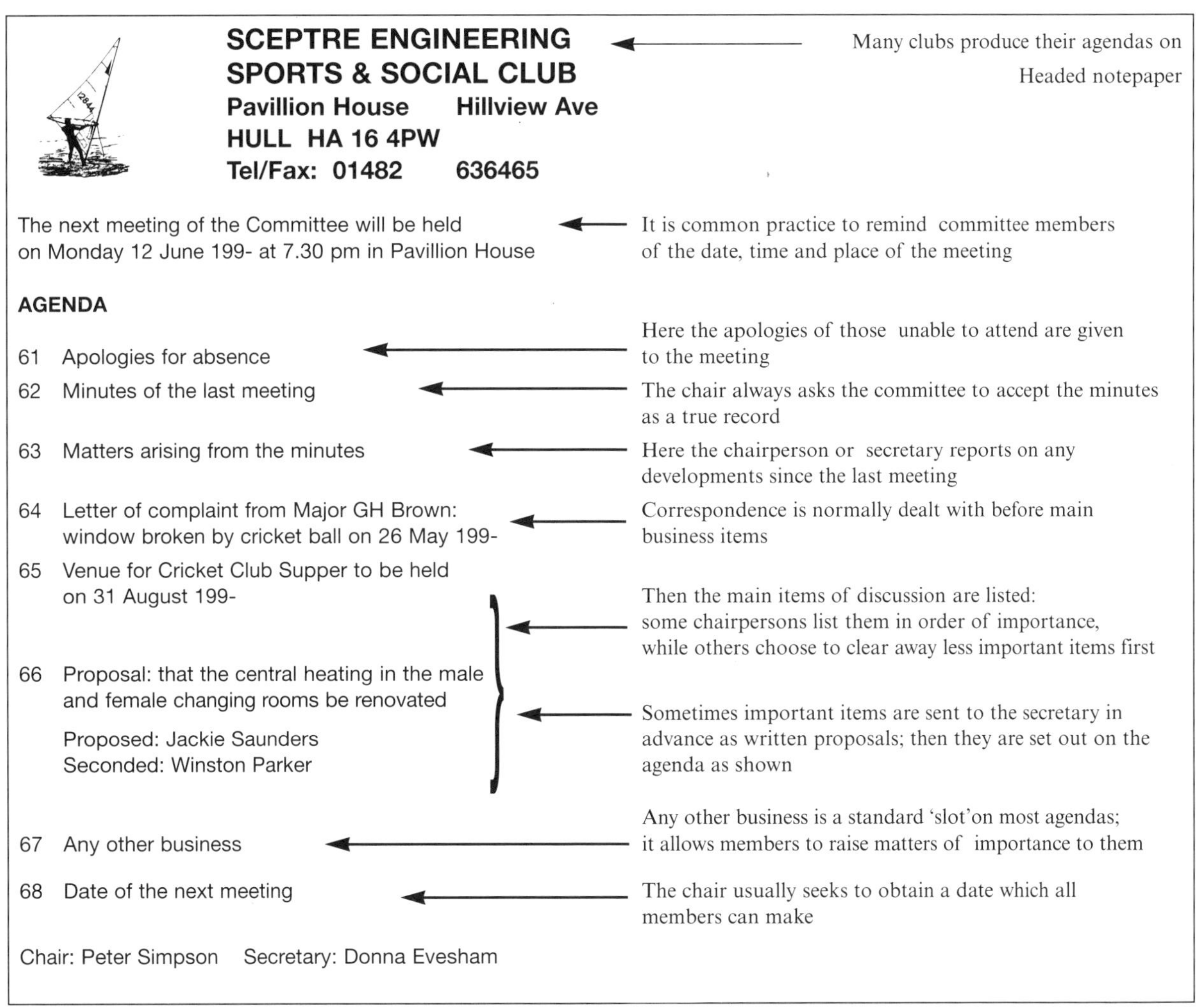

SCEPTRE ENGINEERING
SPORTS & SOCIAL CLUB
Pavillion House Hillview Ave
HULL HA 16 4PW
Tel/Fax: 01482 636465
Many clubs produce their agendas on Headed notepaper
The next meeting of the Committee will be held on Monday 12 June 199- at 7.30 pm in Pavillion House
It is common practice to remind committee members of the date, time and place of the meeting
AGENDA
61 Apologies for absence
Here the apologies of those unable to attend are given to the meeting
62 Minutes of the last meeting
The chair always asks the committee to accept the minutes as a true record
63 Matters arising from the minutes
Here the chairperson or secretary reports on any developments since the last meeting
64 Letter of complaint from Major GH Brown: window broken by cricket ball on 26 May 199-
Correspondence is normally dealt with before main business items
65 Venue for Cricket Club Supper to be held on 31 August 199-
Then the main items of discussion are listed: some chairpersons list them in order of importance, while others choose to clear away less important items first
66 Proposal: that the central heating in the male and female changing rooms be renovated
Proposed: Jackie Saunders
Seconded: Winston Parker
Sometimes important items are sent to the secretary in advance as written proposals; then they are set out on the agenda as shown
67 Any other business
Any other business is a standard 'slot'on most agendas; it allows members to raise matters of importance to them
68 Date of the next meeting
The chair usually seeks to obtain a date which all members can make
Chair: Peter Simpson Secretary: Donna Evesham

Figure 1.8 **Example of an agenda for a committee meeting**

Many committee secretaries produce two versions of an agenda, one for the committee members, and another for the chairperson. Both contain the same business items, but the secretary makes notes on the chairperson's agenda about recent developments, reminders of past decisions or strongly-held views of certain members, etc. These guidelines help the chairperson to run a successful and conflict-free meeting.

The minutes

Different types of committee or meeting adopt different ways of producing the written record of what took place. Many boards of directors' minutes leave out everything except what was decided:

> **123 Expansion into Mainland Europe**
>
> The board decided to support the proposal to open three branches in mainland Europe before the end of 199-, in Paris, Brussels and Berlin.

Such minutes are called **resolution** minutes, since they only record what was resolved (decided). Most social and sports club committees, as well as some in a work organisation, include a summary of the main points of discussion which precede a decision:

> **7. Charity Event to be held on 8 May 199-**
>
> The chair informed the committee that the date for the Charity Event had been confirmed as 8 May 199-. She went on to state that a maximum budget of £300 was available from Association funds. The final decision on what type of event to mount was needed by 30 March 199-. A full discussion ensued, in which Miss Julie Jackson put forward the idea of another pram race. Francis Dickens thought that it was too soon after the one held two years ago, and that large prams were difficult to come by. Mr Pat McCoy suggested a fancy dress, three-legged race around the town centre. There was general support for this idea, but it was eventually considered to be too dangerous, given the excitement which would be generated. Miss Lata Patel proposed that the town race take the form of a giant egg and spoon race, also in fancy dress. This proposal was generally accepted, and the chair undertook to liaise with college management in order to take the proposal forward.

As you can see from the above example, this type of minutes – called **narrative** minutes – compresses a discussion which may have taken some 15–20 minutes into a short paragraph. It is also written in reported speech, a means of expressing factually what took place in a meeting now in the past. Note: the term 'narrative' means 'telling a story', which is what this form of minutes does (see also Figure 1.9).

SCEPTRE ENGINEERING SPORTS & SOCIAL CLUB
Pavillion House Hillview Ave
HULL HA 16 4PW
Tel/Fax: 01482 636465

MINUTES OF THE COMMITTEE MEETING OF 12 JUNE 199-

Minutes	Notes
61 Apologies for absence Apologies for absence were received from Jim Baker and Melanie Young.	Note that many sets of minutes are numbered consecutively for ease of reference
62 Minutes of the last meeting The chair signed the minutes as a true and faithful record after the error in the date of the soccer fixture with Grantham Works Club had been rectified.	Note that if any errors are detected, then the Committeee must agree on what entries to make to correct them; only then can the minutes be signed
63 Matters arising from the minutes The Dog & Duck has confirmed that it could accommodate 36 people for supper on 31 August 199- but would require a firm booking	This item illustrates how information received between meetings is minuted
64 Letter from Major GH Brown The chair asked the secretary to write a letter of apology to Major Brown and to enclose a cheque to cover the cost of repairs and to pay for a bunch of flowers for Mrs Brown.	Some items, like this one, can be dealt with promptly, while others (see below) are discussed at length
65 Venue for the Cricket Club Supper After a lengthy discussion, in which the merits of The Bull, The Angel Hotel and the Dog & Duck were discussed, it was decided to opt for the Dog & Duck, after a vote was taken. The secretary undertook to make the booking.	Some secretaries keep the length of narrative minutes short by not going into the fine details of who said what
66 Proposal to renovate the changing rooms' central heating Jackie Saunders emphasised the bitterly cold conditions in the changing room last winter. Winston Parker reminded the Committee that the club lost several members who complained about the cold and the tepid shower water. The Treasurer advised the committee that there were insufficient funds to renew the system. After a wide-ranging debate, it was decided to seek three estimates for upgrading the system, which the treasurer undertook to obtain.	However, when a formal proposal is made, as here, a secretary may decide that it is important to identify who said what in case of any future problems or disagreements
67 Any other business There was no other business.	AOB items are normally kept short and sweet by the chair, and some committees omit this item completely
68 Date of the next meeting The date of the next meeting was scheduled for Tuesday 14 July 199– at 7.30 pm in Pavillion House.	It is much easier to obtain a consensus date during a meeting than afterwards

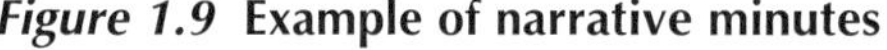

Figure 1.9 **Example of narrative minutes**

As you have probably realised by now, chairpersons and discussion leaders need to possess developed people skills. They must become a cross between a judge, referee, psychologist and football coach! Effective leaders tend to get to know the personalities of their members in order to anticipate likely reactions. They also become expert in reading body language, again to anticipate how participants are thinking and reacting. Needless to say, people in a group-leading role need to be especially good with words, so as to be able to pour oil on troubled waters, to impose a stamp of authority or to encourage people to open up.

WHAT DO YOU THINK?

1 Why do you think some meetings are governed by extensive sets of rules and procedures, but others not?

2 Do you think it better to have officers like chairperson, secretary and treasurer in a committee for at least a year at a time; or would it be better to rotate these posts – say every two or three months?

3 Can you see any dangers arising when no written records are made and circulated after meetings or discussions are held?

4 Some cynical people say that all the important decisions are likely to have been made before a meeting or discussion takes place. What do you think they are driving at?

5 'The best committee is a committee of one!' What criticism of meetings lies behind this statement?

6 Why bother to send out a meeting agenda in advance to members?

7 Can you see any advantages of using narrative minutes to record a meeting's business, as opposed to resolution minutes?

8 Why is so much store set on ensuring that minutes are accurate?

9 Can you think of any reason why some committee chairpersons do not allow Any Other Business items? What would be your own position?

10 What do you see as the role and responsibilities of the ordinary member of a committee who does not hold an office?

SUMMARY OF KEY POINTS

How discussions and meetings are run

Meetings and discussions at work are run according to a wide range of procedures, either more or less formally.

- Some formal meetings have to abide by extensive rules and procedures which are drawn up to ensure fairness, honesty and accuracy. Others are run much less formally, with no printed agendas or minutes to provide advance information or written records.
- Different types of meetings include: board of directors, committee, brainstorming and impromptu.
- The main officers of a committee are: the chairperson, vice-chair, secretary and treasurer; other posts may include membership secretary, social secretary and press-officer.
- an agenda is a printed list of the items which are due to be discussed at a meeting. Agendas are sent to members and, in more detail, to the chairperson.
- Minutes are a set of printed summaries of what was said and decided at a meeting. Some sets of minutes (resolution) only set down the decisions arrived at. Others (narrative) include also summaries of who said what in the run-up to a decision.

SELF-CHECK REVIEW TEST

How discussions and meetings are run

1 List three reasons why discussions take place at work.

2 List two types of meeting which keep written records.

3 Explain how a brainstorming meeting works and what it is used for at work.

4 Outline briefly the duties of a) a chairperson b) a secretary and c) a treasurer.

5 What does the word 'impromptu' mean in connection with meetings?

6 What is the purpose of an agenda?

Continues ▶

7 Explain simply the difference between resolution and narrative minutes.

8 What is the purpose of the agenda business item: 'Minutes of the last meeting'?

9 Why does a chairperson sign and date the minutes of a meeting?

10 What is the purpose of the business item 'Any other business'?

When you have completed the above questions, turn to page 300 to check the answers provided with your own. If need be, revise the appropriate section of Chapter 1 if you got an answer wrong.

The art of active listening

Chapter 1 has so far concentrated on a number of aspects of the spoken word at work. However, no examination of the use of oral communication would be complete without looking carefully into the skills of active listening. Many are the exasperated employees who condemn their bosses by saying:

> The trouble with him is, he never *listens!* Too wrapped up in what *he* wants to say next!

And it is a fact that many people, particularly those who become used to being in charge and issuing instructions or orders, lose the ability over time actually to hear and take in what others are saying, or are trying to say:

> Yes, yes, but what *I* think we need to do is . . .
>
> No, no, Let *me* tell you how we'll solve the problem.

Naturally enough, everyone prefers to take the limelight, to be the one with the good ideas, to dominate others in conversation or discussion. Yet no one has a monopoly of the truth or of wonderful solutions to problems. Wise people, the ones who climb organisational ladders quickly, realise how important it is to acquire active listening skills, because:

- listening to others helps to build team relationships; others warm to those who are genuinely interested in what contributions they have to make

- important facts, suggestions and ideas may affect a listener's views, and thus help him or her to avoid making a mistake, or overlooking a key point
- many heads are better than one; when all members of a group are listened to, it is more likely that good ideas or suggestions may emerge
- careful and concentrated listening (allied to body language observation) enables a listener to get more out of what someone is saying, including hidden messages revealed, for example in what words are given emphasis, and what a person *does not say*
- active listening also enables the listener to remember more of what another says, and for a longer period of time

The above list clearly demonstrates the advantages of adopting an active listening approach, but exactly how is this acquired?

CHECKLIST

Guide to active listening skills

1 Find a seat from which you can see and hear all likely speakers clearly.

2 Make sure notepad and pen are to hand.

3 Watch and listen carefully to the mix of body language and sequence of words of a speaker as they unfold. The two together often indicate very clearly those aspects which the speaker considers most important, as well as those he or she agrees or disagrees with.

4 Note down key points as they are delivered. This firstly helps you to keep your concentration, and secondly to install them in your long-term memory.

5 Ask questions. Do not be afraid to interrupt with a request for further details or for a point to be repeated. If you lose your hold on the meaning of what is being said, you will then very quickly switch off.

6 Avoid temptations to doodle or to start to talk to a neighbour or to watch a gardener outside, etc. Once you have lost a part of someone's delivery, the rest of what is said is likely to become difficult to follow. Also, you will be displaying discourtesy which could affect how others regard you.

7 If need be, ask encouraging questions if a speaker appears to be faltering, so as to show that you have been taking an interest.

8 Use your notes to refresh your mind on what someone actually said, so as to base your responses on fact rather than assertion.

SMALL GROUP SKILLS-BUILDING ACTIVITIES

Developing active listening skills

Task 1 As an individual, and with the help of your teacher, arrange to record a radio programme during the next working week. You should choose a programme which is factual and, ideally, about a work-related topic. All in all, your tape recording should last between 7 and 10 minutes, and should have a clear beginning to it so that your team members can readily grasp what it is about. Note: you may need to give your tape a short, explanatory introduction.

Prior to playing your tape back, you must devise some ten questions about its content, which would suitably check on how well someone else had listened to it and absorbed its main points.

Then, you should play your tape back to the other members of your team, who are to listen to it actively and make any notes they wish. However, they are not allowed to confer at any time. When the tape has finished, ask them each a question in turn to test their active listening skills, and decide who did best.

Task 2 Your class should divide into groups of students, making sure there is an even number of groups. In turns, each group should conduct a discussion lasting some 7–10 minutes. Any of the discussion topics on page 108 may be used, or a group may select one of the following:

1 All students should be given the opportunity to leave full-time education at sixteen plus, but should also have the cost of the equivalent of two years' full-time education credited to them, so that they can 'spend' it at any future point in time, when they have a clearer idea of what vocational path they wish to follow.

2 What is the point of all these technological advances if they result in denying so many people the opportunity to work – ever!?

3 Students and pupils should be given far more say in how they are educated. After all, it is for their future lives, and they only get one go!

While one group is engaged in the discussion, the others should be listening to it actively, making any notes they feel are necessary. At the end of each discussion, and under your teacher's guidance, one of the listening groups should summarise orally the main points that were made. The other listening groups should judge how well the listeners reported back, and whether anything important was missed, etc.

Task 3 After the completion of Tasks 1 and 2, the class should engage in a general discussion on what was learned from them about using active listening skills, and an agreed checklist of key points should be drawn up and copied to each student.

The do's and don'ts of taking part in discussions

This section examines the do's and don'ts of taking part in discussions from the standpoint of an individual participant. It sums up many of the points which have been made in Chapter 1, while adding some additional guidelines on what to aim for and what to avoid. Almost all the points focus on human behaviour and how people react to others, especially in the world of work, with all its unwritten rules and particular forms of employee behaviour.

The do's

In any work involving other people, it always seems much easier to be destructive than constructive:

> We tried that five years ago, and it didn't work then!
>
> Have you even begun to consider how much it would cost?
>
> Produce that design and our competitors will laugh all the way to the bank!

In such ways, initial ideas or suggestions can be torpedoed or stifled at birth by people willing to speak negatively in a convincing way. Therefore the first do is:

1 **Seek as much as possible to be positive and constructive**, and to build on the ideas of others. Aim to be a big enough person to recognise and accept a good idea – even if you did not think of it yourself!

Another aspect of human nature is to make assertions, rather than points based on a logical analysis of facts:

> There's no doubt, no doubt at all, that an exhibition of abstract art will go down like a lead balloon in Clacksworth!

Much more notice would be taken of such baseless assertions, if they could cite some supportive facts:

> ... in Clacksworth! The last time we had such an exhibition – Abstract Art of the 1930s I think it was – takings fell by 45% over the fortnight, and admissions fell by 37% on the average weekly total.

The second do, then, is:

2 Firstly, **be aware when others are making assertions** and pretending that they are facts, and secondly, monitor what you say in order to ensure that you base your own conclusions on facts whenever appropriate.

Because of their personalities, some people simply can never wait to get a word in first in any discussion. However, it is often a much better strategy to let others talk first, so as to obtain a clear impression of who is for and who against any discussion topic, and how strong or weak their arguments are. By biding his or her time, a participant is often better able to counter another person's weak arguments and to provide support for an ally, etc. so the third do is:

3 **Remember that it is sometimes better to listen and wait**, so as to 'suss out' the lie of the land before making a contribution.

Remember, too, the advantages which stem from taking outline notes as others speak, so that you have a confidence-building prompt sheet to refer to as you speak. The fourth do, then, is:

4 Develop and **use the skill of outline note-taking** and **use your notes as a prompt** when speaking.

Although not an exact science, keep in mind the value of looking for and interpreting the body language signals of other speakers. Remember that people in discussions 'speak' in ways other than orally, so the fifth do is:

5 **Be on the look out for body language signals** which may help you to gain additional information about people's views and attitudes.

Lastly, prefer to make your points short and sweet. No one listens to people who drone on and on, but a person who speaks clearly, emphatically and briefly makes a much more telling impression. The sixth and last do, then, is:

6 **Keep your points 'short and sweet'**. Many a good point has been lost as a result of long-winded verbal overkill.

The don'ts

This section started by referring to human nature and the behaviour of groups at work. The first and all-important don't is all about human relations – especially when set in a work hierarchy or pecking-order:

1 **Never put someone down in a group discussion**. Avoid at all costs the temptation to make someone look small or ridiculous by pooh-poohing an idea of theirs, by using sarcasm as a verbal weapon, or exposing their lack of knowledge, etc. They will not forget or forgive such behaviour for a very long time, and may work to turn the tables on you at a future meeting!

The next and equally important don't is all about personal self-control. An old but true saying about discussions and self-discipline is: If you lose your temper, then you've already lost the argument! So, don't number two is:

2 **Do not lose your temper, however much you are provoked**. You will embarrass all present and will in any case cease to make your points convincingly.

As has already been demonstrated, it is dangerous to let your mind wander during a discussion. Murphy's Law states that at the precise moment when a participant is day-dreaming, the chairperson will ask him or her to make a contribution (perhaps deliberately). It will do your image no good at all to splutter: Oh, ah, yes, what was the ah question again? Don't number three, then, is:

3 **Do not allow yourself to switch off or become distracted** – either by other participants or external activities:

As we all realise, listening to others with concentration for an extended period of time is by no means easy. However, we also know that others in a discussion have an equal right to make contributions and that they may come up with the odd good idea! So don't number four is:

4 **Don't allow your active listening to deteriorate**. Use the techniques of observing, making notes, asking questions, etc. to help you stay alert and aware of what is being said.

A fifth and important don't is to allow yourself to become a passenger in a discussion. Passengers are essentially lazy. They are quite content to let others do all the thinking, speaking and deciding. In fact some people are so passive at meetings that they might as well not be in attendance for all the difference they make:

5 **Do not become a passive passenger in meetings and discussions**. Your presence means that others think you have a contribution to make. So make sure you make it!

The last don't is to fail to feed back to managers and co-workers after meetings and discussions. Some people at work hoard information. They keep it to themselves and ration it out in small bits. Presumably such employees feel that they enjoy more status and power by keeping information to themselves. What they fail to realise is that all they are doing is causing the organisation to work at a much lower level of effectiveness, because people are being kept in the dark quite needlessly. Of course, some information exchanged at meetings is confidential, but this should not be used as an excuse for becoming a black hole instead of a message relayer:

6 **Resist the temptation to hoard information obtained at meetings or discussions.** The entire reason for your presence at such events may be to act as the representative of others in your department or unit.

KEY POINT

Aim to be part of the solution!

Becoming an effective participant, and eventually leader, in a meeting or discussion takes a lot of practice. Some people are natural extroverts – they love to be in the limelight and to hog proceedings. Others are much more self-conscious and retiring. So, get to know what your weaknesses are and aim to overcome them. Also, as with many other aspects of working with others to achieve an organisation's aims, keep this thought at the front of your mind whenever you take part in a discussion: *Am I creating part of the problem, or part of the solution here?*

SUMMARY OF KEY POINTS

The do's and don'ts of taking part in discussions

Taking part effectively in discussions is all about understanding how people tend to behave when working in groups and also when working within the hierarchic structure of most organisations.

Do:

- seek to be positive, not negative, and creative, not destructive. Aim to build on the ideas and suggestions of others, rather than to demolish them in favour of your own.
- learn to spot the difference between bold assertion and true facts. Try to ensure that your own contributions do not rely solely on stating your views or prejudices, but use facts to support them.
- develop the habit of patient listening before speaking. It is often better to let others have their say first, so as to be in a better position to counter their arguments or to support them.
- get into the habit of making rapid, outline notes and using them to support you when you speak yourself.
- keep an eye out for informative body language signals, and remember to make use of them when you yourself speak.
- make your points short and sweet rather than long and tedious. You will sound much more expert and people will remember better what you say.

Don't

- ever show someone up or put them down in a group meeting. They will resent it strongly even if they do not show it, and you will almost certainly make a long-term opponent.
- ever lose your temper. Not only will you lose the ability to speak fluently, but you will embarrass others and let yourself down – as well as losing your argument.
- allow yourself to become distracted or allow your active listening approach to be put off by neighbours wishing to gossip, or by your drifting into a day-dream, etc. Instead, make notes, ask questions and observe the body language of the others to help stay alert.
- settle for becoming a passive passenger in discussions with nothing to say, and therefore no contribution to make.
- fall into the habit of hoarding information instead of sharing it. Co-workers will soon spot such a habit, and in any case it only tends to show up an insecure person.

SELF-CHECK REVIEW TEST

The do's and don'ts of taking part in discussions

1 What approach to the contributions of others should a participant adopt, and why?

2 What is the difference between making a statement based on facts and making an assertion?

3 Why is it better sometimes to wait and let others speak before delivering a contribution?

4 How can note-taking help a participant to be effective in discussions?

5 How can an interpretation of body language assist someone taking part in a group discussion?

6 Describe two outcomes to be avoided at all costs when taking part in a discussion.

7 What are the likely consequences of becoming distracted in a meeting?

8 What is meant by describing someone as a 'passenger' in a discussion?

9 Why is it bad practice to hoard information gained during a discussion?

Continues ▶

10 What actions can a participant take to help him or her maintain an active listening approach during a discussion?

When you have completed the above questions, turn to page 301 to check the answers provided with your own. If need be, revise the appropriate section of Chapter 1 if you got an answer wrong.

GENERAL GROUP SKILLS – BUILDING ACTIVITY

General group activity

Read this case study carefully and then discuss the questions which follow.

RIGHT! LET'S MAKE A START

The monthly committee meeting of Newtown Social Club. Present Ron Dixon, chairman; Sally Pierce, secretary; Jack Slade; Eileen Johnston; John Turner; Peter Smith; Pauline Osgood.

CHAIRPERSON: Right! Let's make a start then! Jack, if you're ready . . . Oh, you haven't got an agenda . . .? No, I know, we were a bit late getting them out. Sally, have you got a spare? Oh, well perhaps you could share with Pauline? Good. Right. Apologies for absence. Fred Kemp can't make it. His wife's mother's come down with a nasty bout of 'flu in Leeds, and he's had to drive her up there, though, as he said, the car's not really up to it . . .

SALLY PIERCE: (secretary): (breaking in) I think everyone's received a copy of the minutes, Ron.

CHAIRPERSON: Ah, right. Anyone see anything amiss?

EILEEN JOHNSTON: Well, it would be nice to see my name spelled right, if only once!

SALLY PIERCE: Oh, sorry! My fault again!

CHAIRPERSON: Well, if you're all happy with the minutes, I take it I can sign them as a true record . . .

JACK SLADE: No, hang on Mr Chairman, I'd like to go back on the discussion we had on the annual coach trip to London next month. As I said, I think we should include a stop at Kew Gardens . . . very educational and the admission's very reasonable.

PETER SMITH: Mr Chairman! Surely we're not going all through that again! I thought we'd made the arrangements at the last meeting . . .

CHAIRPERSON: Yes, well Jack, I think we'll have to stick to what we decided. Perhaps next year . . . Now, Matters Arising . . .

JOHN TURNER: I looked into the possibility of our booking the St Mark's church hall for the jumble sale next month but they're already booked for the 25th, so I spoke to Peter who said he would check on St Paul's with the vicar.

PETER SMITH: Oh, er, well, I've been pretty busy at the office lately . . . I'll get on to it straight after the meeting. (whispering to John) Thanks a lot, mate!

Continues ▶

JOHN TURNER: (whispered reply) Sorry! I assumed you'd already found out! CHAIRPERSON: Item Number Three, resignation of Mr Harris, bar steward. I'm sorry to have to report that Charlie's resigned and that we won't have a bar open next week unless we find a replacement as a matter of urgency . . . PAULINE OSGOOD: I didn't know Charlie'd resigned! JACK SLADE: Yes, walked out in a huff I heard. Fed up with the way some members treated him! PAULINE OSGOOD: Well, I'm not surprised. Take that Mrs Hitchcock, for example. Always pushing in at the bar with her 'My good man . . .'	SALLY PIERCE: Why don't we approach Mr Rowbottom? He's retired now but still pretty active. He might be glad of a job. JACK SLADE: What, George Rowbottom! You must be joking! I remember when he used to help out at the Dog and Duck. Hundreds of 'em laid out on the grass, dying of thrist! SALLY PIERCE: All right! You think of someone, then! JACK SLADE: Now there's no need to get hoighty toighty with me, Miss Pierce. Just trying to make a constructive remark, that's all! CHAIRPERSON: Well, perhaps we'd better move on to Item Four, Renewal of the Curtains in the Club Room . . .

(Reproduced from D W Evans, *Effective Business Administration and Communication*, Addison Wesley Longman, 1992)

1 What shortcomings in the way the meeting is administered can you detect?

2 What does Jack Slade try to do when the meeting is discussing the item: *Minutes of the last meeting*?

3 Was Peter Smith right to have become annoyed with John Turner?

4 What do you make of Pauline Osgood's and Jack Slade's response to *Item Number Three: Resignation of Mr Harris, bar steward*?

5 How do you rate the chairperson, Ron Dixon?

Message taking and giving face-to-face and over the phone

The main focus of Chapter 1 has been upon the use of the spoken word in discussions. In addition, the spoken word is often employed at work to pass on messages. In the course of a normal working day, many employees are absent from their desks, workbenches, counters or kitchens. Naturally enough, products and services need to be sold away from the organisation's location, meetings need to be attended and so on. Nevertheless, the business which an organisation builds up continues – and this is where the skills of effective message taking and giving come in.

Spoken word messages in organisations are delivered:

- **face-to-face:** say by a colleague or visitor to the person who is standing in for the absent employee
- **over the phone**: a caller phones in, hoping to speak to the absent employee, but instead has to talk to a substitute
- **via an answerphone message:** a caller may pick up the answerphone message of an absent employee and leave a message; in some organisations, such messages are checked at regular intervals in case of urgency.

In addition, some large and well-equipped organisations may possess a voice-mail facility, which takes in scores of spoken word messages daily and stores them on tape until an employee checks his or her voice-mail box.

The techniques of effective message giving

Giving and taking oral messages is basically straightforward, but simple steps are easily forgotten if the message is urgent or the caller upset, etc. Read the following checklist carefully and absorb each step into your daily routine as a full or part-time employee.

CHECKLIST

How to give effective messages

1 Prepare carefully, *before* entering an organisation's offices, or picking up the telephone. For instance, have details of prices, descriptions, quantities, delivery dates, key person to speak to, etc., to hand before starting to give a message. Bring up any paper files or display any electronic ones before starting. Then you will not waste time or feel foolish by having to find a file in the middle of a conversation.

2 If the message is at all involved and lengthy, write down a set of its key points in a logical order, the most important coming first. Then, as you speak, you can check them off. In this way you will avoid missing any out by accident.

3 If using the telephone, check the number and extension you want carefully. The telephone services estimate that millions of pounds are wasted each year in the UK in misdialling numbers.

4 Seek to speak to your chosen contact, and no one else. We have all wasted precious time explaining complicated messages only to be told at the end:

Continues ▶

Oh, you want Mr Wilson, I'll transfer you!

Before you know it, you have to start all over again!

5 Whoever you speak to, make sure you obtain his or her name, and if need be telephone extension. Some employees hide behind anonymity in order not to have to follow up any requests for action. Moreover, if you fail to obtain a name and have to ring back a week or two later, the first thing another member of staff will ask is:

Who did you speak to?

6 Relay the key points of your message clearly, avoiding gabbling. Repeat important names and numbers without waiting to be asked and give spellings of proper names or unusual words.

7 Emphasise what action needs to be taken and supply a deadline by when you need to have your requests carried out:

I'll need to have your estimate by 7 June 199- at the latest.

8 Ask the message-taker to repeat the main points of the message to you. In this way, you can double-check that it has been correctly received.

9 Remember to thank the person taking your message – especially if it is a substitute for your intended contact.

10 Afterwards, remember a) to log what action was agreed to be taken and by when so as to check out that it has not been overlooked when the time comes b) to keep a note of the name of the person who took your message and c) to put back the documents and files you referred to – you may need to refer to them again.

KEY POINT

Follow-ups are crucial!

If you are the message-taker, do not rely on others to carry out your wishes automatically. It is down to you to monitor and progress-chase any actions promised. So always log the agreed deadline in your diary to act as a memory-jogger. Then you can telephone to ask: *'Hello, I thought I'd call to see when we can expect delivery of .... '*, etc.

The techniques of effective message taking

Taking effective messages is in many ways a mirror-image of giving them. These are the main points to keep in mind:

CHECKLIST

How to take effective messages

1 When at work, always keep a message-pad and pen handy. Scribbled entries on envelopes, cheque-book covers or backs of photocopied documents, etc. nearly always get lost and overlooked. Besides, such practices really are lazy and unprofessional, and will appear so to a visitor or senior executive.

2 Announce who you are at the outset, but do not say exactly what your colleague or manager is doing or where he or she is – it may be confidential, and you have no idea at this stage who the caller is:

Not: Mr Johnson's gone to see his solicitors about the sale of the company. Apparently things are pretty shaky financially. Now how can I help?

But: Mr Johnson is out of the office at the moment. May I take a message?

3 Make it a habit to ensure that, whatever the situation, you obtain this crucial data at the outset:

- name and telephone number (and address if appropriate) of the message-giver, then you can always re-establish contact, say, if you were cut off while on the phone)
- who the message is for, and whether it is urgent

4 When listening to the delivery of the main points of the message, do not feel shy of asking a caller to:

- slow down if speaking too fast
- repeat the last part of the message
- spell a name or word
- repeat numbers of references slowly

Continues ▶

Remember that it is in the caller's best interests to ensure that you take the message down accurately.

5 Use the skills you acquired in making outline notes to aid you in jotting down the main points of the message.

6 When you have taken the message down, ensure you repeat its key points in order to check accuracy and avoid omissions.

7 Thank the message-giver for calling, and assure him or her that you will pass the message on directly.

8 As soon as you are able, and before allowing any other activity to get in your way write out a fair copy of the message and check it carefully for accuracy. Then pass it to its intended recipient's work location. If it is confidential, always ensure you put it in a sealed envelope marked: Confidential. Given the chance, we are all nosey-parkers!

9 Remember to ask the message's recipient as soon as you see him or her if the message has been seen. Do not take it for granted. Take the opportunity of a face-to-face conversation to enlarge the message, stressing its key points.

KEY POINT

Always identify yourself, and smile with your voice!

If you are taking the message over the phone, remember that it is vital to say who you are and what your post is:

'252', Karen Watson speaking, Mr. Patel's assistant. (Pause)

When you finish taking a message – either face-to-face or over the phone – it is important to thank the caller and give your assurances that the message will be passed on promptly. Telephone message-taking is particularly demanding, since a caller cannot see your face. By the same token, clear speaking is essential, as well as the creation of a pleasant and courteous tone.

INCOMING MESSAGE

CONFIDENTIAL ☐ **URGENT** ☑ **FOR YOUR ACTION** ☐ **PLEASE CALL BACK** ☑

TIME: 10.20 AM **DATE:** 12 / 5 / 9-

MESSAGE FOR: MRS GOLDSTONE

MESSAGE FROM: **NAME:** MS J BALL **JOB TITLE** PURCHASE OFFICER
TEL: 0171 123987 **FAX:** 0171 123654
ORGANISATION GLOBAL ELECTRONICS PLC
EUSTON ROAD
LONDON
POST CODE: WCIH EU4

MESSAGE:

Urgently needs to speak to you regarding part of the switch assembly tender – GBL/41624/XK3. Apparently we have missed out a page. Global forgot to include it in the invitation to tender

Ms Ball needs our additions TODAY! All tenders due to be scrutinised tomorrow, 13.5.9-, at 10.00 am.

TAKEN BY: Jimmy O'Connor **EXT:** 2614

Figure 1.10 **Example of a pre-printed message pad**

KEY POINT

Message pads make it easy!

Get into the habit of using the entries of pre-printed message pads like the one in Figure 1.10 to act as prompts while you are taking a message. In this way you will not forget to obtain a key piece of information.

PORTFOLIO BUILDING ACTIVITIES

One-to-one discussions with people familiar to the student and familiar with the subject

Students should take part in the following one-to-one discussions, as the leader of the discussion. Another student, a teacher or supervisor familiar to the student-leader may take on the role of discussion responder (the person who asks questions and prompts the leader as needed).

The discussion leader should be given sufficient opportunity to prepare for two of the following discussions, which should last between 5–7 minutes. The discussion responder should also be given an opportunity to study the topic and to compose questions:

1 What, in your view, could be done to improve further the quality of the information about your GNVQ Foundation course which is sent to students and pupils thinking of enrolling for it?

2 You now possess extensive experience of working as a student in your study centre. How, in your view, could *one* of the following be further improved:

(a) instructions on how to evacuate a room in case of fire or emergency
(b) the way in which students are inducted
(c) guidance on how to get the best out of the library
(d) amenities available to students for sports and social activities
(e) the organisation of the refectory

3 'What changes or additions I would make to my GNVQ programme of study in terms of how it is preparing me for a full-time job.'

4 How I would organise a fund-raising charity event of my choice to be mounted by my department's students.

5 What I learned from my part-time job which will stand me in good stead when I obtain a full-time post.

6 The plus and minus points of the local leisure centre.

7 What our town/city needs to introduce to make the lives of its teenage residents more enjoyable and worthwhile.

8 What I would expect from someone giving me good careers advice.

9 What knowledge and techniques are needed by:

(a) an effective chairperson of a committee meeting

(b) an effective discussion leader

(c) a participant in a discussion who makes an effective contribution

(Select *one* of the above topics.)

10 What women at work have a right to expect and obtain.

Group discussions with people familiar to the student and familiar with the subject

The discussion group may comprise students or a mix of students, teachers, supervisors and work colleagues, etc.

Students for assessment should participate in two of the following discussions, which should last between 7 and 10 minutes. All participants in the group discussion should be given sufficient time to prepare for it and may bring notes to the discussion for reference purposes.

1 What main factors should a teenager keep in mind when selecting a career path to follow?

2 Experts say that young adults today are likely to have to make some three or four major career changes during their working lives. What should be done during their full-time education to help them to prepare for this likelihood?

3 If we are not very careful, in the first decade of the twenty-first century two separate societies will emerge in the UK, one peopled by job-have technocrats and the other by the unskilled and jobless. This could prove to be very dangerous. What should be done – now – to avoid it happening?

4 'A time is not far around the corner when scientists will have perfected the means of providing free energy from the sun, ample food supplies and renewable building materials. People will only have to work if they want to.' Good news, or bad?

5 So far, the state in the UK has managed to provide a basic form of health care and social welfare for its elderly citizens. But statistics show that there are not enough teenagers alive today to earn the money needed to look after the growing number of elderly people who are living much longer and who will survive in much greater numbers from early on in the next century. How can this problem be solved in a way which respects the needs and interests of both the young adults and the elderly people?

6 If the human race is to survive at all, then everyone needs to learn now how to change their lifestyle so they use up far fewer natural resources – especially those which are not renewable! Is this view a pipe-dream, or could it be made to work?

7 'Wherever you turn, whatever you want to do, you'll find a computer system controlling you – at the travel agents, at the bank, at the airport, on the football terraces, in hospital, or driving along a motorway. Bit by bit, our lives are being taken over by faceless people behind computer screens.' True or false? Are computers making or marring our working and personal lives?

8 'Work? I love it! I could stand and watch people doing it for hours!' Why do people work? Is it simply a means to an end – to earn money to live – or would humans be lost without it? What do you think?

9 What, in your view, distinguishes a good organisation to work for from a bad one?

10 If you were a group of directors or trustees of a small work organisation, what skills and qualities would you look for in a person of sixteen plus who applied to you for a full-time post as a support assistant (clerk, operative or sales assistant etc.)?

2 Produce written material

The art of writing is the art of applying the seat of the pants to the seat of the chair.

Mary Heaton Vorse, American writer

What Chapter 2 covers

As the above quotation humorously emphasises, producing written material which is effective is all about getting stuck in and persevering until the writing is right! And so Chapter 2 is devoted to helping you acquire the skills and techniques needed to write effectively at work.

While many business matters are handled in the medium of the spoken word in organisations, it is the written word which is deliberately selected on a number of occasions. Writing is the preferred way of communication when, for example, a long-term record is needed, or a matter needs to be set down in a legal way, or a complex topic needs to be studied and referred to many times.

For these and many other reasons, messages are created and exchanged using the medium of writing and either the paper-based or electronic route for delivery. Chapter 2 examines in detail the skills of writing, from shaping the message into a suitable structure to devising a style for it which will be appropriate for its readers. Keep in mind that not all worthwhile skills can be picked up in a matter of minutes, and take Mary Vorse's excellent advice to heart, as well as the oldie-but-goodie: *Practice makes perfect!*

The main sections of Chapter 2

- Using written documents at work
- Putting written words together – use of English, punctuation and spelling
- How to structure written documents
- How to create formats for written documents
- Creating a suitable style for a document
- How to edit and proof-read a written document

In addition, Chapter 2 includes:

- Sets of discussion topics
- Key tips on good practice
- Opportunities to practise newly acquired skills
- Sets of case studies for discussion and analysis
- Activities for assessment and portfolio building

Using written documents at work

If it is anything, the age we live in is surely the age of the fast response. In all kinds of workplaces, even in buses and on trains, people contact others in a matter of seconds, using either a telephone extension or a mobile phone, or plain, old-fashioned direct word of mouth. So why should a whole chapter of this book be devoted to the written word at work?

As the introduction to Chapter 2 has already outlined, the written word enjoys an important place in the box of communication tools which every efficient worker needs to know how to use well. The following checklist illustrates the main reasons why people at work use the written word in a host of daily routines and tasks.

CHECKLIST

Main uses of the written word at work

- **To set down a written record** of what has been promised, agreed or decided, so that there can be no arguments or misunderstandings at a later date. Examples of such written records include:
  - sales letters supplying details of prices and components
  - estimates and tenders
  - contracts
  - minutes of meetings
  - reports
  - details of personnel employed
- **To inform groups of people in different locations simultaneously:** senior managers in large organisations sometimes need to inform employees in scattered locations about important matters simultaneously, so that rumours do not start or some people feel that they are given second class treatment. Examples of such written messages include:
  - memoranda which make important announcements, say that a sister business has been acquired
  - letters sent out individually to staff offering them a voluntary redundancy package
  - offers to shareholders from an organisation wishing to buy their shares

- **To ensure that a matter is recorded in a way which is legally binding:** many business activities have a legal basis, such as the drawing up of a contract of employment, or an agreement between a firm and its negotiating trade unions on a pay and conditions deal, or an undertaking to purchase products or services. Examples of such legal documents include:
  - *contracts*
  - *tenders*
  - *agreements*
  - *letters of credit (promising to pay a sum on demand)*
  - *detailed planning applications (to build or modify)*
  - *care and section orders (to place a child in care or a mentally ill person into hospital)*
- **To explain a complex set of facts, arguments or alternatives:** some work-related activities are made up of many complicated points which need to be studied carefully in order to arrive at a satisfactory grasp of the whole. Thus employees need to be given data in a form in which it can be picked up, put down, come back to, stored and yet be readily available. Examples of such written documents include:
  - *long reports*
  - *detailed specifications (say for the building of an off-shore oil platform)*
  - *lengthy agreements and contracts*
  - *manuals of instruction (e.g. for a word-processing or spreadsheet package).*
- **To sell or to persuade people to adopt a point of view:** a whole host of written documents are produced in the fields of advertising, selling, public relations and staff motivating. Examples of such written documents include:
  - *sales brochures and catalogues*
  - *advertisements and posters*
  - *news releases*
  - *sales letters*
  - *in-house newspapers and magazines*
  - *memoranda*
  - *bulletins and notices.*

- **To keep a check on administrative processes:** in many organisations, activities take place over extended periods of time, such as selling a product on account. Therefore documents need to be issued and stored which keep track of various processes. Example include:
  - *delivery notes, invoices, statements, agreed discounts offered*
  - *payroll details*
  - *payments made by account customers, etc.*
  - *hours people worked*
  - *quantities of products manufactured*
- **To confirm messages originally delivered via the spoken word:** on a number of occasions, people at work need to supply a written confirmation of what has been promised or agreed by word of mouth. Examples of such documents include:
  - *sales letters*
  - *letters to put right a customer complaint*
  - *job offers*
  - *memoranda to internal staff*

The above list is by no means exhaustive, but it does show clearly the wide range of reasons why people need to produce written material at work. Of course, written material is produced not only as important statements to all staff, but as ordinary, down-to-earth messages written in the course of carrying out a routine task:

Example of a routine, written message

Jack, Mrs Jackson's rung again. She's changed her mind about the bathroom tiles and gone back to her first choice. She would like the Edwardian glazed effect, Model No. CT241 to be delivered by Wednesday noon. Can you ring to confirm? Dannie

Major types of written document used at work

Just as there are many different reasons why the written word is used at work, so there are many different ways of producing it as a document. The chart in Figure 2.1 on page 83 illustrates the main kinds of written document used in the workplace and details some of its main applications.

Figure 2.1 Main types of written word document used at work

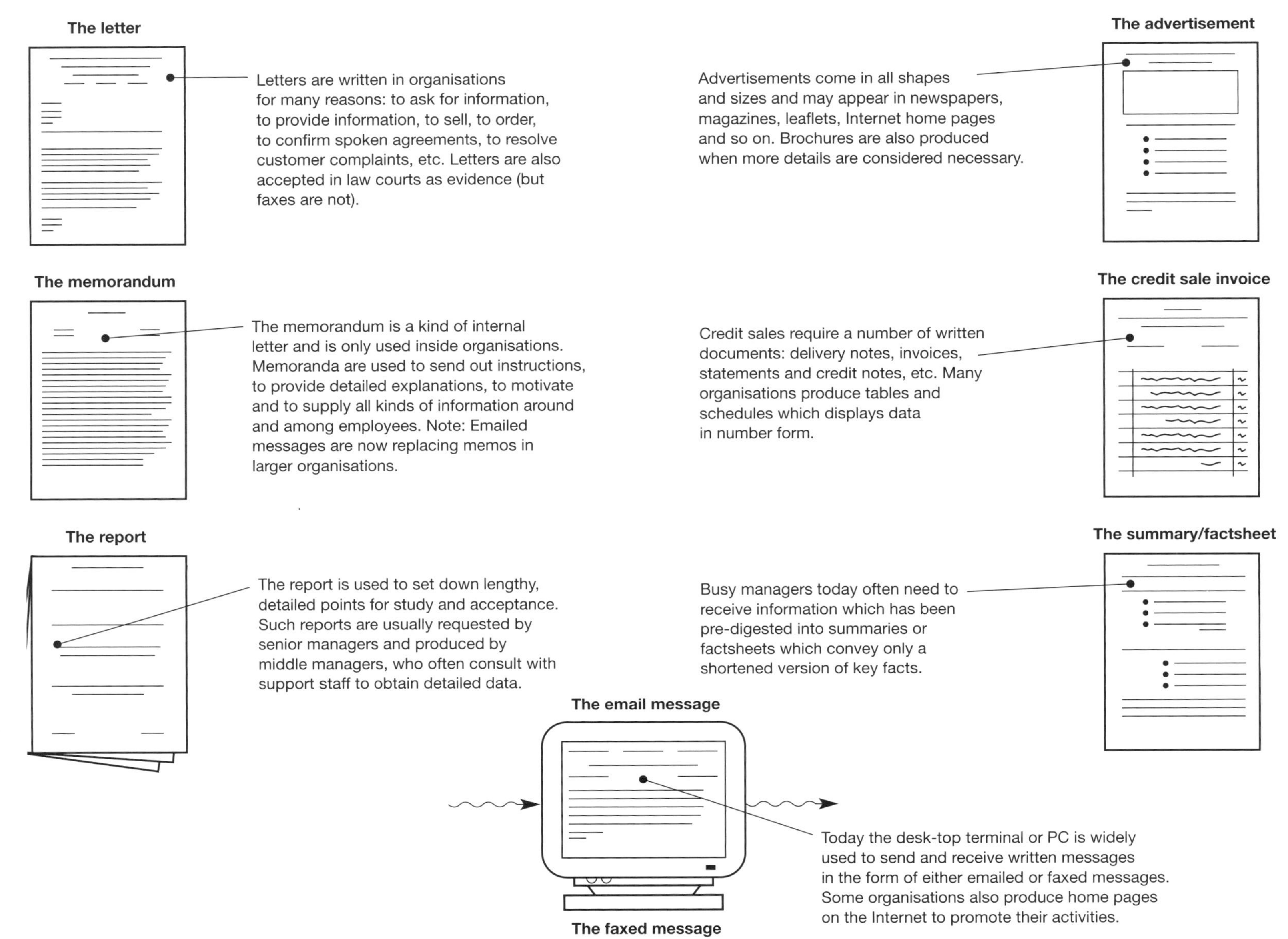

The letter
Letters are written in organisations for many reasons: to ask for information, to provide information, to sell, to order, to confirm spoken agreements, to resolve customer complaints, etc. Letters are also accepted in law courts as evidence (but faxes are not).
The memorandum
The memorandum is a kind of internal letter and is only used inside organisations. Memoranda are used to send out instructions, to provide detailed explanations, to motivate and to supply all kinds of information around and among employees. Note: Emailed messages are now replacing memos in larger organisations.
The report
The report is used to set down lengthy, detailed points for study and acceptance. Such reports are usually requested by senior managers and produced by middle managers, who often consult with support staff to obtain detailed data.
The advertisement
Advertisements come in all shapes and sizes and may appear in newspapers, magazines, leaflets, Internet home pages and so on. Brochures are also produced when more details are considered necessary.
The credit sale invoice
Credit sales require a number of written documents: delivery notes, invoices, statements and credit notes, etc. Many organisations produce tables and schedules which displays data in number form.
The summary/factsheet
Busy managers today often need to receive information which has been pre-digested into summaries or factsheets which convey only a shortened version of key facts.
The email message
The faxed message
Today the desk-top terminal or PC is widely used to send and receive written messages in the form of either emailed or faxed messages. Some organisations also produce home pages on the Internet to promote their activities.

KEY POINT

Seek to suit your style to your reader's needs

When starting to become familiar with the main kinds of written document produced in work organisations, it is all-important to bear in mind that different documents are written for entirely different kinds of reader recipients, which affects both their structure and the style they adopt:

- **customers** expect a friendly, helpful and courteous approach
- **managers** expect short, clearly expressed messages in formats which make them quick and easy to digest
- **external contacts** also expect clearly expressed messages but are also often conscious of their status and sense of importance, and therefore they expect messages to be suitably polite
- **co-workers** are much less likely to stand on ceremony, but do not like to receive messages which effectively 'pass the buck' or which become over-familiar

MOTTO: **Always keep in mind the needs and expectations of your reader**

The format of documents

Not only do written documents vary according to whom they are intended for, they also differ in terms of their appearance. Two terms exist as labels for the appearance of a printed document, which mean the same thing: format and layout. Techniques have evolved in organisations over the years, especially since the arrival of computers, word-processing and desktop-publishing, which enable printed words to be given all kinds of visual effect (see below) and to be supported by various images, especially clip-art (see Chapter 3, page 194).

Basically, how a document is formatted depends upon its purpose. Reports and factsheets, for example, display information in a highly schematised way. The term **schematised** is used to describe the setting out of words on the page. The words might be in bold type, underlined, set towards the right-hand margin or surrounded by white space to make them stand out. A schematic layout helps a reader to grasp lengthy, factual information more easily. Display advertisements also use this technique, together with the use of large text in places to enable selling messages to hit the reader's eye quickly and strongly.

Factors which affect the decision to use the written word

So far, Chapter 2 has concentrated on the main reasons why people use the written word at work and outlined the main forms in which it appears. There are also a number of important factors to be aware of in the workplace which influence whether someone decides to send a message orally, in print, or as a picture or graphic image. In fact, before grabbing for the phone or reaching for the keyboard, the good communicator should always pause to consider:

- What is the nature of the message I want to send?
- Who is it for?
- Is it urgent?
- What is the most cost-effective way of sending it?
- What is the most outcome-effective way of sending it?

Thinking carefully about each of the above questions soon reveals whether or not the printed word is the most suitable medium. For example, if the message is complex and lengthy, then delivering it orally to a group is likely to result in most people soon forgetting most of it. Delivering it as a report is more likely to ensure that the message gets digested, if only a part at a time. Similarly, if the message is for a senior manager, his or her time may be heavily rationed, and so a short summary might prove the best way of getting a message across, since the manager can more easily fit reading it into the daily schedule. But if the message were urgent, then delivering it over the phone or to the manager's answerphone would certainly be more fitting.

Again, if a message is personal and confidential, it would be wrong to deliver it orally in an open office. Either a personal interview in a quiet room is needed, or the message needs to be set down in memorandum form. Also, some messages are simply not right for sending in printed form – except as a confirmation. For instance, a manager always needs to discipline a subordinate face-to-face in the first instance. The same is true when sacking an employee, even if the message is later confirmed by letter.

Not only is time a factor, but so is also the cost of producing and sending the message. For instance, a letter dictated, text-processed and routed to a mailroom for posting in a central office block of a large city organisation is likely to cost between £20 and £30, if all the production costs are truly calculated, including staff time and a proportion of the cost of equipment and materials used. For this reason, faxing printed messages has become a much preferred option. An employee can compose it at a desktop PC and with the help of a modem (often built into stand-alone or networked computers today). This electronic process reduces the costs from pounds to pennies! And, the fax arrives at its destination within a minute or two instead of a day or two.

CHECKLIST

Factors affecting the choice of the written word to send a message

- the nature of the message: long and complicated; not so sensitive as to require a face-to-face meeting
- how available the recipient is (e.g. senior manager)
- the need for confidentiality
- the degree of urgency – both in sending the message and getting a reply
- the need to reach groups of people in remote locations at the same time
- the cost of sending the message
- the need to keep a written record of the message, and/or the need to use a legally accepted medium

Information technology and the written word

The massive expansion of computer systems in work organisations since 1981 has completely changed the ways in which the written word is produced at work. Long gone are the mechanical typewriters of the 1960s, and indeed also their golf-ball and daisy wheel successors of the 1970s.

The invention of the microchip and the skills of electronic engineers have made possible a rapid series of developments in communications equipment and systems.

Today, written word messages can be composed at the keyboard and electronically edited and amended on screen by any trained employee. The need for the shorthand typist has disappeared from most offices and organisations. The same message originator is also able to transmit the message to its intended recipient (even across the world) in a matter of seconds by using modem and telecommunications systems employing telephone lines, satellites or marine cables, or all three!

HOW IT DEVELOPMENTS HAVE SAVED TIME AND MONEY IN ROUTING AN ORGANISATION'S WRITTEN MESSAGES

Paper-based mechanical technology

1

Manager dictates letter to secretary who takes it down in shorthand

2

Secretary transcribes shorthand into a typed letter and addresses envelope

3

Letter waits (for up to three hours) for collection by mail-room clerk.

4

Letter takes some 16–36 hours to be delivered by Royal Mail to UK destination

5

Mailroom clerk delivers letter to intended recipient

Time taken:

15–36 hours
cost: £20

Computer-based, electronic technology

1

Manager or employee composes letter/message on PC or terminal, checks it and edits it until happy with it

2

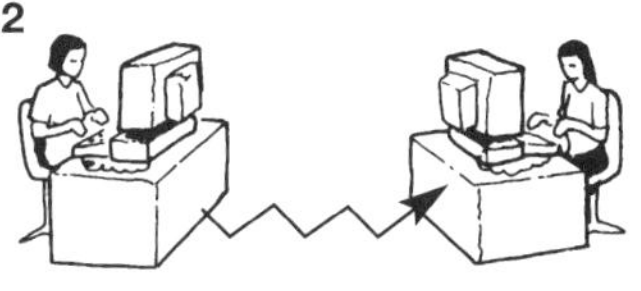

Manager or employee sends letter/message to another computer(s) by means of email, Internet or fax transmitting system

3

Receiving PC/terminal announces arrival of letter/message, with blinking 'NEW MAIL FOR YOU' eye-catcher; Recipient has option to print incoming message on printer

Time taken:

5–30 mins
cost: £3 – £5

Only some twenty years ago, many young women devoted hundreds of hours to learning shorthand. The abler ones became expert in taking down messages at over 100 words per minute. Funnily enough, all their hard-won skills seem pointless, when the letters they produced sat in wire baskets for hours, waiting for a mailroom clerk to collect them! Even though paper-based mail was collected twice each day, it still took (and takes) between 16 and 36 hours for a posted letter to arrive at a UK destination (at a cost of between £20 and £30).

By comparison, letters sent as email or fax messages take far less time and expense to produce, and arrive at their destinations within minutes (or even seconds), thanks to the development of word-processing software, computer hardware and the telecommunication networks, which are all electronically based. The keyed-in message is transformed into a series of electrical pulses which are sent along telephone lines (or in radio waves) at almost the speed of light. At their destination, they are turned back into computer file format for reading from the VDU screen, and may also be printed out if the receiver wishes. The cost of the electronic system (even allowing for the installation of the equipment) is much lower, about £3-£5 per message (e.g. one side of A4).

WHAT DO YOU THINK?

1 What do *you* see as the most important reasons for using the written word at work?

2 'Can't see what all the fuss is about. Writing's a real drag to my mind. Always got by just by speaking to people so far, so why change now? I mean, the phone's got cheaper than ever, know what I mean?' Is this an acceptable approach to writing today, or not? If so, why? If not, why not?

3 In what ways is the printed word better for sending a message, and in what ways worse than using the spoken word?

4 Why do many organisations make so much use of forms for collecting information, when so many people hate filling them out?

5 Will messages printed on paper soon become a thing of the past, as electronic messaging takes over, or will people always want to receive some messages as printed text on paper?

6 Why is it important to keep in mind the kind of person who will receive a written message?

7 Why do some messages – like disciplining or sacking an employee – need to be given orally, face-to-face ?

SUMMARY OF KEY POINTS

The use of the written word at work

People at work use the written word (as opposed to the spoken word or graphic image) for these main reasons:

- to deliver lengthy, complex messages in a way which allows repeated access and reference
- to act as a written record and also as an accepted form of legal evidence
- to monitor administrative processes, such as buying goods on credit
- to persuade or influence people to adopt a point of view
- to confirm spoken word agreements or promises
- to pass messages to others who cannot receive them personally

Naturally enough, the written word is produced in a host of various designs and formats. However, many printed messages take the form of:

- business letters
- internal memoranda
- reports
- advertisements, brochures, posters, newspapers, etc.
- summaries, factsheets
- schedules and forms (e.g. invoices, tables, payroll records)
- faxes, emailed messages, World Wide Web pages

The main factors which affect the choice of the written word (or its spoken or image alternatives) as the medium in which to send a message are:

- nature of the message
- need for confidentiality
- need for urgency
- need to reach people in remote locations simultaneously
- need to keep a written record which is also legally acceptable
- extent of availability of intended recipient

SELF-CHECK REVIEW TEST

Why written documents are produced at work

1 List four reasons why written documents are produced at work.

2 List six main types of written documents regularly used at work.

3 List four different types of person likely to receive a document produced at work.

4 Explain briefly five factors which affect the decision to use the written word at work to send a message.

5 Explain briefly how Information Technology has simplified the ways in which written documents are produced.

When you have completed the above questions, turn to pages 302 to check the answers provided with your own. If need be, revise the appropriate section of Chapter 2.

INDIVIDUAL SKILLS-BUILDING ACTIVITIES

Exploring the use of the written word at work

Task 1 Arrange to interview two people who work in different types of organisation – say a private sector company and a local council department. You should seek to interview two people you know, such as a relative, neighbour or family friend. Your task is to find out what sorts of written documents they send out and receive at work and what sort of messages they contain. Try to find out also what your interviewees like most and what they like least about the paperwork (or email messages) which they have to deal with. Make notes of what you find out to support you in a general class discussion about the various uses of written documents in a range of different organisations. Arrange, with your teacher's help, to summarise the main points of your discussion as a written source of reference.

Task 2 In the course of the next working week, try to obtain a sample of the documents illustrated in Figure 2.1 page 83 (and any others which can be made available). Make use of the goodwill of your parents, relatives and friends, but also ensure that they know you do not wish to obtain any document of a confidential nature. Bring your collected documents to your baseroom, and with your teacher's help, arrange an exhibition of them, focusing on displaying as many different types as possible.

Then, make time to examine the displayed documents and to note down what you noticed about them in these areas:

- the kind of paper they were printed on (e.g. cheap or high quality)
- the use of colour, and/or techniques of word-processing such as bigger or smaller print sizes and use of different fonts
- the size of the paper used
- the kind of message printed, and what the intentions of the author were

Having made your notes, take part in a class discussion on the main features of the exhibition, and whether any general conclusions can be made, such as the use of high quality paper and coloured inks for business letters seeking to sell goods or services to customers.

Putting written words together – use of English, punctuation and spelling

Choosing and using the right words

Already in Chapter 1, you have carried out useful work on some aspects of the use of English and spelling which will stand you in good stead now. The first important point about choosing and using the right words in written English is that, for the most part (save sometimes in advertising), the use of familiar language and slang is not acceptable. So let us be sure what is meant by the terms 'familiar language' and 'slang'. Familiar language is the kind we tend to use among family and close friends, and tends to be spoken rather than written:

> Hey, Darren, chuck us the tomato sauce across mate! Thanks.
>
> She's a real giggle! Does her hair like Tina Turner, just to be different – she says. But I reckon it's to draw attention to herself. She really fancies herself that one!
>
> Heard Blur's latest? It's wicked! Played it at the disco last night. It's got a really catchy rhythm, know what I mean?

Familiar language often includes slang or colloquial words and expressions: *chuck us across, mate, a real giggle, fancies himself, wicked, catchy, know what I mean?*

All of us use familiar language and slang terms in many situations in which they are entirely appropriate and enable us to communicate ideas in a colourful and interesting way. However, the world of work relies upon a different kind of language, based upon a different type of vocabulary and structure of ideas. It is not always easy to know whether a word is used as slang or in a familiar way and is therefore not suited to, say, a business letter or memorandum. We do, of course, know inwardly that many of the expressions we use *are* slang:

He's giving me a lot of *aggro.* But I don't rate him. He hasn't got the *bottle.*

Chill out, man, *stay cool!* Don't give me *any of your lip.*

I felt really *gutted!* It's *the pits.*

How do we know the difference between the formal language of the written word at work and colourful slang like that illustrated above? A great deal of the time we are unconsciously aware of the two quite separate languages we use when speaking and writing. But many of the materials we read are of no help at all. Some newspapers make deliberate and effective use of slang. *The Sun* used slang very effectively to create a mood, when it disagreed with a certain M. Delors, a Frenchman who was at the time the chief of the EU commissioners in Brussels:

UP YOURS, DELORS !

What can be done to avoid using unsuitable slang and familiar language when writing at work? Firstly, it helps enormously to do more reading. Reading regularly a good quality newspaper and magazines works wonders in developing an active vocabulary, so that alternative words and expressions readily come to mind.

Secondly, making a note occasionally of a useful phrase or choice of words used in a document at work also helps to build up a string of acceptable ways of stating ideas in print. Again, when in doubt, ask a colleague for an opinion. But often the best option is to consult your dictionary. A good, recently published or new edition English language dictionary will indicate (usually by *sl* or *slang* or *colloq.*) if a word is a slang word, and may provide illustrations for it being used in a slang or in a colloquial way.

KEY POINT

Slang and work rarely mix

Keep your use of slang and familiar expressions for the times you enjoy with family, friends and socialising. Be on your guard when using the written word at work to check that the vocabulary you employ is suited to the task. And whenever in doubt, ask, or check up in your dictionary.

Head or heart words

When choosing and using words in writing at work, there is also another aspect to be aware of. Within the broad area of language suited to written materials at work are two quite distinct kinds of English language:

- **language which is factual, neutral, logical, unbiased and precise used, for example in:**
  - *(a) descriptions of science experiments*
  - *(b) reports investigating problems*
  - *(c) factsheets*
  - *(d) instruction manuals*
- **language which is emotional, one-sided, persuasive and which seeks to arouse feelings**
  - *(a) advertisements*
  - *(b) sales letters*
  - *(c) electioneering pamphlets*
  - *(d) editorial articles in newspapers*

Here are some illustrations of the two types of words shown as alternatives. Notice how we all tend to respond in a different way to the two different types of vocabulary.

Factual, neutral	Emotive, persuasive
residence	home
state	country
exterminate	murder
lethal	deadly
spectator	fan
irate	angry
interrupt	butt in

Interestingly, the words in the right-hand column stem from Anglo-Saxon, Old German and Old English roots, while those in the left-hand column all derive from Latin. After the Romans conquered and colonised England in the first five centuries AD, the learned and educated people – Romans, monks and British chieftains – used Latin. Later, after waves of invasions by Vikings, Norsemen, Saxons and Angles and the Norman French invasion of 1066, two languages were in use, one based on Latin and Norman French, the other on a mix of north European languages, such as Anglo-Saxon.

In this way, Latinate words were used in churches, to administer the law and to govern and those used in the farms around the castles and forts tended to be Germanic or Scandinavian. The Latin/French language tended to contain words which were **many syllabled and abstract in meaning,** e.g. *illegitimate, compulsory.* Germanic and Scandinavian words were more often **single or double syllabled and direct in meaning,** e.g. *fresh, live, dead, hedge, land.*

English, as we would recognise it, did not emerge as the language used by all people in England until about 1400 – not that long ago! And even today, we find that longer, abstract words are used to convey a meaning which is impersonal and factual, and that they often stem from Latin. In contrast, the words which are used to arouse and persuade derive from the simpler Anglo-Saxon, Norse and Danish languages. In current English there is room for both types of language, but it is important to be aware of the likely effect of using, say, *destroy* or *eradicate*, *break* or *fracture*, *airy* or *aerated*, *hilly* or *undulating.*

KEY POINT

Use short words rather than long ones

Experts on the use of English have, for many years now, advised writers to prefer short words rather than long ones, and to use vocabulary based on the Germanic and Norse languages (i.e. the language which emerged as English) rather than those stemming from Latin (or Greek). The basis of this good advice is that the use of too many multi-syllabled, Latinate words in sentences turns readers off. They lose the thread of the meaning of the sentence, and their interest is not excited by words which are not colourful or easy to follow.

Consider the following examples:

> Sara cogitated upon her dilemma and pondered upon the two alternatives which confronted her. If she embarked upon precipitate action, she might very well engender precisely the consequences she sought to evade. Correspondingly, if she procrastinated, her inactivity might also generate a scenario she would deplore.
>
> (Content: sixteen multi-syllabic, abstract words deriving from Latin)
>
> Sara thought hard about her problem, and weighed the two options before her. If she acted too fast, she could very well bring about just what she was trying to avoid. On the other hand, if she did nothing, the outcome could be to bring about exactly what she did not want.
>
> (Content: four double syllabled Latinate words, the rest stemming from Old English)

Instant activity: Can you identify the words which come from Latin in both examples? Count up in each example the number of words used with three or more syllables and decide which example is easier to follow and why.

Word of warning: While it is certainly true that shorter, simpler words convey meaning much more easily and promptly, it is sometimes essential to use a longer, multisyllabled word, even if it derives from Latin, if it is best suited to the job.

Examples

> The researcher carefully *extracted* 200 milligrams of the *liquid* with a *sterilised syringe*.
>
> The nurse gave the *authorised* dose of the *medication* to the *patient*.
>
> According to the accident inspector's *analysis* the *fracture* in the wing was caused by *metal fatigue*.

As the above examples indicate, when a message needs to be conveyed in a language which is precise, factual and impersonal, then technical, specialised words need to be selected which best do the job, leaving the reader in no doubt at all about the meaning of what has been written.

INDIVIDUAL SKILLS-BUILDING ACTIVITY

Choosing and using the right words

Examine the following sentences carefully, and then select what you believe to be the most suitable word to fill in the blanks from those listed.

1 Because of his failure to (a)... to the warnings given at the disciplinary (b)...the personnel manager (c)... that John Brown (d)...

(a) take on board, respond, agree (b) get together, session, interview, meeting (c) figured, decided, reckoned (d) would have to go, would have to be sacked, would have his employment contract terminated.

2 With the help of a (a)..., the engineer (b)... that the (c)...was (d)... by a (e)... (f)... on the case of the missile.

(a) magnifying glass, microscope, telescope
(b) discovered, found out, calculated
(c) hold-up, fault, delay
(d) triggered, occasioned, caused, down to
(e) teeny, tiny, minute, really small
(f) bump, mound, projection, extra piece

3 The (a)... patient was (b)... as a result of (c)... arthritis, which (d)... most of his (e)... . He was therefore given (f)... doses of (g)... to (h)... the (i)... .

(a) old, ancient, elderly
(b) bed-bound, bed-ridden, restricted to bed
(c) long-standing,ongoing, chronic, enduring
(d) effected, afflicted, affected, aggravated
(e) limbs, bones, joints, parts
(f) constant, regular, continuous, occasional
(g) drugs, medicine, medication, tablets
(h) assist, lessen, decrease, drop down, reduce
(i) gyp, hurt, pain, affliction

Bear in mind, when discussing your selections with your class members, that in some instances either of two words from a list could be acceptable. Also, in order to extend your active vocabulary, decide with your teacher's help why some of the words listed are unsuitable for the job and how they tend to be used.

Grammar and syntax revisited

Before moving on to this section, it will help if you spend a little time revising pages 28–33 in Chapter 1 which examine the natural order of English word clusters which form sentences. You already know how to check whether a sentence you have composed is, in fact, grammatically correct. Remember the need for all true sentences to contain a subject and a finite verb. Remember, too, that extensions are often added to such simple constructions to provide extra meaning and interest.

CHECKLIST

Quick revision of grammar

- Doer words in sentences are called **subjects** and are either **nouns** or **pronouns.**
- Action words in sentences are called **finite verbs,** and need to possess: a number (singular or plural), a person (first, second, or third) and a tense (present, past, future or conditional = would....).
- Extension words (or phrases) which add meaning to a finite verb are called **adverbs**; extension words (or phrases) which add meaning to nouns or pronouns are called **adjectives**.
- The word or word cluster which *receives* the action of the subject is called an **object.**

Quick example:

SUBJECT — **FINITE VERB** — **OBJECT**

The knowledgeable travel agent strongly recommended a low-cost, flexible holiday.

knowledgeable = ADJECTIVE; agent = NOUN; strongly = ADVERB; recommended = VERB; low-cost, flexible = ADJECTIVES; holiday = NOUN

Note the word *travel* is also in reality an adjective stating what sort of agent, but we tend to use the term *travel agent* as a single word.

Prefer well chosen nouns and verbs to adjectives and adverbs

When composing written sentences, it pays to choose nouns and verbs which are particularly expressive, and communicate exactly what you wish to say. Inexperienced writers tend to select nouns and verbs which do not convey much meaning, and then they try to add the meaning they want by placing adjectives and adverbs next to the nouns and verbs as the following example illustrates:

> The *broken up* and *rusting* ship was being hit *constantly* and *unrelentingly* by *stormy, mountainous* waves. (over-use of adjectives and adverbs)
>
> The derelict wreck was being pounded by towering seas. (better selection of words to express meaning)

The choice of the word *wreck* communicates much more than ship, and *derelict* conveys the idea of gone beyond recall or repair. Also, *pounded* expresses by itself a continuous process, thus doing away with the need for *constantly* and *unrelentingly*. Similarly, *towering seas* are likely to be both *mountainous* and caused by a *storm*.

Expressing ideas in longer sentences

Chapter 1 introduced the technique of connecting two or more ideas (constructed as short, simple sentences) into longer ones by using linking words called **conjunctions,** and this section takes this technique further.

Consider these three, connected ideas, expressed in short sentences:

1. The train to London was over twenty minutes late.
2. Peter just managed to keep his 11.00 am appointment in Kensington.
3. He hailed a taxi immediately on arriving at Paddington.

As they stand, they do convey the three ideas clearly, even if they do read as the work of an inexperienced writer. What a more practised writer would do is to join them together with conjunctions in this way:

> *Although* the train to London was over twenty minutes late, Peter just managed to keep his 11.00 am appointment in Kensington *because* he hailed a taxi immediately on arriving at Paddington.

The main impact of this three-part sentence lies in Peter's managing to keep his appointment. The sentence starts with a conjunction, *although*; this is used to introduce what is in fact a dependent clause, because it depends on the main point: Peter kept his appointment. Another dependent clause is introduced by *because*, which explains why Peter managed to keep his appointment. By holding back the main clause – *Peter just managed to keep his 11.00 am appointment in Kensington* – the writer forces us to read on, and thus maintains our interest and wish to find out more. If all two or three clause sentences started with the main clause, we would tend to skip over the dependent ones.

KEY POINT

Use conjunctions to create interest

Remember that these conjunctions introduce equal, main clauses:

and, but, next, then, yet

and that these conjunctions introduce clauses which are dependent on a main clause for their meaning to become clear:

although, though, even though, because, as, since, that, which, who, where, when, until, so that, in order that, with the result that, if, whether.

The best advice is to vary the length of sentences and to mix those made up of several clauses with those which are simple (single clause) sentences. Also, if main clauses and simple sentences which contain the key points are held back in a passage of writing, they will take on extra emphasis. For example:

Not: We have decided to give you the job, even though there were over 500 applicants, because we think you are best qualified.

But: Even though there were over 500 applicants, because we think you are best qualified, we have decided to give you the job.

Not: Today Jack Green was selected for the Great Britain Olympic athletics team. Just over a year ago, he badly tore a ligament in his left leg. He was laid off for some six months as a result. He gave up his full-time job last March to train full-time to achieve his dream.

But: Just over a year ago, Jack Green badly tore a ligament in his left leg. He was laid off for some six months as a result. He gave up his full-time job last March to train full-time to achieve his dream. Today Jack Green was selected for the Great Britain Olympic athletics team.

In both example sets, the second version is much more interesting to read, since our expectation is built up as we are forced to wait for the key point to emerge.

INDIVIDUAL SKILLS-BUILDING ACTIVITIES

Creating longer sentences and improving sentence structures and vocabulary

Task 1 Use as appropriate the conjunctions listed on page 99, and make any other changes you think suitable to re-write the following passage as a more varied and interesting series of sentences.

> It was hot. The heat was dry. They had climbed up from swamps below. The swamps made their clothes drip in the humidity. They had escaped from the furious tribesmen. The tribesmen were angry. They considered that the explorers had walked across their forbidden, holy ground. The explorers reached a shady plateau. The climb had been hard. They were exhausted. They had no rations or blankets left. They had fled in a great hurry. Now it seemed they had forgotten the first rule of survival. It was always hammered home in training that an explorer must always carry the essential tools for survival on his person. Now they did not even possess the means of lighting a fire. The explorers began to fall out. This seemed likely to make their survival even more doubtful.

Compare your version with that of others in your class, and decide who has produced the most interesting one and why.

Task 2 Unjumble the following sets of words and write them down as the sentences they once were.

1 vase dropped The has cleaner priceless clumsy Ming the.

2 lost in depressed the their cup in They mood had team were a because.

3 corner a into old crashed the Careering lamp-post around banger a.

4 flying because it Although she colours had hard with examination well the was she studied passed.

5 with night Whatever Caroline very Roger hold decided future that might elope to the.

Task 3 Rewrite the following passage more interestingly by cutting out as many adjectives and adverbs as possible, and by replacing the nouns and verbs with more interesting ones as you think appropriate.

> The old, weather-beaten man picked up his collection of plastic bags wearily, and walked slowly up the long, winding road until he reached the top. The clouds gradually but steadily moved away, and a hot, dazzling sun came out, which started after a while to dry his damp, steaming clothes, which had become wet and cold when the heavy burst of spring rain had suddenly arrived over the collection of small, beautiful and old country houses.

Common errors in using English

The following section examines a range of errors which are commonly made by writers of English. Take pains to learn from the mistakes of others, commit the correct versions to memory, and you will have already come a long way in improving your writing skills!

The horrific howlers

The rogues and vagabonds of incorrect English usage never seem to die. They seem to grow up again like dragon's teeth with each new writing generation of young people. They do not exist and have never existed in the world of grammatically correct writing, so delete them *now* from your mind and pen!

a lot

There were ~~*alot*~~ of tourists walking along the promenade.

Thank you

~~*Thankyou*~~ for your letter of 21 April 199-.

sincerely

... to hearing from you. Yours ~~*sincerley*~~

all right

Will it be ~~*alright*~~ if the curtains are delivered a day later than requested?

definitely separate

I confirm that the goods will ~~*definately*~~ arrive in ~~*seperate*~~ boxes.

should have

I realise now that I ~~*should of*~~ told you earlier.

Agreement of the subject with its finite verb

One of the most common mistakes is to mix up the number of a noun and its verb (number here means whether a noun or verb is singular or plural), for example:

was

The collection of toy soldiers ~~*were*~~ included in the exhibition.

The error occurs because of confusion over which noun – *collection* or *soldiers* – controls the finite verb. Because *soldiers* is nearer to the verb, *were* is used instead of *was*. But it is the *collection* which is the subject. *Of soldiers* describes it. The mistake is most often made with nouns used as subjects which are called collective nouns:

herd of elephants   set of golf clubs   suit of cards

Golden rule: If the subject is singular, so is the finite verb; if it is plural, so is the finite verb!

Should, would and could

Problems sometimes occur when the verb *to be* is used in its *should* form. They stem from the way in which Anglo-Saxon verbs (from which *shall* descends) are used. Like modern French or German, Anglo-Saxon verbs used to decline, or change in the first, second or third person. We are left with:

I shall   you will   he, she, it will   we shall   you will   they will

I should   you would   he, she, it would   we should   you would they would

The matter is further complicated by the different use of *should* to mean *ought to*, for example:

You *should* pay her a visit before it is too late   = ought to

And notice when *would* means *willing to*:

I should be grateful if you *would* accept payment by Visa = are willing to

Golden rule: When you wish to convey *ought to*, use *should* across the board: I, *you, he, she, it, we, you, they should*. When you wish to write a statement in which one action or view depends upon another, use *I should* ... if you *would* ...

I *should* be very pleased if you *would* remember this golden rule!

Another similar word which trips up the unwary is *could*. It stems from *can*, meaning to be able. For example:

I *should* be truly amazed if you *could* lift that iron anvil = to be able to lift it

Many writers mix up *could* and *would* in this way:

would = be willing to

I should be grateful if you *~~could~~* post this letter for me.

Was and were

One form of the verb *to be* exists to communicate a sense of uncertainty, or what we might call an if-factor.

If I *were* you, I should be careful how you make the complaint.

If they *were* clever, the would create an export market for such a good product.

Some English oral dialects permit the use of: If I *was* you. But remember that after such *if* constructions, *were* is the correct form of the verb to be.

Overloading prepositions

As you already know, prepositions are those short but important words which are used to form some verbs: to put *up with* to look *down on*, to come *up to*. Prepositions are also used a great deal to introduce nouns or pronouns in a way which explains a direction or relationship:

down the road   *up* the hill   *over* their heads   *from* the west

face *to* face   hand *over* hand   *over* to him   *across* to them

Sometimes in writing, we use two verb forms form together before a single preposition:

She was neither prepared (to) nor willing to support the proposal.

This is fine if both verbs take the preposition *to*, but we run into trouble if the two verbs take different prepositions:

He decided to stick up (for) and to stand by his old friend in a time of trouble.

Here the writer tries to make *by* cope with both *stick up* and *stand*. The result is that in the first half of the sentence, the *He* appears to be a highwayman!

Split infinitives

The infinitive form of a verb is always preceded by the word *to*. We use infinitives extensively in sentences:

Do you wish *to go* now, or do you want *to stay* for lunch?

Problems can occur when we seek to add an adverb to give more meaning to such infinitives:

She decided to *quickly* leave the meeting and make the phone-call.

Grammar experts say it is better to place such adverbs outside the infinitive, which should be thought of as a single word:

She decided to leave the meeting quickly and to make the phone-call.

Dangling or loose participles

A participle is the name given to a part of the verb which ends in either *-ing* or *-ed*. Occasionally, unintended humour results from errors in their use:

Strolling along the road, the loose roof-tile knocked his hat off.

Tired and depressed, the brochure brightened up her outlook with colourful pictures of a Mediterranean holiday.

Dangling participles become separated from their proper subjects. It was not *the tile* but *he* who was strolling along the road. *The brochure* was neither tired nor depressed. It was *she* whom it brightened up. The error arises from too much compression in the sentences. We need to put back the key subject words:

As *he* was strolling along the road...

She felt tired and depressed, but the brochure brightened up her outlook ....

Lay or *lie*, *born* or *borne*, *accept* or *except*, etc.

There are quite a few double-trouble verbs which are easily confused. For example the verbs *to lay* and *to lie* are used quite differently. To lay takes an object: *The chicken lays an egg. The builders are laying a tarmac drive. To lie* is different. It cannot take an object, only a verb extension: *He lies in bed all day. She was lying on the grass, reading a book*. So the following are wrong:

lying lain

She was ~~laying~~ on the grass. He had ~~laid~~ there in the sun all day.

Similar confusions occur with *to bear* (a child, fruit or to carry) and *to be born*, when used in the past tense:

She has borne a beautiful girl. He has borne the burden cheerfully.

But: I was born in the lovely month of May.

Other double-trouble pairs to beware of include:

verbs: accept, except affect, effect allude, elude

nouns: access, excess compliment, complement counsel, council principle, principal forward, foreword

adjectives: dependent, dependant continuous, continual oral, aural unreadable, illegible

mixes: counsel, council desert, dessert gage, gauge assent, ascent lose, loose wholly, holy

INDIVIDUAL SKILLS-BUILDING ACTIVITY

Sorting out double-trouble words

Research into each pair of the above double trouble-words and jot down in your notebook the differences in their meanings and uses. Test out your class members when you have all completed this activity.

Who and *whom, that* and *which*

The only people who confuse the use of *who* and *whom* are those who a) are unable to recognise a word in a sentence used as an object and b) do not know the form of *who* to use after a preposition. To explain:

The word *who* is another version of *I, you, he, she it, we* or *they*. We use it either to ask a question: *Who are you*? or to save repeating the same noun or pronoun:

This is the wonderful tailor *who* made John's suit so well!

When the noun or pronoun is an object (which receives the action), *who* turns into *whom*:

He trusted the salesman *whom* he knew.

Use this simple test to decide whether to use a *who* or a *whom*:

Golden rule: If the word *who* can be replaced by *he/she*, then it stays as *who*. If the word can be replaced by *him/her*, then it should be *whom*.

That is the man *who/whom* I saw at the scene.

I saw *him* = whom is correct

Another golden rule to remember is that whenever the word *who* is preceded by a preposition, it is always *whom*: *to whom*, *from whom*, *with whom*, *by whom*, etc. For example:

This is the woman *to whom* the praise should really be given and *on whom* I totally rely.

Keep in mind, too, that after prepositions like *to, from, by,* etc, the correct versions of the personal pronoun are:

I should like to thank you all for the lovely retirement present you have given to my wife and *me* (not *I*, since the full version is: to my wife and *to me*).

The words *that* and *which* are often interchangeable:

This is the book *that/which* I am reading.

However, the conjunction *which* must be used if it defines the one which precedes it:

This is the sailing dinghy *which* you wanted to try out.

More and most

If we wish to compare one thing with another, most often we simply need to add *-er* on to a word:

The discount would be *larger* at Bickfords than at Snellings.

and if the best rating is to be given (termed the superlative), then most of the time we add *-est* to a word:

Yes, but Frasers give the *largest* discounts.

So far so good. But some writers get carried away by their desire to impress. They add a *more* or a *most* to a word already doing its job quite happily and correctly:

I think it is *more easier* to learn a foreign language in the country in which it is spoken.

That's the most loveliest dress I've ever seen you in!

Golden rule: Avoid the temptation to add a *more* or a *most* where they are not needed, but remember, too, that some words, like beautiful, splendid, attractive, etc., do not take an *-er* or and *-est*, and so *more* and *most* are needed: *most* beautiful, *more* attractive.

Most words ending in *-ly* need to take *more* or *most* to create a sense of better or best:

more slowly most expertly more gently most quickly

Less and fewer

It is surprising how many people who should know better confuse these two, similar words. Here, the simple rule is that if the noun being described is taken to be a single item, then *less* should be used:

There is *less* water in the bucket now, due to evaporation.

But where the item being described can be viewed as made up of a number of parts, then *fewer* should be employed:

There are *fewer spectators* staying on, now that a draw looks inevitable.

KEY POINT

Word building requires *organisation!*

It never fails to surprise communication teachers and writers that, while students are more than willing to make notes on new subjects of study in the areas of, say, science, manufacturing, information technology, leisure, tourism and care, etc., they tend to believe that they can develop their communication skills through a kind of magical in-breathing!

As the poet rhymed: *No way José*! It takes just as much effort as any of the subjects mentioned above. But what does help, directly and quickly, is the practice of noting down how certain words and phrases are used (correctly) in the newspapers and magazines you read. By copying an example of good and correct practice into your notebook, you will help yourself to memorise it, so that you, too, can use it with confidence – perhaps even to amaze and astonish your co-students and teacher!

Unfortunately it is simply not possible to include guidelines on all the areas of correct English usage within the scope of this textbook, and so you should make an early opportunity now to carry out the following activity:

STUDENT PAIRS ACTIVITY

Locating English usage reference sources

Carry out your researches in your study centre's library, resources/self-based learning centre and local libraries to find out what sources of further study and reference exist to help you develop the skill of using English correctly. Make a checklist of them and share in a class briefing what you and your partner discovered, making sure you create a resource reference sheet in your folder.

SUMMARY OF KEY POINTS

Putting written words together

- Selecting appropriate types of words and expressions is extremely important in the workplace, since what is perfectly acceptable in spoken word conversations among friends (slang and colloquial use of English) is almost never suited to written material at work.
- Writers of documents tend either to want to inform and measure factually, or to persuade and convince. Therefore, they pick and choose from two quite different 'head or heart' kinds of vocabulary. Be sure you think carefully about the aims of your own written documents and select your words accordingly.
- Readers of printed documents at work find it much easier to take in and to understand short, rather than long words (monosyllabic/multisyllabic). Always prefer to use shorter words, but remember that a series of sentences made up entirely of short, one- or two-syllabled words can read like the work of a pre-teen writer.
- Use your knowledge of grammar, word structuring and correct use of English to write messages which not only convey your meaning clearly, but also according to accepted use. Whatever people may tell you, correct spelling and punctuation and accepted use of English do very much matter at work. So persevere – practice really does make perfect!

WHAT DO YOU THINK?

1 Should documents in the workplace be written in a way which avoids using slang and colloquial words and over-friendly expressions? Or doesn't it matter?

2 Why, in your opinion, do some words pull at our heart-strings, and others appeal only to our heads?

3 Is it possible to create messages which deliberately appeal to our emotions, by selecting cunning ways of putting words together? Is so, what sort of words? And can you think of any examples?

4 What do you think about the approach to developing writing skills which includes identifying the jobs certain words do, such as subjects and finite verbs? Does it help? If so, why? If not, why not?

5 What tips can you supply on how to avoid making mistakes in using English? Example: If you are not sure whether to write station*e*ry or station*a*ry for notepaper, envelopes and compliments slips, etc., think of *e* for *e*nvelopes and use that form and you will always get it right!

6 Is it really important to spell and use English correctly, or does it not really matter, as long as you get the main gist of the written message across at work? If it does matter, why does it? If not, why not?

INDIVIDUAL SKILLS-BUILDING ACTIVITY

Practice in using English correctly

Correct the errors you spot in the following sentences by writing them out correctly

1 Thankyou for your kind donation to our charity. I know alot of our elderley residents will definately appreciate some extra comforts.

2 The full set of cigarette cards were priced at £50.

3 I would indeed be most grateful if you could post me a catalogue as soon as possible. Yours sincerley Jack Smith.

4 Going into the classroom, the case with her new pen fell to the floor. Luckily, she found it still laying there when she rushed out, having suddenly mislain it.

5 'I just don't know how to thank you for the lovely present what you have given to my partner and I!'

6 The customer who he had served with the hair-drier was standing there looking more angrier than anyone he had ever seen!

7 If you took more care, you'd make less mistakes!

8 'No, please, I'm alright. If I was you, I'd see if there's anyone further down whose more badly injured than myself.'

9 I don't know whether to quickly mend it myself, or to take it to a professional restorer. I suppose a proper repair would give the best affect.

10 The printing of the text in the forward of the book was so small as to be almost unreadable.

SELF-CHECK REVIEW TEST

Use of English, punctuation and spelling

1 Why is the use of slang and colloquial language unsuited to most work documents?

2 Explain briefly the difference between 'head' and 'heart' words.

Continues 

3 What is meant by a) a multisyllabic word b) a monosyllabic word? Which is easier to understand?

4 Outline briefly why most of the multisyllabic words in English stem from Latin.

5 Provide the technical terms for a) a doer word b) an action word c) a word which links together clauses within a single sentence.

6 Correct the following:

(a) A column of ants were marching through the jungle.
(b) I received alot of get-well cards. Thankyou all very much.
(c) I would be grateful if you could send me the catalogue.
(d) Feeling on top of the world, the mountains stretched in front of her.
(e) I decided to register with the doctor who you advised.
(f) I'd like my GNVQ course better if there were less activities to do!

When you have completed the answers to the above questions, check them against those provided on page 302. Revise those sections of Chapter 2 where you got an answer wrong.

How to structure written documents

The wide range of written documents regularly used in organisations has already been surveyed on page 83. This section examines the accepted ways in which the most frequently used written documents are structured. The documents examined in detail are:

- the business letter
- the memorandum
- the report
- the advertisement
- the set of instructions
- pre-set formats: forms and datacards

Common areas in the structure of all written documents

It may sound obvious, but all effective documents need to have a clear:

Beginning ⟶ **Middle** ⟶ **End**

Studying one of these three key structure sections at a time will explain why their connection is logical, but perhaps not as obvious as you may have thought.

The beginning of a document

An effective beginning of any written document has a clear, single aim: to put the reader quickly into the picture by providing answers to the five Ws:

Who? Why? What? When? Where?

Effectively, the five Ws put the letter, memorandum or report, etc., into a context by explaining very briefly:

- What the document is about
- Who is involved
- When its key events took place
- Where they took place
- Why the document is being written, and what outcomes it expects.

By supplying answers to the five Ws in an initial paragraph or section of a written document, its writer enables any reader to grasp quickly 'what it is all about'. Thus briefed, the reader is able to absorb the more detailed content of the middle section much more clearly and easily. The example in Figure 2.2 illustrates how this technique works.

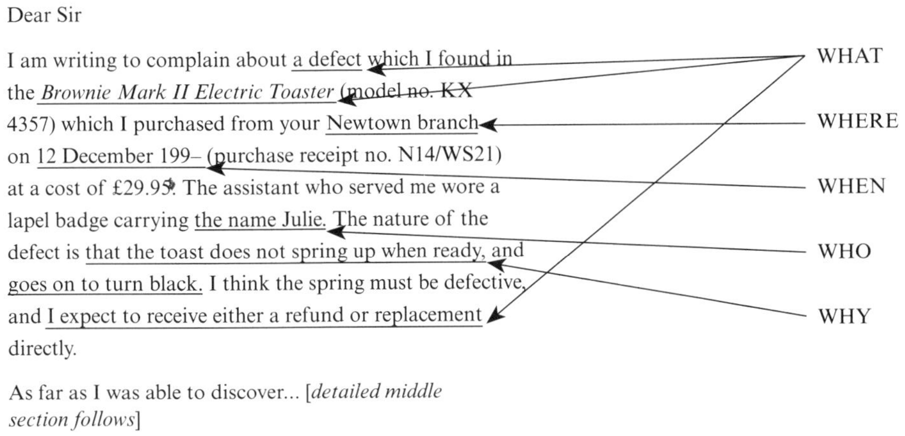

Dear Sir

I am writing to complain about a defect which I found in the *Brownie Mark II Electric Toaster* (model no. KX 4357) which I purchased from your Newtown branch on 12 December 199– (purchase receipt no. N14/WS21) at a cost of £29.95. The assistant who served me wore a lapel badge carrying the name Julie. The nature of the defect is that the toast does not spring up when ready, and goes on to turn black. I think the spring must be defective, and I expect to receive either a refund or replacement directly.

As far as I was able to discover... [*detailed middle section follows*]

WHAT
WHERE
WHEN
WHO
WHY

Figure 2.2 **Example of a consumer's letter of complaint**

The middle of the document

The task of the middle section of a written document is to set down the main details of a message. In a report, the middle section may be made up of several sub-sections, each one supplying the main points concerning a specific area. A business letter's middle may consist of two or three paragraphs which carry out the same job. The most important skill needed to construct a suitable middle for a document is to make sure that it is clearly structured, as the following examples illustrate:

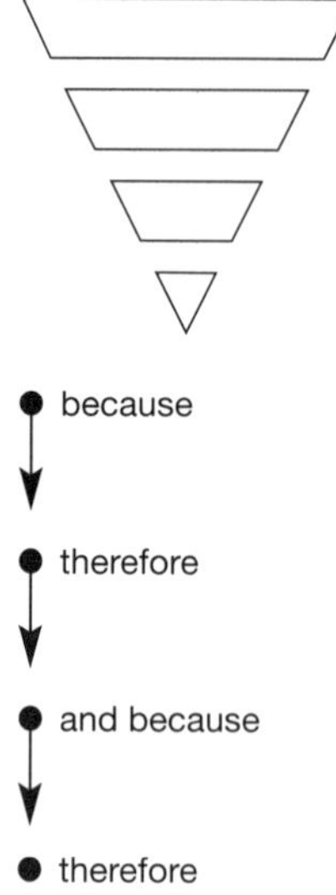

■ **Most important point/area first – least important last:** This middle structure follows a sequence in which the most important topic or point is detailed first, with each following point moving down, from the most important to the least important.

■ **Logical sequence of points:** This kind of structure follows a sequence of points, where one point is linked logically to the one which precedes it:

You ordered a Mark IV Zenith washing machine with beige and coffee colour finish.

We import these models from Italy.

They are transported by container ship to Southampton Docks. Currently there is an industrial dispute at the Docks, and your washing machine cannot be unloaded for the time being.

But we do have a white finished model in stock, which we could deliver directly.

Please telephone to advise whether you wish to accept the white model, or wait for the beige and coffee coloured one.

■ **Chronological sequence of points:** Some middle structures set down a sequence of points which follow on through a time period, such as the details to an outing organiser of a coach mystery tour, or of a five capitals European holiday.

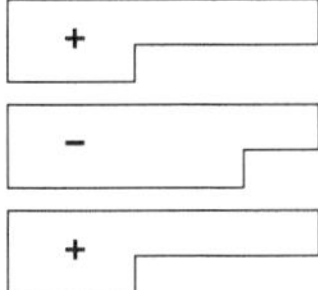

- **The pros and cons structure:** If a letter, report or memorandum is communicating two (or more) sides of an argument or discussion, then its middle is likely to take on a sequence of points which balances the pros and cons or plus and minus points:

  On the one hand +

  But, on the other –

  Then again, +

  However, – etc.

The main aspect to remember when constructing a middle part of a document is that each report section, and each paragraph of a letter or memorandum, deals with one main point at a time. Within the section or paragraph, several sub-points may be included to add meaning to a main point, but in order to convey meaning simply and clearly, keep in mind:

One section = **One main point** plus some sub-points

One short paragraph = **One main sentence** plus some sub-sentences

Example of a section within a middle part of a report

3.3 <u>Causes of Damage to the Office Floor</u>

The major cause of damage to the office floor was found to be water escaping from the underfloor mains pipe, which has badly affected some 60% of the total floor area. Some discolouration of the parquet tiles around the edge of the flooring is the result of drips from radiator controls, which have been left to dry naturally, thus taking the stain from the wood blocks. In some areas (under desks in the main), metal tipped heels on the shoes of staff have scored the wood floor. Affected areas will require the blocks to be replaced.

KEY POINT

Always pre-plan your structures

Whatever structure you decide is most suited to the middle section of any document you are composing, keep in mind the need to explain key points in a clear and logical order. Remember, too, that to create such a sequence of points you will most certainly need to *set them down in an outline list of note points*, and not off the top of your head as you write! *Continues* ▶

The acid test for a middle section is to read back over it and to ask yourself: Have I included all the major detail points which my reader needs to know? At the same time, check to see that you have not repeated any point (and delete the repetition if you have), and that you have not wandered away from you points list by including too much detail, or by becoming long-winded.

The end of a document

The final section of a document has one or more of these tasks to fulfil:

- **to provide a brief summary of the main points of the middle section** (the conclusion section in a report), or to re-emphasise the key point of the message (in a letter or memorandum)
- **to provide a decision** – if the middle was examining pros and cons, do the pros have it on balance, or the cons?
- **to make a clear request for action to be carried out** (by the reader) **by a clear and given deadline** (especially in letters)
- **to supply a courteous close** (only in the business letter).

Example of the Conclusions section of a short report

4 CONCLUSIONS

The fracture of the water main running beneath the floors of the Administration Department has resulted in extensive damage, requiring an estimated £17,500 to make good. The floor of the records office will need to be dug up to repair the fracture and then replaced, while in the adjacent offices, parts of the wood block floors will need to be taken up and fresh blocks laid, suitably stained and polished. Some electrical underfloor wiring has been damaged in the stockroom, and this will need to be renewed. The repairs are expected to take approximately two weeks to complete, but staff should be able to work from the Department by sharing work-stations in unaffected locations on the ground floor.

Example of the end section (final paragraph) of a business sales letter

I am pleased to confirm, therefore, that an introductory discount of 10% is available on the new *Chefmaster* range of cooking utensils detailed above, on all orders over £250.00. To qualify for this special offer, I shall need to receive your written order no later than Friday 29 March 199-. Having been fortunate to be given a guided tour of the factory making the new

Chefmaster range, I can personally assure you of the extremely high quality of their construction. I know you will not be disappointed and very much look forward to receiving your order.

Yours sincerely

Example of the closing paragraph of an internal memorandum

The chairman of the Board of Directors has therefore decided to address all head office staff in the cafeteria at 5.00 pm on Thursday 12 July 199-. In view of the importance of his announcements, all staff not required to answer telephones or carry out safety duties (who will be notified in advance) are required to attend this meeting. Any member of staff unable to attend must speak to his or her departmental manager directly in this regard.

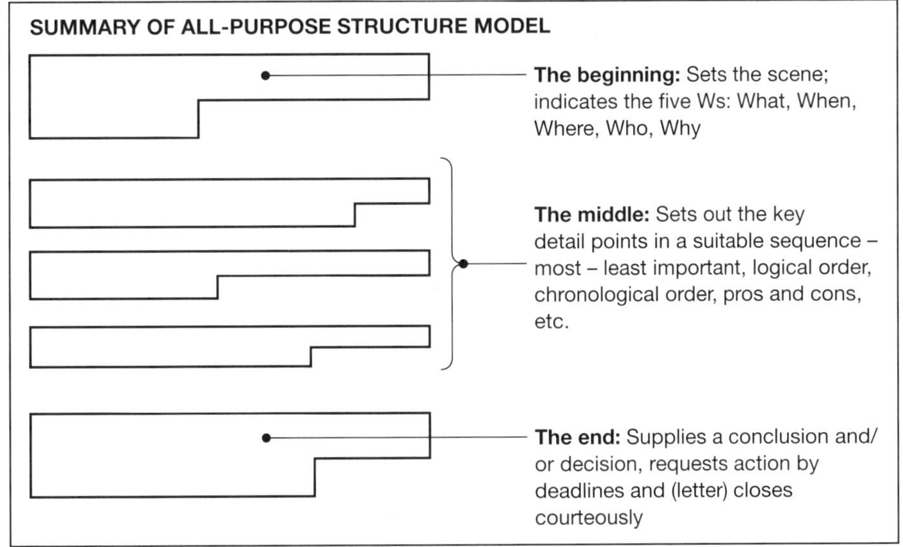

SUMMARY OF ALL-PURPOSE STRUCTURE MODEL
The beginning: Sets the scene; indicates the five Ws: What, When, Where, Who, Why
The middle: Sets out the key detail points in a suitable sequence – most – least important, logical order, chronological order, pros and cons, etc.
The end: Supplies a conclusion and/or decision, requests action by deadlines and (letter) closes courteously

WHAT DO YOU THINK?

1 Are the five Ws of a document's beginning really needed, or are they not? What do you think?

2 This section has illustrated these structure models for the middle sections of workplace documents: a) from most to least important, b) logical sequence of points, c) chronological sequence of points, d) pros and cons. Can you suggest and outline any other types of structure for the middle of a document which could also serve as a useful model?

3 Many writers of business letters finish the end section with closings like these:

I should be grateful if you would *kindly* send me your catalogue of bathroom suites.

I look forward to hearing from you.

Please accept my thanks for your prompt service.

Do not hesitate to contact me if I may be of *any further help.*

Why do you think that such closing sentences are so often employed? What is the writer's purpose in selecting the words in italics?

4 In many letters and internal memoranda, middle sections are made up of several short paragraphs instead of one or two long ones. Why?

5 Sometimes, writers of longer workplace documents insert headings above sections or paragraphs. What purpose do you think they serve?

SUMMARY OF KEY POINTS

How to structure written documents

- How a written document is structured depends, of course, on the kind of message it contains. However, a useful, all-purpose approach to constructing documents is the **Beginning ➝ Middle ➝ End** one, where the beginning answers the five W questions **Who? Why? What? When? Where?** – which set the scene and enable the reader to grasp quckly what the 'meat' of the document will be all about.
- The middle parts of a document communicate the meat of its message, and there are several useful structure models for middle sections to lean on: **most to least important, logical series of steps, pros and cons,** etc.
- The ends of documents are also very important to organise correctly, since they provide the last chance to get the document's most important point across. This may be to **make a request for someone to do something, provide a decision or answer to a query, sum up briefly the main points of the message and so on.** In letters, it is always important to close politely. But remember that some kinds of letter, like those seeking to obtain payment of long outstanding bills, while not ever descending into rudeness, are most unlikely to close: *With All Good Wishes!*

STUDENT PAIR SKILLS-BUILDING ACTIVITIES

Creating outline document structures

Task 1 Last Saturday morning you went into town with some friends for a wander around the shops and to drink a coffee. You were browsing among the Rock and Pop CDs in Your Kinda Music (a music centre), and discovered to your delight a re-issue of a CD recording of your favourite group. You paid £7.49p for it and could not wait to get it home to hear it all through. You stuffed the sales receipt in a pocket. Its receipt number was YKM/4/934. Andy Brown, who served you, said that you were lucky to find it, since he thought they'd sold out, as it was in high demand.

When you got home, you sped up the stairs to your room and put the disk into your hi-fi stack. Tracks one and two were brilliant, but just into track three, you heard a throbbing noise, which, from experience, you realised meant that the CD had stuck. You took it back to the store the following Monday lunch-time. Another assistant played track three and it played through without any problem. But when you got home, the same fault occurred!

You were puzzled at this, because your hi-fi stack, a reputable Canwood Ultimate Microstack, is only some two months old, and still in warranty. Coincidentally, you also purchased it from Your Kinda Music exactly two months ago today.

Compose a set of points (but not the full prose version) which would form the basis of a letter of complaint to the manager of Your Kinda Music. Make use of the guidelines on document beginnings, middles and ends to help you in structuring your set of notes. When you have finished, swap your version with those of some co-students in your class and see who can learn what from whom in terms of devising a suitable structure for this letter.

Task 2 Arrange, with your teacher's help, to swap your set of notes with those of a co-student. Then read the following:

Assume you are the manager of Your Kinda Music. You have received the letter (actually the set of points) making the complaint about the CD and the hi-fi stack. Normally, hi-fi equipment under warranty and with suspected faults has to be sent back to the manufacturers for inspection. It so happens that a senior Canwood technician is based at your store this week giving a training course to some of your staff. She has agreed to look at the hi-fi stack if it can be brought into the store.

Compose a set of points for a letter to send to the complaint-maker, which offers to have the hi-fi stack inspected, etc. You will need to have the warranty certificate brought in also.

When you have finished Task 2, swap your note points again with your co-student and see what sort of answer you received, and which version you believe is the better set of points and why.

Task 3 Your teacher has asked you and your co-student to produce a set of instructions which explain clearly (to new GNVQ Foundation students) how to produce and submit an activity for assessment, which is intended to form part of your portfolio. You have been requested to produce them as a set of points in a clear structure for your teacher to check before you write out a full version.

Your instructions should consist of some 12–15 steps which have to be taken. You should take care to ensure that you use the correct names for any forms which have to be completed, and that the points you devise are put into a logical and suitable order.

When you have completed your set of points, compare it with the ones produced by other student pairs, and decide which set is likely to result in the most effective set of instructions.

Task 4 As you are both quite experienced GNVQ students now, your head of department has asked you to carry out the following activity:

> 'I want to produce an informational leaflet about the good features of our GNVQ Foundation programme to give to potential students at careers evenings, talks to school pupils, etc. So, I'd like you to research a set of key points which could be included in a two-sided A4 leaflet to inform intending students about your course.
>
> Perhaps a good way to approach this would be to ask around your GNVQ group to find out what sort of information you and your fellow students found most helpful – or would have found most helpful if it had been made available to you.
>
> When you have collected enough suitable material, I should be most grateful if you would set it down in note form in a suitable structure, as a set of points with a beginning, middle and end. I can then see the sort of approach you took, without your having to produce a leaflet in full.'

With your partner, first carry out the research suggested, and then produce a set of notes for the leaflet in a suitable sequence and structure.

SELF-CHECK REVIEW TEST

How to structure written messages

1 Why are five Ws important to the beginning of a written message?

2 Describe briefly two ways of structuring the middle of a message.

3 Why are the middle sections of a letter or a report split into several short paragraphs or sections?

Continues ▶

4 What sort of information would you expect to find in the end section of a letter?

5 And what sort in the conclusion section of a report?

When you have completed the above questions, turn to page 303 to check the answers provided. If need be, check the relevant section of Chapter 2 to revise any aspect you got wrong.

How to create formats for written documents

In many ways, the kind of structure adopted for any written document controls the format it will possess. For example, a letter which uses the beginning, middle and end type of structure will take on an appearance like this, since it is likely to contain some five or more paragraphs in all:

Dear Mrs Smith

Yours sincerely

However, there are a number of additional features of format (the way a document is set out down the page) which you will need to learn and remember, since – for ease of creation and production – most organisations follow widely accepted format models. Such styles, when used in the same way across an entire organisation, are called

house styles. This section, then, examines in detail the accepted current formats for:

- the letter
- the memorandum
- the short report

In addition, it covers the areas of effective layout (e.g. for advertisements) where there are no hard and fast rules, and also the use of various features of modern word-processing packages, such as the use of various sizes of typeface (called fonts), bold type, capital letters and so on.

The format of the letter

Some years ago, writers in organisations used to employ several different formats for business letters, including some with indented paragraphs and centring:

Dear Sir,

Xxxxxxxxxxxxxxxxxxxxxxxxxxxxxxxxxxxxxxxxxxx
xxxxxxxxxxxxxxxxxxxxxxxxxxxxxxxxxxxxxxxxxxxxxxxxxx

Xxxxxxxxxxxxxxxxxxxxxxxxxxxxxxxxxxxxxxxxxx
xxxxxxxxxxxxxxxxxxxxxxxxxxxxxxxxxxxx

Yours faithfully,

Mrs D. Smith

Such letters also included commas and full stops in addresses and to indicate word-endings and abbreviations, etc. You will probably be pleased to learn that computer-based technology has made the formatting of business letters much simpler! Once it became possible to return either a typewriter's carriage (which effectively rolled down a line a time) or a word-processor's cursor a line at a time to the left-hand margin of the next line, then everything changed. For a start, every new entry in the letter was placed against the left-hand margin, including the address of the recipient and the *Dear Sir ... Yours faithfully* entries. Also, the practice of ending address lines, etc., and abbreviated words with commas or full stops was promptly discontinued, being regarded as unnecessary and a waste of time.

As a result, the letter format used almost everywhere today looks like the one shown in Figure 2.3 on page 121. The name given to this type of letter format is **fully blocked, open punctuation**. Remember that the main body of the letter is normally punctuated.

Letter	Notes
GLOBAL TRAVEL SERVICES LIMITED ***15-17 HIGH STREET MIDCHESTER*** ***MIDSHIRE MS 2 1TA*** ***TEL: 01234 567890 FAX:01234 123456***	Pre-printed letterhead Company logo
12 May 199-	Start of text-processsed letter
Miss T Sanderson Appletrees 3 Downland Ave Midchester Midshire MS14 3RD	Note that the address includes no punctuation
Dear Miss Sanderson	The salutation
18-35 BEACHCLUB HOLIDAYS Thank you for your letter of 10 May 199-, in which you request a current holiday brochure of 18-35 BeachClub Holidays.	The letter's subject-heading is in bold type, so stands out
I am pleased to enclose a copy of the current holiday catalogue, which contains detailed information about summer holidays in Europe. Also, for your information, I have included a copy of 18-35 BeachClub's latest brochure for holidays in the USA and Caribbean.	Each of the letter's paragraphs starts against the left-hand margin
With regard to your enquiry about paying for your holiday in instalments, I regret to advise you that we are unable to provide you with this particular service. Our terms of sale need you to pay a 10% deposit on the cost of a holiday and the balance no later than eight weeks prior to your departure.	Note the use of double spacing to separate each paragraph, so as to make the letter's message easier to digest
You may be able to negotiate a personal loan with your bank or with National Credit, 48 High Street, Midchester (Tel: 01234 543210), whom I can recommend.	This letter's structure responds to the main enquiry first and then deals politely but clearly with the position regarding payment.
I shall be pleased to supply further advice and to make a firm booking for you when you have had an opportunity to browse through the brochures. In the meantime, please do not hesitate to call me if I may be of any further help.	As this is a sales reponse, the letter ends on a very helpful and courteous note
Yours sincerely	The complimentary close
MS Jennie Carstairs Holiday Adviser	The printed version of Jennie Carstairs name is included for clarity, as well as her job title
encs	Note the inclusion of a reminder reference for the brochure enclosures

Figure 2.3 **Example of a fully-blocked open punctuation letter**

Key rules for accepted letter format

The following section takes you step by step through the set of key rules to follow for producing an accepted business letter format. Throughout, the format model followed is that of the fully-blocked, open punctuation format.

1 **Paper size:** In the UK, letters are printed on A4 paper. The paper most often used is called bond paper which is a label for its quality, and it measures 297 millimetres down and 210 millimetres across. Letters are always produced with the longer paper side vertical, which is called portrait style. (The alternative is called landscape style.) Letters are printed on one side of the paper, and only make use of the pre-printed letterhead for the first page, because of its cost. Further pages are printed on plain bond paper.

2 **The pre-printed letterhead:** Letters sent out of organisations always display a pre-printed letterhead, which is the name given to that part of the letter's appearance which displays the name, full postal address, telephone, fax, Internet and telex numbers and addresses. It often also includes a logo. This is an image which is designed to communicate what the organisation is and does. Logos are intended to act as visual memory-joggers, and famous ones include British Rail's two-way rails the mongrel dog listening to an early gramophone record (His Master's Voice), *Coca-Cola* and so on. Sometimes a strip of the foot of the notepaper used for letters displays details of company directors, the legal address of the organisation and so on.

For the purposes of letter formats, consider these top and tail areas out of bounds, and leave a good sized margin of at least two line spaces above and below them.

3 **Margins:** All business letters contain their processed text within a kind of frame formed by four margins: left, right, top and bottom. These make clear the extent of the printed message and provide a visually attractive frame for it. Staff who use word-processing software frequently either make use of pre-set letter margins, or set up their own, according to the house style they use. Typical left- and right-hand margins vary between two and three centimetres in width. A bottom margin is also likely to be at least two centimetres above any printed text or edge.

All the letter's text-processed message must remain within these four margins at all times.

4 **Order of letter entries:** The various entries which make up a business letter follow a fixed running order from top to bottom:

(a) **Status of the letter,** *e.g. Private & Confidential, Personal etc.*

(b) **Letter references** of the letter being replied to (*Your ref*) and the one being written (*Our ref*), e.g. *Our ref DWE/ JJ/AWL 24.*

A reference commonly includes the author's initials and those of the text processor *(DWE/JJ)* and then any other helpful filing reference: letter number 24 to Addison Wesley Longman publishers.

(c) **Date:** In the UK, the date is printed in the order day, month year, and the month is always given in full, e.g. *24 November 199-* and never as 24/11/9-.

(d) **Recipient's full postal address:** Whenever possible, include the name and job title of the recipient. If the name is not known, then start with the job title: *The Leisure Centre Manager.* **Tip:** – if using both, drop the ***The*** of the job title:

Mrs Diana Richards
Leisure Centre Manager

Omit all punctuation from the address, save for apostrophes in street names, e.g. *King's Walk.*

Some organisations set out the name of the town in capital letters to aid postal sorting:

MAIDENHEAD
RG24 6AJ

and then enter the post code beneath which is an essential part to include on the envelope if it is to be routed quickly. Whenever possible, seek to limit the recipient's address to five lines, so as to avoid using up too much writing space for the message,

(e) **The salutation:** A letter's salutation is its greeting: Dear ... Such salutations take one of two major forms:

- *Dear Sir* or *Dear Madam*

This greeting is considered to be most formal, and is used when writing to someone whom the writer does not know, or who occupies a senior post.

Dear Sir/Madam is *always* paired with *Yours faithfully* (see below).

- *Dear Dr/ Mr/ Mrs/ Miss/Ms Smith*

This salutation is considered more informal and is used when the letter writer knows the recipient, or wishes to establish a friendly tone, as in a sales letter.

Dear Dr/Mr/Mrs/Miss/Ms is *always* followed by *Yours sincerely.*

(f) **The subject heading:** This is a brief title for the theme or subject of the letter. It is usually set in bold capital letters, so as to stand out, which helps support staff who route incoming mail to departmental staff.

(g) **The body of the letter:** This takes the form of the paragraphs which contain the message. Note that they are separated by double-line spacing and in the fully blocked format are not indented:

Not: Xxxxxx	**But:** Xxxxxxxxxxxxxx
xxxxxxxxxxxxxx.....	xxxxxxxxxxxxxx....

Always punctuate the letter's body normally.

(h) **The complimentary close:** This is the name given to the Yours ... signing off entry. Complimentary closes are paired with salutations in this way:

Dear Sir/Madam ...Yours faithfully

Dear Dr/Mr/Mrs/ Miss/Ms ...Yours sincerely

Firmly embed in your memory: Always a small f or s, and -lly (two ls), -erely (-er-*e* -ly).

(i) **The enclosure reference:** This is shortened either to *enc* (one enclosure) or *encs* (two or more enclosures).

(j) **The copies to reference:** Sometimes a letter's writer wishes to inform additional people as to its contents, and so uses the reference: *copy to*: or *copies to*: followed by the names of the recipients:

copy to: Jean Brown, Customer Services Manager

5 **Continuation sheets** Some letters extend over more than a single page. In order to connect them if their sheets become separated, each further or continuation sheet displays details of its author, date of production, number of page and topic:

2

Jennie Carstairs
18-35 BeachClub Holiday Enquiry
12 May 199-

a firm booking for you when ...

INDIVIDUAL SKILLS-BUILDING ACTIVITY

Developing knowledge of letter formats

Task 1 Use your initiative to find out:

1 how to supply an informal salutation to a knight

2 how to supply a formal salutation to a partnership of two or more partners

3 how to format a postal address in a city such as Liverpool, Birmingham or Bristol

4 what information is provided in a postcode

5 who is allowed to open a letter with an envelope marked *PERSONAL*

6 how an opened letter marked *Confidential* should be handled

Task 2 Find out the names and sizes of the common types of envelopes used to contain letters, and also what a window envelope is and how its use may affect the format of the letter put into it.

Task 3 Find out what these terms stand for:

1 *manilla* envelope
2 *recorded* delivery
3 *blind* copy
4 *mail-merged* letters
5 a *circular* letter
6 *redirected* mail

The memorandum and email message

At this time, the life-span of the internal memorandum produced on paper is coming to an end. IT systems which enable computers to be networked are now becoming widely established in larger organisations. As a result, many staff are able to send email messages instead of paper memos. The email message has the advantages of being:

- much faster to produce: an employee with a terminal can quickly key in a message personally
- very much faster to send
- much simpler to send simultaneously to groups of staff
- easy to read and delete, to store electronically or to print on paper
- capable of attaching computer-produced files (e.g. of reports or letters) to email covering notes and sending them together.

However, the paper memorandum is likely to survive for a few more years, and so it is worth learning how to format one.

The format of a paper-based memorandum

Traditional memoranda are in essence internal letters, and indeed, their main bodies are set out in the same way as letters, so we only need to examine their 'memoheads' and one or two points of difference.

1 The memohead: The memohead of a memorandum is simply an area in which essential data is displayed to enable it to be routed to its intended recipient, to be filed and retrieved. A typical memohead looks like this:

MEMORANDUM ①

TO: Works Manager ② **DATE:** 3 June 199- ③

FROM: Assistant Marketing Manager ④ **COPIES:** Marketing Manager ⑤

SUBJECT: TIMETABLE OF LAUNCH OF NEW FITNESS ROOM EQUIPMENT ⑥

① Note that the bold type in the above illustration represents those parts which are printed on pads or reams of paper. Against each of these indicators, a typed or text-processed entry is made.

② The recipient of a memorandum may be identified either, as above, by job title only, or as:

John Brown

Works Manager

The title Dr, Mr, Mrs, Ms, etc., is always omitted.

③ The date is displayed exactly as for the letter.

④ The identity of the sender is set down exactly as for ② above.

⑤ Either the names or the initials of additional receivers of the memorandum are displayed against *Copies:*

⑥ The subject of the memo is displayed just as it is in the letter, and serves the same purpose.

2 Further features

- *Continuation sheets are produced in the same way as for letters.*
- *Some memo writers like to read their memos after they have been produced, and initial them to indicate that it is in order for them to be despatched.*
- *Some organisations colour code paper copy memos – say:*

  Yellow: for information only

  Pink: for filing/ sender's copy etc.
- *Unlike the business letter, memoranda do not start or finish with a Dear... Yours... . Only the body of the memorandum appears under the memohead. However, it is set out like the letter's body, with double spacing between each paragraph.*

Sometimes memoranda (and letters) may include a section which communicates data in number form, say as a table. In this case it is likely to be centred:

Xxxxxxxxxxxxxxxxxxxxxxxxxxxxxxxxxxxxxxxxxxxxxxxxxxxxxxxxxxxxxxxxxxx xxxxxxxxxxxxxxxxxxxxxxxxxxxxxxxxxxxxxxxxxxxxxxxxxxxxxxxxxxxx:

FIRST QUARTER'S OUTPUT

Kilos	**North Region**	**Midlands**	**South Region**
Ice Cream	234,540	357,492	323,971
Lollies	121,459	187,987	165,989
Sundaes	97,234	81,932	35,967
TOTALS:	365,233	627,411	525,927

Xxxxxxxxxxxxxxxxxxxxxxxxxxxxxxxxxxxxxxxxxxxxxxxxxxxxxxxxxxxxxxxxxxx xxxxxxxxxxxxxxxxxxxxxxxxxxxxxxxxxxxxxxxxxxxxxxxxxxxxxxxxxxx ...

Also, memoranda and letters may display an introductory title above a paragraph to help the reader grasp its meaning:

Reasons for Decline in Sundaes Production (South Region)

Xxxxxxxxxxxxxxxxxxxxxxxxxxxxxxxxxxxxxxxxxxxxxxxxxxxxxxxxxxxxxxxxxxxx xxxxxxxxxxxxxxxxxxxxxxxxxxxxxxxxxxx:

MEMORANDUM

TO: Carol Abrizzi Personnel Manager **DATE:** 31 January 199-

FROM: Richard Hill Assistant Production Manager **Copies to:** Production Director
Works Manager

SUBJECT: **ARRANGEMENTS FOR INTERVIEWS OF MODERN APPRENTICESHIP SCHEME (PRODUCTION) ENTRANTS**

Thank you for your revised list of applicants for the company's Modern Apprenticeship Scheme spring intake. I can confirm that the Production Department is able to offer eight apprenticeship places.

I have spoken to Sam Brooks (Production Director) and Anna Wilcox (Works Manager), and am also able to confirm that they have both kept free the whole of Tuesday 12 February 199- for the proposed interviews.

Also, I had a meeting yesterday with the shopfloor supervisors I mentioned, who have all readily undertaken to act as mentors/counsellors for the eight apprentices.

You asked me to take into consideration the applications in terms of the company's policy as an equal opportunities employer. I am pleased to say that the Production Department will be happy to take on any selected female apprentices and can also provide you with the assurances you requested about providing suitable restroom, changing and toilet facilities, etc.

Lastly, would you please let me know when you expect to send across the files of all forty-five applications for our senior mangers to consider.

RH

Figure 2.4 **Example of a memorandum**

The format of an email message

There is no single way of setting out an email message. In fact, its format is likely to be dictated by the way in which programmers design that part of the communications section of the software. They

FILE EDIT VIEW FORMAT TOOLS TABLE WINDOW SEND HELP

TIME: 0930 **DATE:** 12/3/9- **INFO COPIES**: PERS MGR

MESSAGE TO: INVESTORS IN PEOPLE TEAM **STATUS**: URGENT

FROM: GAIL BREWSTER QUALITY SYSTEMS MANAGER

MESSAGE:

I've decided to call an urgent team meeting of the IIP Team for:

WEDNESDAY 13 MARCH 1700 HOURS
IN STAFF TRAINING SUITE

Only three weeks remain before the visit of the assessor, and from your latest progress reports, we've a mountain to climb.

Three-line whip, so - please ensure you can be there!

CONFIRMATION: MESSAGE RECEIVED: TIME:
MESSAGE BOX OPENED: YES/NO TIME:

Figure 2.5 **Example of an email message**

may design a screen which looks rather like a paper memohead, but with additions, as in Figure 2.5 above.

Email technology enables groups of people to receive a message at the same time (in a matter of seconds of depressing the send button). Note the inclusion of time boxes, to enable a recipient to check how long a message has been in his or her mail-box. Also notice that the same technology enables an email message sender to know whether the message has arrived (at the terminal) successfully, and if its recipient has opened the mail-box and read it.

Sets of instructions

Sets of instructions are often displayed on noticeboards in organisations. They need to be logically structured and clearly written (see Figure 2.6 on page 130).

HOW TO EVACUATE THIS ROOM IN CASE OF EMERGENCY OR FIRE

1 RAISE THE ALARM BY SETTING OFF THE ALARM **5 METRES TO THE LEFT** OF THE DOOR TO THIS ROOM

2 IF THERE IS TIME, CLOSE ALL WINDOWS

3 LEAVE IMMEDIATELY. DO NOT TAKE ANY BELONGINGS WITH YOU AS THESE MAY HAMPER A SAFE EVACUATION

4 CLOSE THE DOOR OF THE ROOM ON LEAVING

5 **TURN RIGHT** AND MAKE FOR THE FIRE ESCAPE AND STAIR WELL AT THE END OF THE CORRIDOR. IF THE STAIRS ARE NOT SAFE TO DESCEND, USE THE FIRE ESCAPE THROUGH THE FIRE DOOR. **DO NOT USE THE LIFT UNDER ANY CIRCUMSTANCES**

6 DO NOT PANIC. WALK AND DO NOT RUN OR PUSH OTHERS. ALERT OTHERS AS NEEDED BUT DO NOT SHOUT OR CRY OUT, CAUSING OTHERS TO PANIC.

7 TAKE CARE OF ANY SPECIAL NEEDS STUDENT. A CARRYING HARNESS IS SITUATED BY THE MID-CORRIDOR ALARM BELL FOR PARAPLEGIC PEOPLE

8 MAKE FOR ASSEMBLY POINT D (SEE MAP BELOW) AND WAIT FOR A REGISTER TO BE TAKEN

9 DO NOT STRAY TOWARDS ANY BUILDINGS

10 **WAIT AT THE ASSEMBLY POINT** FOR FURTHER INSTRUCTIONS. DO NOT LEAVE THIS POINT, OR EMERGENCY SERVICE STAFF MAY RISK THEIR LIVES THINKING YOU ARE STILL IN THE BUILDING

College Safety Officer Room D Block 234 2/10/199-

Figure 2.6 **Example of a well structured set of instructions**

Word-processing software: templates

Great strides have been made in developing helpful features in many word-processing packages. In formatting terms, one of the most useful features provides a range of templates to use when creating a particular kind of document. A template is a kind of framework which enables the author to key text into pre-set positions on the page. The software then converts the text into a larger or smaller point size, capitals, etc., so that the end product is produced automatically as, say, a business letter, memorandum or schematically presented report.

STUDENT PAIR SKILLS-BUILDING ACTIVITY

Researching word processing templates

Research into the range of templates which a leading word-processing package offers, and print out some examples to use as visual aids in delivering a 3–5 minute talk to your class which explains their use.

The short report

Routine reports

In workplace organisations, there are basically two kinds of report. The first type could well be called a routine report, since it is used to provide feedback about routine happenings which occur regularly. For example, a salesperson usually has to report to his or her line manager once a week on how successful, in sales terms, the week has proved. To meet legal requirements (under the Health & Safety At Work Act 1974) all organisations are obliged to ensure that accident report forms are completed immediately after an accident. In terms of plant and equipment maintenance, reports have to be made out on a routine basis when a machine is serviced or checked, and so on.

To save the time of staff and to avoid wasted effort, routine reports are almost always made out on forms which have been specifically designed for the purpose (see Figure 2.7 on page 132). As a result, managers ensure that the precise information they need is made available.

Routine reports used at work which use pre-printed forms to store and display information include:

- the accident report
- the sales report
- the medication delivered report
- the plant/equipment safety check report
- the maintenance engineer's visits made report etc.

The advantages of using a pre-printed form for collecting and displaying the data of such reports are as follows:

- The form designer has already carried out the first thinking about what sort of data is required, and in what order; all the reporter needs to do is to complete the form as instructed.

Global Electronics plc | Company Safety Oficer | Form No. Acc 12X/3/94

ACCIDENT REPORT FORM

REPORT COMPILED BY: ____________________ TIME:__________ DATE: __/__/__

JOB TITLE: ______________ DEPARTMENT: ____________________

DATE OF DESPATCH OF COPY TO SAFETY OFFICER: ____________________

FOR OFFICE USE: __________ ENTERED IN ACCIDENT REPORT LOG: ______________

1 ACCIDENT OCCURRED AT (TIME): ____________ON DATE: __/__/__
AT LOCATION: Enter precise location and address if not on company premises:

2 DESCRIBE NATURE OF ACCIDENT Outline briefly who was involved, how it happened and your views as to the reason for it:
PERSON(S) DIRECTLY INVOLVED:____________________

DETAILS OF ACCIDENT:____________________

APPARENT CAUSE OF ACCIDENT: ____________________

DETAIL AS PRECISELY AS POSSIBLE THE NATURE OF ANY INJURIES:

Figure 2.7 **Example of a routine report**

- The information set down on the report form ensures (over a period of time and with revisions of the form's design) that nothing important can be left out – but if omitted, can be speedily spotted and followed up.
- All the data collected in each question or section of a report form is of a similar nature, which makes it much easier to analyse by means of database software; for example, an analysis of safety inspections of identical lathes or drilling machines over a period of

time could well throw up the fact that the same part is failing again and again, and lead to investigations into its design and construction.

- Completing a report form takes much less time than writing out a one-off report, starting with a blank sheet of A4 paper.

Designing a report form requires a logical approach and the ability to amend sections after carrying out tests. The following checklist illustrates the main points to keep in mind when designing a report form.

CHECKLIST

Main techniques of report form design

- Careful decision-making is needed to ensure that only relevant and important data is collected.
- Thought and several drafts are needed to ensure that:

  (a) data is requested in a logical sequence of questions or requests for information

  (b) sufficient space is given for meaningful data to be entered in boxes or spaces or along lines
- Care also needs to be taken to ensure that the questions asked are not ambiguous (capable of being misunderstood) and that all wording and instructions are simple and clear.
- Thought needs to be given, too, to making sure that data is not asked for more than once (which tends to irritate the form filler).
- Draft report forms should be edited by several experts to ensure that they have been kept as simple and short as possible, that they will deliver the data sought and that they cannot be misunderstood.
- After the design has been completed, a prototype or Mark I form should be tried out on typical users, and their feedback obtained on the design and how it may need to be amended in the light of its practical use.

STUDENT PAIR SKILLS-BUILDING ACTIVITY

Designing and testing a report form

Task 1 As a student pair, and with the help of your teacher, select one of the following form-designing subjects:

1 A form to check on the individual progress a Foundation GNVQ student is making (over four-weekly intervals), and to highlight any particular needs the student has.

2 A form to survey the degree of satisfaction with the current range of services and products of the refectory/cafeteria, and to identify (in order of preference) the kinds of food and drink students would like to be available, and when.

3 A form to survey the type and extent of social and sports activities which are currently made available to students by the study centre, and to identify degrees of satisfaction with them, as well as detailing in order of popularity (from a later analysis) what new or changed activities should be introduced, where and when.

4 A form to survey the spending and saving habits of the students in your class; this survey should include details about finances either earned or supplied as pocket money, and what typical amounts are spent weekly on what items, and what saving practices are followed (if any). Students selecting this topic must, with their teacher's help, devise a system of collecting the data anonymously.

Task 2 When you have designed your chosen form to your satisfaction, arrange to test it out upon a suitable sample of students in your study centre (i.e. between ten and fifteen students). Set a deadline of no more than five working days for its completion and return. When the completed forms have been returned, assess the degree of success of your particular design in supplying the data you wished to collect. Identify also any parts of the form which could be improved. You will need to interview your sample of reporters to do this.

Task 3 When all report forms have been designed, tested and the results assessed, hold a general class discussion of what general points have been learned from the activity. Arrange to set down a summary of these points and to store them in your work folder.

One-off, investigatory reports

While some events in organisations can be effectively reported upon using a pre-printed report form, this is not so for all the reporting situations which arise at work.

Middle and senior managers are regularly required to submit reports about a one-off situation which is unique and unlike any other. The following checklist illustrates a typical range of these situations:

CHECKLIST

Typical management one-off reporting situations

- Something has gone wrong: sales are sliding dangerously in a retail branch; a mysterious illness is attacking residents in a nursing home; holiday bookings are well down for a popular Mediterranean resort this year, so far; wastage rates are climbing for some unknown reason in a large production process.
- A new product or service has been launched by the competition and we need to assess the likely impact on our own, similar product/service.
- The organisation is planning to introduce a highly important change, say of moving lock, stock and barrel some 250 miles away, or of introducing a paper-free office system. Extensive consultation among employees is needed.
- Due to the recession, sales are falling and the organisation needs to identify some ways of making major savings in operating.

As the above examples illustrate, managers sometimes have to carry out a great deal of research and then to provide the results of their investigations in a detailed report. Moreover, junior support staff may, occasionally, be obliged to produce a short, written report upon a one-off topic, such as:

- problems being experienced in operating a newly installed piece of equipment
- responses to a new system of working, recently introduced
- feedback on the effects of a recent burglary upon files, stores, work materials, etc., for which the support employee is responsible

As we have already discovered, an all-purpose way of structuring a written document is to use the beginning – middle – end approach. And indeed, just such a structure is employed when producing a short report. The short report itself may take on several slightly different formats, according to the kind of details supplied. For example, a simple, short report may consist of three main section headings, each followed by several paragraphs.

REPORT

For: The Head of Department Date: 18 August 199-

INVESTIGATION INTO RECENT INCREASES IN STAFF ABSENCES

By: Jane Green Administrative Assistant

Copies To: Personnel Manager

Figure 2.8 Example of a report's title page

Example of the three-section report format

INTRODUCTION

Xxxxxxxxxxxxxxxxxxxxxxxxxxxxxxxxxxxxxxxxxxxxxxxxxxxx xxxxxxxxxxxxxxxxxxxxxxxxxxxxxxxxxxxxxxxxxxxxxxxxxxxxx xxxxxxxxxxxxxxxxxxxxxxxxxxxxxxxxxxxxxxxx

Xxxxxxxxxxxxxxxxxxxxxxxxxxxxxxxxxxxxxxxxxxxxxxxxxxxx xxxxxxxxxxxxxxxxxxxxxxxxxxxxxxxxxxxxxxxxxxxxxxxxxxxxx xxxxxxxxxxxxxxxxxxxxxxxxxxxxxxxxxxxxxxxxxxxxxxxxxxxxx

Xxxxxxxxxxxxxxxxxxxxxxxxxxxxxxxxxxxxxxxxxxxxxxxxxxxx xxxxxxxxxxxxxxxxxxxxxxxxxxxxxxxxxxxxxxxxxxxxxxxxxxxxx xxxxxxxxxxxxxxxxxxxxxxxxxxxxxxxxxx

INFORMATION

Xxxxxxxxxxxxxxxxxxxxxxxxxxxxxxxxxxxxxxxxxxxxxxxxxxxx xxxxxxxxxxxxxxxxxxxxxxxxxxxxxxxxxxxxxxxxxxxxxxxxxxxxx xxxxxxxxxxxxxxxxxxxxxxxxxxxxxxxxxxxxxxxxxxxxxxxxx

Xxxxxxxxxxxxxxxxxxxxxxxxxxxxxxxxxxxxxxxxxxxxxxxxxxxx xxxxxxxxxxxxxxxxxxxxxxxxxxxxxxxxxxxxxxxxxxxxxxxxxxxxx xxxxxxxxxxxxxxxxxxxxxxxxxxxxxxxxxxxxxxxx

Xxxxxxxxxxxxxxxxxxxxxxxxxxxxxxxxxxxxxxxxxxxxxxxxxxxx xxxxxxxxxxxxxxxxxxxxxxxxxxxxxxxxxxxxxxxxxxxxxxxxxxxxx xxxxxxxxxxxxxxxxxxxxxxxxxxxxxxxxxx

CONCLUSIONS

Xxxxxxxxxxxxxxxxxxxxxxxxxxxxxxxxxxxxxxxxxxxxxxxxxxxxxx
xxxxxxxxxxxxxxxxxxxxxxxxxxxxxxxxxxxxxxxxxxxxxxxxxxxxxxx

Other types of short report, however, make more use of what is called **schematic layout**. This means setting out a report which employs these display techniques:

- **indentation:** this is a term used to describe the moving of an entry or block of text at least one tab stop nearer to the right hand margin. Tab stops form part of the formatting commands of word-processing software. They can be set so as to create internal page margins, from which to start text entries.

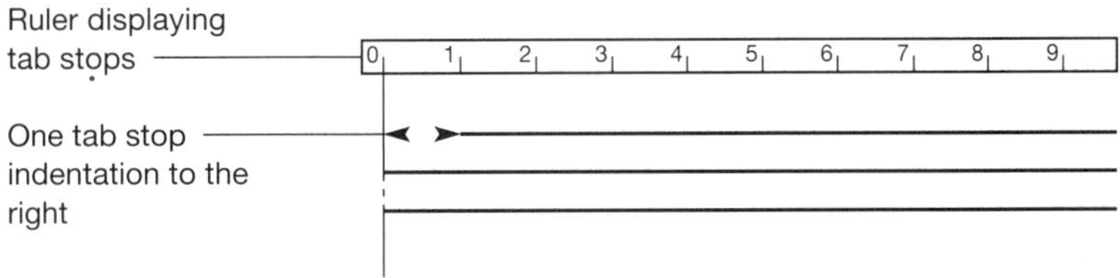

- **centring:** in order to make a piece of text or a table etc. stand out from the normal run of the report's paragraphs, it may be centred:

Xxxxxxxxxxxxxxxxxxxxxxxxxxxxxxxxxxxxxxxxxxxxxxx:
Xxxxxxxxxxxxxxxxxxxxxxxxxxxxxxxxx
xxxxxxxxxxxxxxxxxxxxxxxxxxxxxxxxx
xxxxxxxxxxxxxxxxxxxxxxxxxxxxxxxxxxxxxxx

- **number referencing:** a set of numbers (which follow a sequence) is given to the section headings and certain points in the text to enable the report's readers to quote it in a memorandum or letter, and so to pinpoint the item quickly and accurately:

2.0 INFORMATION

Xxxxxxxxxxxxxxxxxxxxxxxxxxxxxxxxxxxxxxxxxxxxxxxxxx

2.1 Xxxxxxxxxxxxxxxxxxxxxxxxxxxxxxxxxxxxxxxxxxx
xxxxxxxxxxxxxxxxxx. Xxxxxxxxxxxxxxxxxxxxx

2.2 Xxxxxxxxxxxxxxxxxxxxxxxxxxxxxxxxxxxxxxxxxxx
xxxxxxxxxxxxxxxxxxxxxxxxxxxxxxxxxxx

- **use of bullets or numbers to list points and to make them stand out:**
- Xxxxxxxxxxxxxxxxxxxxxx Xxxxxxxxxxxxxxxxxxxxxxxx
- Xxxxxxxxxxxxxxxxxxxxxxxxxxxxxxxxxxxxxxxxxxxxxxxx

1 Xxxxxxxxxxxxxxxxxxxxxxxxxxxxxx
2 Xxxxxxxxxxxxxxxxxxxxxxxxxxxxxxxxxxxxxxxxxxxxxxx

- **use of white space:** sometimes, two or more line spaces, as well as wider margins, are used to make an entry stand out more visibly:

  Xxxxxxxxxxxxxxxxxxxxxxxxxxxxxxxxxxxxxxxxxxxxxxxxxx xxxxxxxxxxxxxxxxxxxxxxxxxxxxxxxxxxxxxx:

  - Xxxxxxxxxxxxxxxxxxxxxxxxxxx
  - Xxxxxxxxxxxxxxxx Xxxxxxxxx

  Xxxxxxxxxxxxxxxxxxxxxxxxxxxxxxxxxxxxxxxxxxxxxxxxxx

As well as using the above schematic layout techniques, report writers use other features available on current word-processing packages to make specific text entries stand out and catch the eye:

- USE OF CAPITAL LETTERS

  U S E   O F   C A P I T A L S   D O U B L E   S P A C E D
- Use Of Initial Capital Letters (making the first letter of each word a capital).
- **USE OF BOLD CAPITAL LETTERS**

  Bold Initial Capitals or lower case words.
- *USE OF ITALICS FOR CAPITALS,*

  Italic Initial Capitals or lower case words
- Use of underlining

  (Either the whole piece or individual words) and of double underlining

KEY POINT

Formatting reports effectively

Follow these guidelines for formatting text in short reports:

- Use bold for main title and main section headings.
- Use initial capitals (with or without underlining) for sub-headings.
- Use italics for the names of places, books, titles of works, etc.
- Perhaps use a larger printer's point size for a main title, but otherwise stick to the same capitals and lower case point size throughout.

Continues ▶

- Even though they are available, resist the temptation to use several different fonts in the report. Stick to an accepted one, such as *Times New Roman* or *Helvetica.*

INDIVIDUAL SKILLS-BUILDING ACTIVITIES

Developing document formatting and composing skills

Task 1 Revise the guidelines on short report formatting and text presentation on pages 135–138, and then see how many of the techniques described you can identify in the report in Figure 2.9.

REPORT

FOR:	**Mr F Dixon**	**Head of Department**	**Date: 25 March 199-**
BY:	**Ms D Andrews**	**Administrative Assistant**	**Copies To: Section Heads**

INVESTIGATION INTO POSSIBLE SECURITY RISKS IN THE DEPARTMENT

1.0 INTRODUCTION

Following upon the break-in and theft of an extensive range of items from the Personnel Department's offices on Thursday last, I was asked by Mr Dixon, Head of Department, to carry out an investigation of current possible security risks in the Department and to submit a short, written report to him, with a copy to the Personnel Manager, by Friday 27 March 199-.

The report's terms of reference were to check the satisfactory operation of company security systems as well as the level of security regarding both company and staff's materials and personal possessions. The report's brief also included the making of appropriate recommendations.

2.0 INFORMATION

2.1 ***Areas of Investigation***

The following areas were investigated:

- In-house alarm and intruder security systems
- Procedures carried out by staff for entering and leaving the Department at start and close of work
- Awareness on the part of staff of Departmental procedures for locking away confidential materials, and of logging off computers securely

Continues ▶

- Use of lockable drawers in desks, locks on filing cabinets and general security procedures.
- Views of section heads and individual staff on Departmental security

2.2 ***In-house Alarm and Intruder Security Systems***

With the help of the Maintenance Engineer, all installed sound and visual alarm systems were test-operated and found to be fully satisfactory. The three closed-circuit cameras installed were also found to be fully operational and no problems were discovered with the video-tape recording system.

A test, using a contact not known to staff, resulted in this person being able to enter the premises and penetrate as far as the Department's offices without being stopped or questioned. This took place between 1.00 pm and 1.30 pm on Tuesday 21 March 199-.

2.3 ***Staff Procedures for Entering and Leaving the Department***

In general terms, these procedures were found to be satisfactory. Ample evidence was found of the section heads operating an effective rota for unlocking and locking the main entrance to the Department at start and close of work. The pull-down bars of the emergency fire exits were found to be operating satisfactorily while maintaining strong locks from any external entry attempts.

2.4 ***Security of Company Materials and Staff's Personal Possessions***

2.4.1 ***Company Materials***

Some shortcomings were found in certain sections (Maintenance and Contracts) where confidential documents had been left on desks overnight. Also, three filing cabinets were found to have been left unlocked on two mornings when checks were carried out.

2.4.2 ***Staff Personal Possessions***

A mixed picture emerged here, with some staff keeping their clothing and personal possessions securely locked away at all times in drawers and lockers, while others left handbags, purses and clothes in full sight and unattended.

2.4.3 ***Computer Security***

Security procedures in this area proved to be most satisfactory, and staff interviewed spoke highly of the recent training programme on computer security organised by Personnel.

Continues ▶

However, two members of staff (Frank Johnston and Rita Charles) stated that they were not sure about how to leave their PCs secure while still switched on, during a temporary absence, and relied on the screen-saving display.

2.5 *Discussions on Security with Heads of Section and Staff*

At a meeting of section heads, concern was expressed about the ease with which unauthorised persons could penetrate the premises, as well as about the ongoing lack of security guards between the hours of 1730 and 2130. They also stressed that they frequently reminded staff about leaving personal possessions lying around.

Support staff complained about not being issued with keys to the Department and about having to wait around until the duty section head arrived. All were upset about the recent break-in, which has most certainly caused a change in attitude generally. The most serious view, commented upon by most staff interviewed, concerned the establishment of an informal route through the Department to Accounts. All felt that a stop should be made to this development, since not all Accounts staff were known and so readily recognisable.

3.0 CONCLUSIONS

The following conclusions are drawn from the investigation:

- In-house security equipment is functioning satisfactorily, especially in terms of out-of-hours security.
- Security concerning visitors during the day was found to be lax and ineffective, especially in terms of reception's responsibilities.
- A reasonable level of Departmental security exists regarding the locking away of confidential materials, but staff in Maintenance and Contracts were found to be lax at times.
- Most staff take care of their personal possessions, but some are careless,
- Computer security is generally of a high standard. Arrangements have been made already to address the problems revealed by Frank Johnston and Rita Charles.
- Staff interviewed expressed concerns about the unsatisfactory level of security regarding unauthorised visitors and the through-route to Accounts.

Continues ▶

As a result of the investigations carried out for this report, the following recommendations are made:

3.1 The lax security at reception should be investigated as a matter of urgency and appropriate steps taken.

3.2 The developing habit of using the Department as a short-cut to Accounts should be directly stopped.

3.3 Improved surveillance between 1730 and 2130 should be considered as a matter of priority.

3.4 A reminder should be sent to all staff over your signature which emphasises the need to keep confidential and sensitive materials secure at all times, as well as to bring home to staff the need to take care of personal possessions and to use the secure lockers provided.

3.5 Despite some staff's unhappiness, the practice of opening and closing the Department by means of a rota of section heads should continue.

Figure 2.9 **Example of schematically formatted short, formal report**

Task 2 Bear in mind before answering the following questions that the *information* section of the report is shorter than it would be in reality, so as to save space in this text for other study material.

Study the model report carefully and then write down your answers to the following questions:

1 Would it be possible to use the memorandum format for this kind of report?

2 What is the purpose of numbering some sections in the report? Should the points highlighted with bullet points have been numbered instead? If so, why? If not, why not?

3 Can you think of any other formatting techniques which could have been used to make the report easier to read and absorb?

4 Why did the *Information* section start with a list of the areas investigated? What do you think is the point of this approach?

5 If you check the report's sentences carefully, you will find that they are written in the passive, a construction which uses the verb *to be* and a verb's past participle:

Ample evidence *was found*

concern *was expressed*

checks *were carried out*

What effect on the style of the report does this use of the passive have?

6 How many times does the report writer use the word 'I' in the report? Why is this?

7 What is the effect of writing in short paragraphs within the three sections of the report?

8 In your view, how successful are the techniques of using: *capital letters*, ***bold***, *italics* and *underlining* in making the report easier to read and understand?

9 How accurately do the conclusions summarise the information points? How justified are the recommendation points, given the evidence unearthed? How important is it for conclusions and recommendations to reflect accurately the detailed information obtained for a report?

10 Why does the report writer use the word *should* and not *must* in the recommendations part of the report's *Conclusions*?

The advertisement

Basically, there are two kinds of advertisement which organisations produce themselves or ask a newspaper's advertising staff to produce for them:

- the classified advertisement
- the display advertisement

The classified advertisement is the type which appears in columns of fairly small print in a newspaper, under headings like: *Personal, For Sale, Wanted, Pets, Boats and Boating.* For the most part, they consist of a mix of capital letters and an abbreviated lower case text:

MIRROR DINGHY Sail No: 22,343
Wooden constr. Well preserved,
includes trolley and trailer. V. good
sailing record. £485 o.n.o

Since a local or national newspaper prints such advertisements according to its own house style of layout and font, there is not much which can be done to vary the format of published classified advertisements.

The display advertisement

On the other hand, the display advertisement offers much more scope for producing a creative, eye-catching format. This section, therefore, explains the key features of effective formatting and design for display advertising.

First of all, it should be emphasised that the development of both word-processing and desk-top publishing software has greatly extended the ability of even small organisations to produce in-house advertisements which appear most professional, thanks to the features of borders, shading and tinting and the inclusion of clip-art images. In addition, software can provide the facility to import any kind of image into the design by means of an electronic scanner, which converts an image into an electronic signal a computer can pick up and store.

There are any number of ways of formatting an effective advertisement, but most display advertisements embody these main features of design:

CHECKLIST

Key features of effective display advertisement design

- a bold, eye-catching headline or slogan
- one or more images (photos, cartoons, line-drawings, clip-art images, etc.) to provide visual appeal
- use of sub-headlines and short, snappy phrases to convey the message
- use of strong colours and white space to attract the tired eyes of, say, commuters in buses or tubes, or stuck in traffic-jams

KEY POINT

Successful advertisements stick in the mind

An effective display advertisement is one which communicates a simple message quickly and in a way that enables its readers to remember it.

There are no set rules when it comes to the formats of advertisements. Indeed, we have been deluged by so many advertisements by the time we reach adulthood, that we tend, instinctively, to turn the newspaper page quickly to avoid them, or are able to stare at them for minutes on end during a bus or underground journey without even taking them in! For this reason, designers of advertisements today are constantly seeking to produce unusual effects which do manage to capture our attention, such as an entirely white and blank full page in a broadsheet newspaper with a message in tiny print set in one corner. Similarly, photographs may be made to lie by, for example, placing Mrs Thatcher's head on Mr Major's shoulders, etc.

Such tricks of the trade need all the resources of an advertising department's creative unit. Nevertheless, simple yet effective advertisements can be produced by following these guidelines on layout.

CHECKLIST

Guidelines for producing an effective display advertisement format

- First, think carefully about the main effect you wish your advertisement to have on its readers. Are they to make an immediate response (e.g. telephone a number and enquire about a product or service) or simply recall a catchy slogan or image as part of a promotion to get new customers to recognise a product's packaging?
- Decide on the size of your advertisement. Note that some magazines and newspapers sell advertising space in terms of: entire, half, quarter and eighth page sizes. Remember that A5, A4 and A3 paper sizes can be readily copied on departmental photocopiers, which is why they are popular for in-house advertisements. Consider how you will use such paper – whether in portrait or landscape position.
- Explore the range of images which are available to you and which would provide suitable visual appeal; think carefully how you will install them on your design sheet (e.g. by using scissors and paste on an original photograph, by importing as a clip-art file, or by hand-drawing). Think, too, about the time and effort needed to include certain types of image in a display advertisement, and therefore about which is most likely to prove cost-effective.
  - Work out in advance the draft wording of:

Continues ▶

(a) a main slogan or headline

(b) the sub-heading and key points of the message of the advertisement

- Consider carefully how you wish to communicate the key action request of the advertisement (e.g. the classic: *BUY SOME NOW!*).
- Experiment with various mixes of headline, image and text until you arrive at a pleasing format (see Figures 2.10, 2.11 and 2.12).
- Produce the first, draft version of your display advertisement.

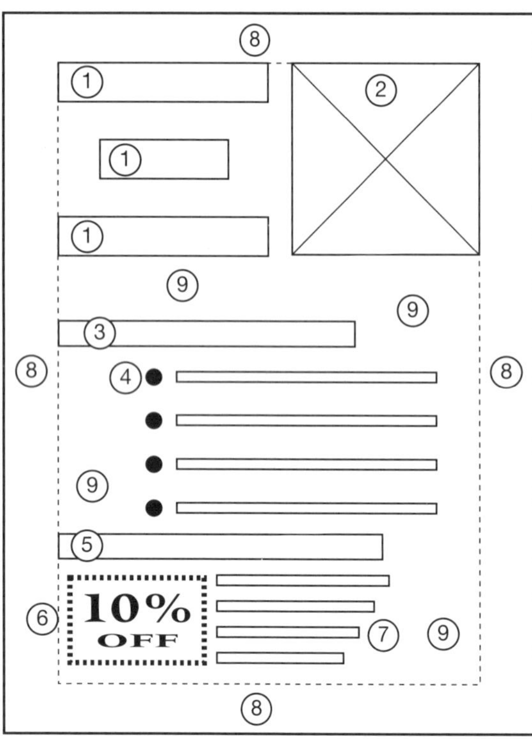

Key to display advertisment format A4 portrait size (e.g. for mail-order plants and bulbs)

1. Boldest, eye-catching slogan (e.g. SPECIAL SPRING 199– PLANT & BULB OFFER)
2. Colour photograph of a border of roses and perennial plants
3. Sub-heading for key sales points (e.g. CHOOSE FROM THESE SELECTED OFFERS:)
4. Bulleted details of the four special offers
5. Sub-heading introducing How to Order section
6. Special discount offer token if order sent within 7 days
7. Address for order
8. Margins set around advertisment
9. Use of while space to make text and images stand out

Figure 2.10 **Example of the format of an A4 size portrait display advertisement**

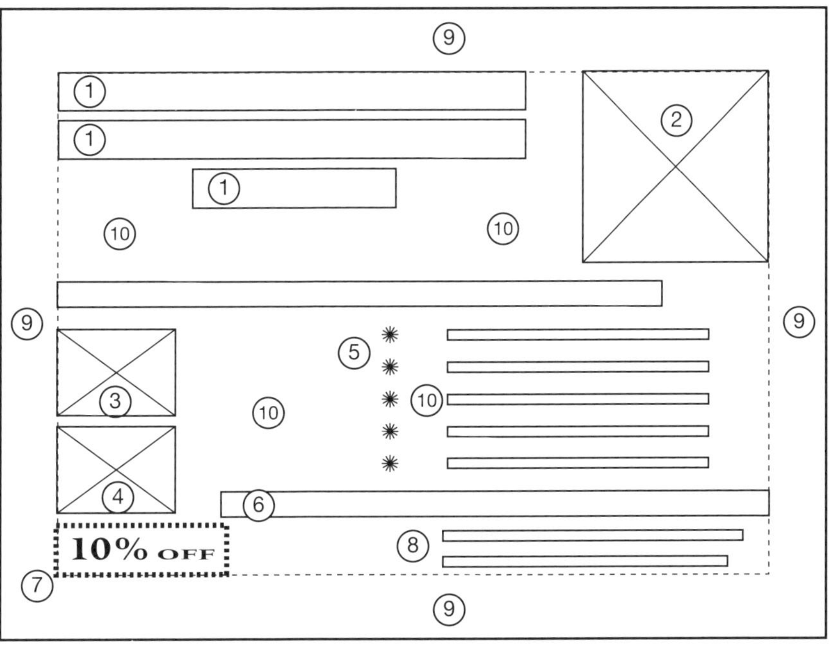

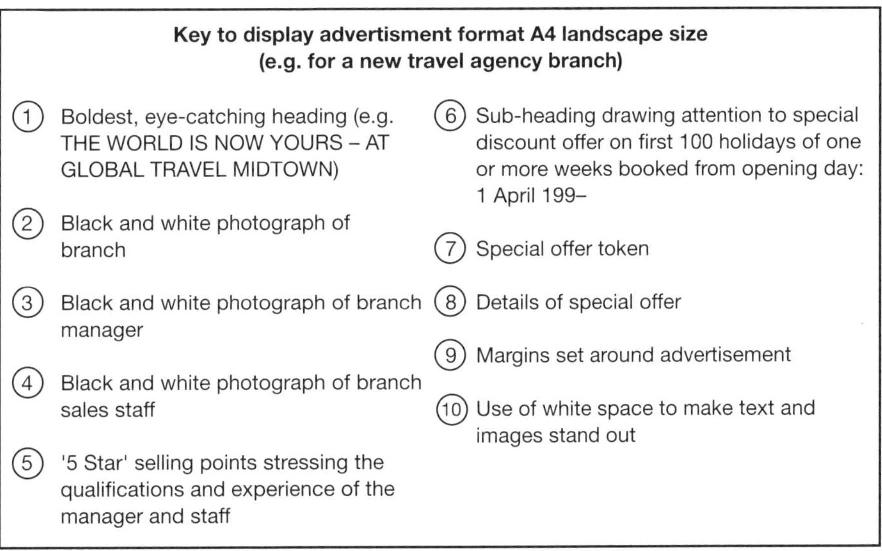

Key to display advertisment format A4 landscape size (e.g. for a new travel agency branch)

(1) Boldest, eye-catching heading (e.g. THE WORLD IS NOW YOURS – AT GLOBAL TRAVEL MIDTOWN)

(2) Black and white photograph of branch

(3) Black and white photograph of branch manager

(4) Black and white photograph of branch sales staff

(5) '5 Star' selling points stressing the qualifications and experience of the manager and staff

(6) Sub-heading drawing attention to special discount offer on first 100 holidays of one or more weeks booked from opening day: 1 April 199–

(7) Special offer token

(8) Details of special offer

(9) Margins set around advertisement

(10) Use of white space to make text and images stand out

Figure 2.11 **Example of the format of an A4 size landscape display advertisement**

BASIN STREET JAZZ CLUB

10-12 WHARF QUAY BRISTOL PHONE/FAX 0117 987456

JUST THE HOTTEST NIGHT SPOT IN TOWN! FOR JAZZ AND RAZZMATAZZ!

RESIDENT BAND: JIMMY RAY AND HIS LITTLE RAYS OF SUNSHINE

VOCALIST: KAY WINTERS

GUEST BANDS	TUESDAY	7 JUNE:	CHUCK NEWBERRY'S
	WEDNESDAY	8 JUNE:	MODERN JAZZ
	THURSDAY	9 JUNE:	QUINTET
	FRIDAY	**9 JUNE:**	**MIKE McGARRY AND THE MOONSHINERS**

SATURDAY 10 JUNE: **CHICAGO FATS ALLSTARS**

- ORIGINAL DIXIELAND JAZZ AT ITS BEST!

SUNDAY 11 JUNE: ALLCOMERS TALENT EVENING

TICKETS HALF PRICE!

DANCE TILL YOUR KNEES ACHE! FULLY LICENSED BAR

HAPPY HOUR 8-9PM DAILY

ADMISSION: 8-11.00 PM ALL RIGHTS RESERVED ENTRY: 7-10.00 PM £5.00

10-11.00 PM £7.50

Figure 2.12 **Example of the format and design of a display advertisement**

WHAT DO YOU THINK?

1. What do *you* think are the four most important features of effective document formats?
2. Does it really matter if a comma or full-stop is included (in error) in the recipient's address in an open punctuation letter?
3. Why is that most organisations decide to adopt and follow current conventions and practices of document formatting?
4. 'It's high time all the cobwebs were blown away from the finicky procedures surrounding formatting! Hang loose and do your own thing. If you can read it, that's all that matters. After all, it's your document, isn't it?' Do you agree?
5. Why do you think some managers always take care to ensure that they read the memoranda that their support staff have produced, before allowing them to be routed around the organisation?
6. Email written messages are generally much more chatty and less 'hung up' on layout rules than their paper-based counterparts. Why should this be so?
7. What do you see as the pros and cons of the pre-printed report form as opposed to the 'blank-sheet' investigatory short report when it comes to effective reporting?
8. In your opinion, is all the time and effort put into formatting written documents according to currently accepted practices worthwhile?
9. Some communication experts reckon that producing a good written report is about the most difficult communications skill. What do you think?
10. As consumers and employees, are we really as influenced by the format and design of a display advertisement as the experts would like to think?

SUMMARY OF KEY POINTS

How to format written documents

- While there are no absolute rules for formatting written documents at work, a set of long-standing and agreed conventions have existed for many years, which most organisations agree to follow.
- Developments in information technology have caused these conventions to be changed and will certainly continue to bring about further changes.

- The essentials of effective document formatting are: (a) to help make it easier for the reader to grasp information easily and promptly (b) to help identify which parts are most important in the document and which less so (c) to provide a pleasing layout which captures the reader's interest and attention.
- The invention and development of word-processing and desk-top publishing computer software has brought enormous advantages to effective document formatting by (a) enabling clip-art and scanned-in images to be used, and (b) providing a wide range of fonts, print sizes and textual features (e.g. bold, italics, underlining).
- Some document formats, such as those of pre-printed forms, are designed to enable information to be entered simply and in ways which help the end-user to collect and analyse data.
- The format of the short report and display advertisement are most demanding to produce, and an effort must be made to acquire the skills of schematic layout (see pages 137–138) and display advertisement design (see pages 145–148).

SELF-CHECK REVIEW TEST

How to create formats for written documents

1. Explain briefly the main features of the fully blocked, open punctuation letter.
2. Complete the following: Dear Madam ... Yours — Dear Mr Smith ... Yours —
3. What are the entries made in a letter to remind its reader that a) something has been sent with it and b) someone else has also received it?
4. Why do letters include *Our ref* and *Your ref*?
5. Why do many letters include a subject heading?
6. List the parts of a memohead, against which text is entered.
7. Memoranda also start with *Dear* ... and finish with *Yours* .... Right or wrong?
8. Explain briefly what is meant by a schematic layout.
9. List three common section headings used for a three-part short report.
10. List three different ways of making text stand out in a report.

Continues 

11 Outline briefly what an email message is and how it works.

12 List three main features of the format of a display advertisement.

When you have completed the above questions, turn to page 303 to check the answers provided with your own. If need be, revise the relevant section of Chapter 2 for those answers you got wrong.

INDIVIDUAL SKILLS-BUILDING ACTIVITIES

Developing skills in document production and formatting

Task 1 The following passage is a business letter which an accounts manager has decided to send to a customer who has received goods on credit, but who has defied all efforts to persuade him to pay for them. Your task is to format the letter in the accepted fully blocked, open punctuation layout, as well as to punctuate it correctly.

> our ref jg sp 24aps 12 october 199- mr a p smith proprietor chatsmore rest home 24 brockenhurst way lymington hants ly12 pt4 dear sir overdue account £892.24 in spite of the copy statement and reminders sent to you on 3 april 199- 21 april 199- and 7 may 199- your account for february 199- still remains outstanding enclosed please find a final statement as previously stated the period of credit extended to you was agreed as one calendar month from receipt of statement unless the above overdue account is settled in full within seven days i shall be compelled to undertake the necessary legal action to recover the debt yours faithfully john green accounts manager

Task 2 Your parents have just won a family holiday (lasting three weeks) in a newspaper competition. The holiday takes the form of a Caribbean cruise in the first three weeks of January. According to the informational literature that has been sent to you, some aspects of the holiday are educational, such as a tour of the old forts on Jamaica and various lectures on ship about the culture and geography of the islands you will visit. Carry out the following two activities:

1. Write a well-formatted letter to your teacher which seeks permission to be absent from your study centre for the first two weeks of the forthcoming spring term.
2. As your teacher, text-process a memorandum to your head-teacher which explains the situation and request which your letter has detailed. Assume that your teacher is not sure about granting permission and is asking the head to give his/her advice and a decision. Also, assume that your teacher is

sympathetic to your request, especially about swapping UK grey winter skies for the sun and warmth of the Caribbean! Produce a suitably formatted memorandum on an A4 sheet.

Task 3 A number of students in your class are keen to put on an event which would be based in your study centre, and which would raise money for extending and updating the equipment (hi-fi, computer games pcs, hot drinks vending machines, etc.) in your student common room. Your teacher has raised this interest with the senior manager of your study centre, who has asked you to produce a short report, which meets these terms of reference, supplied by your head:

> The idea sounds fine, but I should like to receive a short, written report within ten working days, which details the idea chosen for the event, explains how it would be run, estimates what support from us would be needed, and which includes a forecast of a) the cost of putting on the event, and b) the amount of money raised for the equipment.

Research and then produce a suitably formatted short report which meets the above terms of reference.

Task 4 Having completed the report for Task 3, now design and produce a suitable display advertisement to be posted on your study centre walls and noticeboards which will suitably promote the event you researched and persuade staff and students to take part and give generously.

Note: you can produce the display advertisement either on an A3 or A4 sheet of paper. It should include at least one example of an image. You are free to decide what coloured paper and inks, etc., you will employ, and should use your initiative in this regard.

Creating a suitable style for a document

This section of Chapter 2 concentrates upon the skills needed to create a style which is suited to the purpose of a written document. Already in this chapter, we have learned that there is a great deal of difference between the language (words and expressions) used to convey factual information and the language used to persuade people.

By the same token, the situation in which a document is produced – grave, serious, congratulating, amusing, etc.–also has a great effect upon the style in which its message is conveyed. Again, the profile and background of the people who are expected to read the document will also have a bearing on its style.

The following checklist illustrates the major influences upon the style in which a document is written at work.

CHECKLIST

Major influences upon a document's style

- **The background or situation:** A sensitive writer is careful to ensure that there is no mis-match between the style of a document and the background against which it is written. For example, it would be highly inappropriate for a letter confirming that its recipient has been made redundant to include a jokey reference to him or her 'having more time now to play golf.'
- **The nature and relationship of the document's recipient:** Quite naturally, some people who receive written documents from organisations enjoy a special relationship, such as a customer or tax officer. A writer to such people will take especial care to keep a customer happy, and not to offend the tax officer! By the same token, a junior employee writing to a senior one will make sure that a courteous tone is maintained, so as not to affect his or her prospects.
- **The intention of the document:** Virtually all written documents have a specific aim – to sell, recover a bad debt, to inform, to reply to an enquiry. The aim of any document will directly affect its style. For instance, a sales letter to a business's account customers is bound to adopt a warm and friendly tone, to stress the value of the sales item, to emphasise the ease of ordering and the support surrounding any given order, etc. On the other hand, a final letter seeking to recover a long-outstanding debt will be much more terse and formal.
- **The personal profile of the recipient:** If, for example, the recipient is as expert and experienced as the writer in a memorandum's or report's subject, then the language used can be full of technical terms and specialist abbreviations; if not, then the writer will need to select much simpler, everyday language and do more explaining. In a similar way, a writer must consider carefully whether a reader might have different views and beliefs from his or her own.

As can be readily imagined, it pays not to leap into print (a common danger among email users) when needing to produce a written document, before having given due thought to creating a suitable style for it.

The following section supplies a set of guidelines which will help you to create a suitable style for the documents you produce at work.

CHECKLIST

Guidelines for creating a suitable style in a written document

1 Consider before starting any writing the following alternatives:

What is the essential aim of this document? Is it to:

- *provide a set of detailed and factual information points?*
- *supply feedback on an event or situation to a manager, which will mix facts and personal views or reactions?*
- *persuade the recipient to adopt a particular view or attitude?*
- *put across neutrally a set of balanced pros and cons, while allowing the recipient to make up his or her mind without pressure?*

It is essential to be clear on a document's key aims if a suitable style is to be created in it.

2 Consider carefully the relationship which you will establish (through the writing of the document) with your recipient.

What is the essence of your relationship with the recipient?

- *supplier – customer*
- *support staff member – line manager*
- *employee – senior manager*
- *employee – external official contact (e.g. bank manager, accountant, factory inspector, county council fire officer)*

The nature of the relationship will influence directly whether a suitable style should be formal and impersonal, friendly and direct, helpful and courteous etc.

3 Consider whether the recipient will share your own views and attitudes or whether, perhaps because the recipient's age or experience is different from your own, you need to adapt your style so you will not offend him or her.

The following memorandum to the managing director (a male in his sixties) which was sent by a group of junior staff in their twenties is an example of an unsuitable style:

> **SUBJECT: REQUEST FOR A CHANGE TO THE WAY THE ANNUAL CHRISTMAS STAFF PARTY IS RUN**
>
> ... As you will be only too aware, last year, a lot of younger staff left the party early because of the boring music. This was even more irritating to them because the elderly staff did not even dance to it, but just stood around drinking and smoking. And half of them – as usual – complained that it was far too loud.
>
> We would all like to have a disco instead of the same old Jack Baker Quartet and the golden oldies of the fifties and sixties, and hope you will come to see our point of view...

The writers of the above memorandum undoubtedly have some cause to seek at least a mix of entertainment. But how responsive is the MD likely to be to the message, worded as it is?

SUMMARY OF KEY POINTS

How to create a suitable style in written documents

- Before starting to write a document, consider carefully how the background of the topic, the relationship between the recipient and you, the essential aim of the document and the profile of its reader(s) are most likely to affect the style needed for it to work.
- Also, before starting, and while writing, keep in mind your choices – factual and neutral words, or persuasive ones which change people's views.
- Keep firmly in mind the needs of the recipient(s) – whether technical language will be understood, and where care needs to be taken not to offend by mistake, because someone's likely views and outlooks were ignored.

INDIVIDUAL SKILLS-BUILDING ACTIVITY

Creating a suitable style

Re-write the above memorandum extract in a style which you think would be more likely to achieve the writers' aim. Compare your version with those produced by other students in your class.

GENERAL GROUP SKILLS-BUILDING ACTIVITIES

Assessing written styles

Task 1 Read the following extracts carefully, and make notes on what you think is suitable or unsuitable in terms of the styles in which they are written.

1 Letter to a small business proprietor from a sales executive:

...I regret that I have to cancel our appointment for next Monday at 10.00 am, as I have to see an important customer. I will get back to you in due course.

2 Letter to an elderly council house resident who has telephoned the district council's offices to ask for a leaking tap to be repaired:

Your orally communicated message of 3 March 199- regarding the fluid emission from the faucet in your scullery is acknowledged. It is with regret that I have to advise you of a temporary deferment of the rectification of this deficiency, due to the indisposition of a majority of the Council's hydro-management technicians, who have succumbed to gastro-enteritis. A resumption of customary support services is anticipated by Monday next.

I trust this will serve to clarify the matter.

Note: You may need to use your dictionary for **2**.

3 Memorandum to all departmental staff on the staff holiday rota

Dear All

Before he went off on his winter holiday, the boss asked me to do him a favour and give you the low-down on what he thinks about the way you lot are sorting out your summer holidays. I'm sorry to tell you that he was fair gutted at the diabolical selfishness you all showed when filling out his holiday form. There has been a zilch response for the months of March and October – surprise, surprise! And – you're gonna love this, 99% of all staff think they're gonna get off for the month of August. They'll be lucky, know what I mean?...

4 A display advertisement for a personal computer

POTENTIAL COMPUTER USERS ARE INVITED TO CONSIDER THIS PROPOSAL

The Apex Computer Manufacturing Company has recently completed the launch of its new Domicile Computer, which is now available for inspection by potential purchasers. This highly innovative model embodies an optimal, yet straightforward specification, including: 16mb EDO RAM, 1.5gb HD, Stealth 64 video VRAM with 2mb, 256K Pipeline Burst Cache, 6- speed CD ROM drive, and a 28.4 V34 Standard modem.

As the above specification clearly indicates, there is no justifiable rationale for selecting an alternative purchase.

5 Extract from a short report on a Health & Safety survey:

INFORMATION

2.3 Then I thought it would be useful if I had a chat with the people in production. After all, they're the ones who are pretty much in the firing line, when it comes to health and safety. Anyway, I popped over on Thursday last, during their mid-morning break, which was a good time for me, since Thursday mornings are my least busy, especially now that Mavis is back off holiday. Bert Hoskins had kindly got the group together, so we got stuck right in. When I say we, I really mean they, because there was no shortage of feed-back, I assure you! Well, Ernie Stackford (who runs the press) said that, to his mind, but meaning no disrespect, which he particularly wanted me to ensure I did not forget to mention, which I have not, too little attention is being paid at the moment to the dangers of leaving equipment switched on, but with nobody around. As he quite rightly pointed out ...

6 Letter of complaint about a faulty vacuum cleaner:

I have never been served by such a daft dolt in my life as the one who went through the motions of selling me the vacuum cleaner at your Midfield branch last Saturday.

What particularly annoyed me was the poster on the wall which read 'The Customer Is King!' Serf would be more like it, given the lack of attention I received during the first twenty minutes I was in your store. And, to cap it all, the wretched vacuum-cleaner broke down the first time I tried to use it. And I was all the more angry because your pushy manager persuaded me to buy foreign rubbish – as it has turned out.

I therefore look forward to your maintenance engineer calling as soon as possible, but before Friday, when I am holding a party for the Association of Electrical Retailers.

Task 2 In a general class discussion, decide what is right and what is wrong in style terms about each extract, and why – in particular – a style may be very unsuitable.

Task 3 On your own and with your teacher's guidance, re-write one of the above extracts in what you consider to be a more suitable style. Seek your teacher's help if you are not sure about the meaning of some of the more long-winded and complicated words used in some extracts.

How to edit and proof-read a document

So far in Chapter 2, the emphasis has been placed on producing written documents which achieve a specific aim, which are effectively structured, which are presented in an accepted format, and which use English appropriately. In this final section, the time has come to examine the techniques of editing and proof-reading documents.

In many ways, editing and proof-reading can be compared to a group of soldiers who carry out a last spit and polish session on their uniforms and equipment before taking part in an important parade. Before the widespread use of IT software, this was a tedious and time-consuming process. For example, a manager would compose a report, say, which a typist would then have to produce in several drafts, having to type each draft out afresh. There was no way of storing the report as an electronic file able to handle additions, deletions and changes where they occurred, while the bulk of the document remained unchanged. A single word change on an A4 sheet meant that the whole page would have to be retyped!

Today, thank goodness, editing and proof-reading take place very differently. Now, the same manager is likely to compose the first draft personally using a word-processing package. Depending on his or her document presentation skills, the manager will either carry out all the necessary editing and proof-reading, or pass the draft report to a skilled word-processing operator for completion. The first draft can be given to the operator in two simple, labour-saving ways:

- as a file on a 3.5 floppy disk which has been copied from the manager's computer
- as an electronic file sent via email on a computer network

Either way, there is no need to print it out on paper.

Editing techniques

Editing text well is a technique learned from experience and practice. However, these guidelines will help you to set off to a good start:

CHECKLIST

Guidelines for effective text editing

When editing text, continually ask yourself these questions:

- Does the title accurately summarise the theme of the document?

Continues

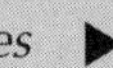

- Are the sections/paragraphs in the best running order, or should a change be made?
- Can any sentence (or part of it) be changed to convey the same meaning in fewer, simpler words?
- For documents possessing a schematic layout: Can any part be better displayed and/or referenced?
- Are there any repetitions which can be cut out, without destroying any key meaning?
- Are there any awkwardly constructed ideas which need to be re-phrased?
- Would the insertion of an example help to make a general point clearer? Should any examples be deleted, because they are over-long?
- Should paragraphs be given headings to make their content clearer? Should any long paragraphs be cut in two?
- Should any words in the text be in bold type, italicised or underlined (e.g. people's names, titles of works, key words)?

Techniques of proof-reading

There are two kinds of proof-reading to become familiar with: one which is involved with a paper original and the other with a computerised electronic file.

Proof-reading a paper manuscript

The following checklist provides you with the essential guidelines to follow when revising a manuscript which is hand-written or printed on paper.

CHECKLIST

Guidelines for proof-reading a paper manuscript

- If you are the author, put the document to one side for a day or two if possible. You will proof-read it much more clearly after a break from it, and detect errors much more readily.

Continues ▶

- There are three quite different kinds of error which writers make when producing a document:
  (a) errors of composition, e.g. using words incorrectly, getting a construction wrong and so on
  (b) errors in writing or text-processing which mean words are set down incorrectly
  (c) errors of spelling and punctuation

It pays to be on your guard for these various types of error, as, for example mixing *one* and *you* in a construction, transposing *likely* into *liekly*, using *principal* when it should have been *principle*, or omitting an apostrophe before an *s*, etc.

- There is no single, correct way of proof-reading a document. For instance, some people like to read it through two or three times, concentrating on a different aspect each time, for example, looking firstly for errors in composing sentences, then for spelling and punctuation errors and finally for what the Americans call typos or text production errors. Others focus on a paragraph or section at a time.
- Use whichever approach you feel comfortable with, but do read slowly, and without distraction or interruption. A word from a colleague is enough to make you lose your place and perhaps to overlook a glaring mistake.
- Proof-reading of early draft documents is made much easier if they are set out with double line spacing, so that corrections can be easily written above words or phrases which are then crossed out clearly.
- All changes to text should be entered on the page in a contrasting coloured ink, say red for correcting text in blue or black ink.

The following checklist illustrates some of the most frequently occurring errors which writers tend to make when creating a written document.

CHECKLIST

Common errors which occur in writing documents

- **omissions:** when ideas are coming thick and fast, it is easy to leave out a word or words in a sentence:

Continues ▶

The order which had already dispatched was sent in error, but it was late to recall it

Here, *been* dispatched and *too* late have been omitted in error; watch out for omissions like these, for they are sometimes quite hard to spot. Also, it is very easy to omit a phrase or a whole line of text when, say, copying a quotation from another document, as the eye moves back and forth.

- **errors in sentence construction:** it is also easy – when composing longer sentences – to mix up two different constructions, which then create confusion:

  Despite the increase in customer orders, and although the firm's summer holidays were at their peak, which resulted in all production records being broken.

- Here the writer is trying to say that in spite of two difficulties, the firm still managed to break its production record. But because of the length of the build up, a key middle section has been overlooked:

  ...at their peak, *the whole factory staff worked incredibly hard,* which resulted...

  The clause *the whole factory ... incredibly hard* was in the author's mind, but never got on to the paper!

- **final letters of words are 'clipped off':** again, in the creative process, the final letter or letters of words can be omitted:

  final for finally gettin for getting conscious for consciousness etc.

- **errors of punctuation:** these are very common, such as writing it's (it is) for its (of it), apostrophes in the wrong place for single or plural words: womens' shoes (wrong) women's shoes (correct), the omission of a question mark at the end of a sentence – especially long ones, etc.

- **errors in spelling commonly occurring words:**

Wrong	**Right**
occuring	occurring
seperately	separately
independant	independent (when it means not relying upon)
stationary	stationery (for paper and envelopes, etc.)

Proof-reading a word-processed file on a computer screen

Proof-reading text displayed on a screen presents another crop of pitfalls to watch out for. The following list indicates some of the main ones:

CHECKLIST

Pitfalls of text displayed on a screen

- **omissions:** words and even sections can be very easily left out in error as the result of using some of the editing features of a word-processing package. For instance, a section of text might be cut to the clip-board with the intention of pasting it in lower down a page, which the author then forgets to do. Again, the author may use the line spacing key to create an area in which to insert a line of text; in so doing a section is pushed down to the next electronic page which is not included in the printing command, so never sees the light of day!
- **deletions made in error:** a common mistake occurs when an author highlights a section of text in order to delete it, but allows the black ribbon to run across more text than was intended, which disappears just as swiftly!
- **printing command errors:** whole pages of text can easily be overlooked if a mistake is made in entering the printing command. If pages 5–10 are keyed in, when the correct numbers were: 5–12, the two pages of text could be missed out (a good reason for always entering the page numbering command for longer documents).
- **over-reliance on spell-checking features:** as experienced authors know only too well, relying totally on running a computer's spell-check on a document is a recipe for doom! Computers are incredibly fast, but equally simple-minded checkers of spelling. As long as a word is spelled correctly, fine. Never mind if it is the totally wrong version for a given context:

  The personal manager sited they're draught plan, witch should of shown a strait sided bench for the quire.

Nothing wrong here, says spell-checker! Ho-hum! But, in fairness, a spell-checking feature is very good at identifying typos. But you still have to decide for yourself which one of several alternatives offered to substitute.

KEY POINT

Be your *own* spellchecker!

It pays to become your own, fully self-reliant spell-checker!

SELF-CHECK REVIEW TEST

Creating a suitable style for a document; proof-reading and editing a document

1. List three major influences upon the style in which a document is written.
2. What aspects of the reader of a document should its writer keep in mind when creating a style for it?
3. Describe briefly the main purposes of proof-reading a document.
4. What is meant by the American term *typo*?
5. List four types of common error which often need correcting by proof-reading.
6. Write down three questions it helps to keep in mind when editing a document.

When you have completed your answers to these questions, check your answers with those on page 304. Revise the relevant sections of Chapter 2 for those answers you got wrong.

INDIVIDUAL AND GROUP SKILLS-BUILDING ACTIVITIES

Developing proof-reading skills

Task 1 Read through the following sentences carefully, and then re-write them, correcting any errors in spelling and punctuation you detect:

1. I have written to the Manager of the Norbury Hotel enquiring what accomodation he has available on 6 November.
2. There is unfortunately no acess to the roof from this floor.

3 The reps will definately be occupied elsewhere on that date.

4 Without exagerating, sales have trebled this month.

5 Is it really necesary to be an efficient proof-reader?

6 Of all our branches, throughout the country, it is the best stocked boys department.

7 In five year's time, when I will be 28 will there be any secretaries still using typewritters?

8 Yesterdays post was not taken to the Mail Room because Mary's off sick.

9 Transport, food, clothes, household goods, and raw materials will all be more expensive as a result of the increased price of oil.

10 This is the typists office. Is this yours? No, its the accounts office.

Task 2 Form into two or three class teams. Study the following sentences carefully to identify and correct any errors you find. Then choose one and challenge another group to write it out on the board correctly. Give the group five points for getting a sentence all right. Deduct a point for each error or oversight. Deduct three points for each error the challenging team cannot correct! Your teacher is referee.

1 Will you take the minutes at the finance comittee meeting.

2 A letter should conclude with 'Yours sincerly' when it begins with 'Dear Mr or Mrs'.

3 Would you arrange for all my calls to be transfered to extension 212, Miss Burton?

4 The memorandum was ommitted from the delegates' envelope.

5 The cost accountant drew up the management accounts'.

6 Each recipient should be informed of the timetable rearangements.

7 She accnowledged that Tom was group leader.

8 The telephone gave a wierd buzz and crackled into life.

9 Each visitor was recieved with due ceremony.

10 The Ajax sales representive had a psychology advantage over his competitor.

11 For that special ocassion – Moondew – a perfume can't forget!

12 Paperclips staples and typewritter ribbon made jumbled mess on the desk top.

(Activities reproduced from D W Evans, *Communication at Work*, 2nd edition, Addison Wesley Longman, 1987.)

PORTFOLIO-BUILDING ACTIVITIES

Produce four pieces of written material on straightforward subjects

1 A letter to a local organisation

Part of your GNVQ course is a week's work experience at a local organisation. This week is due to take place in two months' time. As part of your Communication programme, your teacher has asked you to identify a suitable organisation to contact in order to seek their help in providing you with a week's work experience. You also have to find out who would be the best person to write to in your selected organisation. The aims of your letter are to introduce yourself, to outline the nature of your GNVQ course, to explain what sort of work experience would be most suitable, and to ask for an interview if your request can be granted.

Compose a suitable letter – either hand-written or text-processed. Your letter should not exceed one and a half sides of A4, and should conform to the fully-blocked, open punctuation format.

2 A letter to your local careers centre (your teacher will supply the address and contact)

Your local Careers Centre has recently been reorganised. It now provides advice both on full-time careers in a wide range of occupations and on further study opportunities in schools, FE colleges and sixth forms and universities. You have been giving careful thought recently to your options after completing your GNVQ Foundation course. You want to find out what opportunities are available to you in either local full-time employment or further education in the broad area of your GNVQ vocational course.

Compose a suitable letter – either hand-written or text-processed. Your letter should not exceed one and a half sides of A4, and should conform to the fully-blocked, open punctuation format.

3 Compose a memorandum

Assume that you are the administrative assistant of Mrs Asha Patel, who is the refectory manager in your study centre.

Over the past two months, Mrs Patel has become increasingly annoyed by the decline in manners and consideration shown by students during the lunch-break in the refectory. This is how Mrs Patel expressed her frustration to you earlier today:

> 'I've finally had it with these kids! I mean, if it's not chucking beakers of water about, it's flicking mashed potato with forks, or trying to stick bread lumps on the ceiling. And despite all the notices, do they return their trays? Of course not, the lazy little tykes! And the cheek of some of them. Gladys Worsnip has twice threatened to walk out! Imagine trying to lay on 200 meals without your senior cook!
>
> I thought after the last admin staff meeting, I was supposed to get a regular daily rota of teachers to patrol the refectory. Some hope! Haven't heard a word about it since.'

And so it went on, as Mrs Patel got all her worries and stress off her chest. But, she ended up by asking you to compose a memorandum to the Headteacher/ Principal, setting out the nature of the problem, reminding him/her of the promise of help, and stressing what would be likely to happen soon if nothing was done.

Compose a suitable memorandum – either hand-written or text-processed. Your memorandum should not exceed one and a half sides of A4, and should conform to the fully-blocked, open punctuation format.

4 Compose a display advertisement

Your department at your study centre is holding an Open Day for parents, local employers and potential students on the 15th of next month. Your GNVQ class is putting on a suitable display to exhibit the range of work you are doing. Accordingly, your head of department has asked you to design a display advertisement (on one side of A4) which will form part of a general Open Day handbook, given to visitors on arrival. The aim of your display advertisement is to encourage visitors to visit your display and to give them (in a tempting way) some details of what they can expect to see. Note: your advertisement should include at least one image which suitably illustrates the text.

5 Compose a leaflet

Recently, a number of accidents have occurred in your study centre, in both specialist study and general access areas. Some have been caused by carelessness, such as people running along corridors or pushing violently through swing doors and hitting someone on the other side. Others have been caused by misusing tools or equipment in workshops, and by failing to follow basic safety precautions, such as wearing safety-glasses.

As a result, you have been asked to devise a leaflet (on one side of A4), which can be displayed on noticeboards, handed out, etc., which brings home to all users of your centre the dangers – to themselves and others – of failing to take due notice of the health and safety regulations and practices which are in place, and for that matter, outlined in the Centre Students' Handbook.

Compose a suitable leaflet on one side of A4 (hand-written or text-processed) which will meet the aims of your brief. It should include at least one suitable image.

6 Producing a short report

First carry out your research, and then produce a suitable short report (hand-written or text-processed in not more than three sides of A4) on *one* of the following topics:

(a) the range of full-time employment opportunities which exist in your locality in your vocational area, what sort of qualifications are needed, and what long-term career opportunities are available

(b) the nature of sporting and recreational activities available to teenagers in your locality, what strengths and weaknesses they possess, and how they might be extended in the future

(c) the availability of care and accommodation for the elderly residents in your local community, its strengths and weaknesses and how it might be best improved or further developed

(d) what developments based on information technology have been made by local manufacturing businesses in your locality, and how they are likely to develop during the coming five years

(e) how IT has changed the ways in which a small or a large business operates in your locality, and how it is likely to change further in the next five years

7 Designing a form

Your head of department has asked you to design a new application form for students wishing to join the GNVQ programme you are following. It needs to be clear and simple to complete, as short as is practicable, but capable of logging key details. First discuss with your teacher the likely areas of information needed, and then design a suitable form on no more than two sides of A4.

8 Designing a form

Assume that you are the leader of a local youth club, which is very popular. There is a waiting list, and places (when vacancies arise) are made available on the basis of what the would-be joiner can contribute to the club. Design a form which would prove suitable as an application for membership form on not more than one and a half sides of A4.

9 Designing a notice

A group in your study centre has decided to form a task-force to carry out voluntary work for elderly and infirm local residents at weekends, such as doing their shopping, clearing leaves, cleaning windows or running errands. The commitment would be for one or two hours on two weekend days each month. Design a suitable notice for display on your study centre noticeboards which outlines the idea and asks for volunteers.

10 Devising a set of instructions

Carry out your researches first, and then devise a set of instructions to meet one of the following briefs:

(a) how to use a computer in your study centre safely and with consideration for other users

(b) how to contact a first-aider in an emergency

(c) how to produce and submit for assessment a Foundation GNVQ portfolio activity

(d) how to find a study resource in your study centre's library, and how to take it out on loan.

11 Proof-reading two paragraphs and a letter

Proof-read and reproduce the following paragraphs and letter correctly:

(a) Its a well known fact that tourism is one of Britains expanding industry's this explains why more and more school leavers aply for catering and tourism courses at there local colleges or for aprenticeship in the industry.

(b) A well written buisness letter gives a good impresion of a firm. It proclaims it eficient and painstating in it's corespondance, which indicates a firm worth dealing with. The responsability for this good impression rests mainly on the text processors shoulders.

(c) Dear Mr Simpson

Enquiry for adjustable typists chairs

I am writing to enquire whether your company stocks adjustable typists chairs which might proof suitable for use in my company's General Office. At present some forteen audiotypists and word processing operators are employed in the office and of recent months I have recieved a number of complaints regarding the shortcomings of the chiars in use, some of which have been in use for over twelve years.

I have inspected the working hieghts of the desks used by the typists and find that this varies from 3.2 to 3.6 meters. The chairs would therefor need to be adjustable in a range of heights. Also, some of the ladies have criticised the suporting panels which support thier backs, and I should like to enquire if your chairs are helpfull in this regard?

The offices decor is predominately green and yellow and I wonder if you could suggest a colour which would blendin with our wall paper and carpets I should be gratefull if you would contact me with a view to arrangeing for one of your representatives' to call so that we would discuss the matter further.

I look forward to hearing from you.

Yours faithfully,

(Activity 11 reproduced from D W Evans, *Communication at Work*, 2nd edition, Addision Wesley Longman, 1987)

3 Use images

Draw me a picture!

Anon

What Chapter 3 covers

When baffled, either by an oral explanation or someone's written words, we often exclaim 'Draw me a picture!' in an attempt to obtain a form of communication which will make everything clear. And indeed, **images** – a word used to describe all kinds of pictures: maps, charts, tables, diagrams, sketches, cartoons, photographs, etc. – do just that. They help to make talks, presentations, articles, advertisements and reports, etc., much easier to grasp, by expressing ideas not in words, but in two- or three-dimensional shapes.

Developing the skills needed to construct effective images is just as important as developing speaking or writing skills, as you prepare for a full-time career. Thus Chapter 3 focuses entirely on the skills and techniques which support image making. You will need to develop a different kind of eye, one which can put together a visually pleasing design of people or things in a frame, and also one which can display number information visually, in the form of, say, graphs, pie-charts and bar charts.

The main sections of Chapter 3

- The major uses of images in organisations
- Images with a number content (tables, graphs and charts)
- Images with a space content (diagrams and maps)
- Images with a shape content
  - Photographs
  - Sketches and cartoons

In addition, Chapter 3 includes:

- Sets of discussion topics
- Key tips on good practice
- Opportunities to practise newly acquired skills
- Sets of case studies for discussion and analysis
- Activities for assessment and portfolio building

The major uses of images in organisations

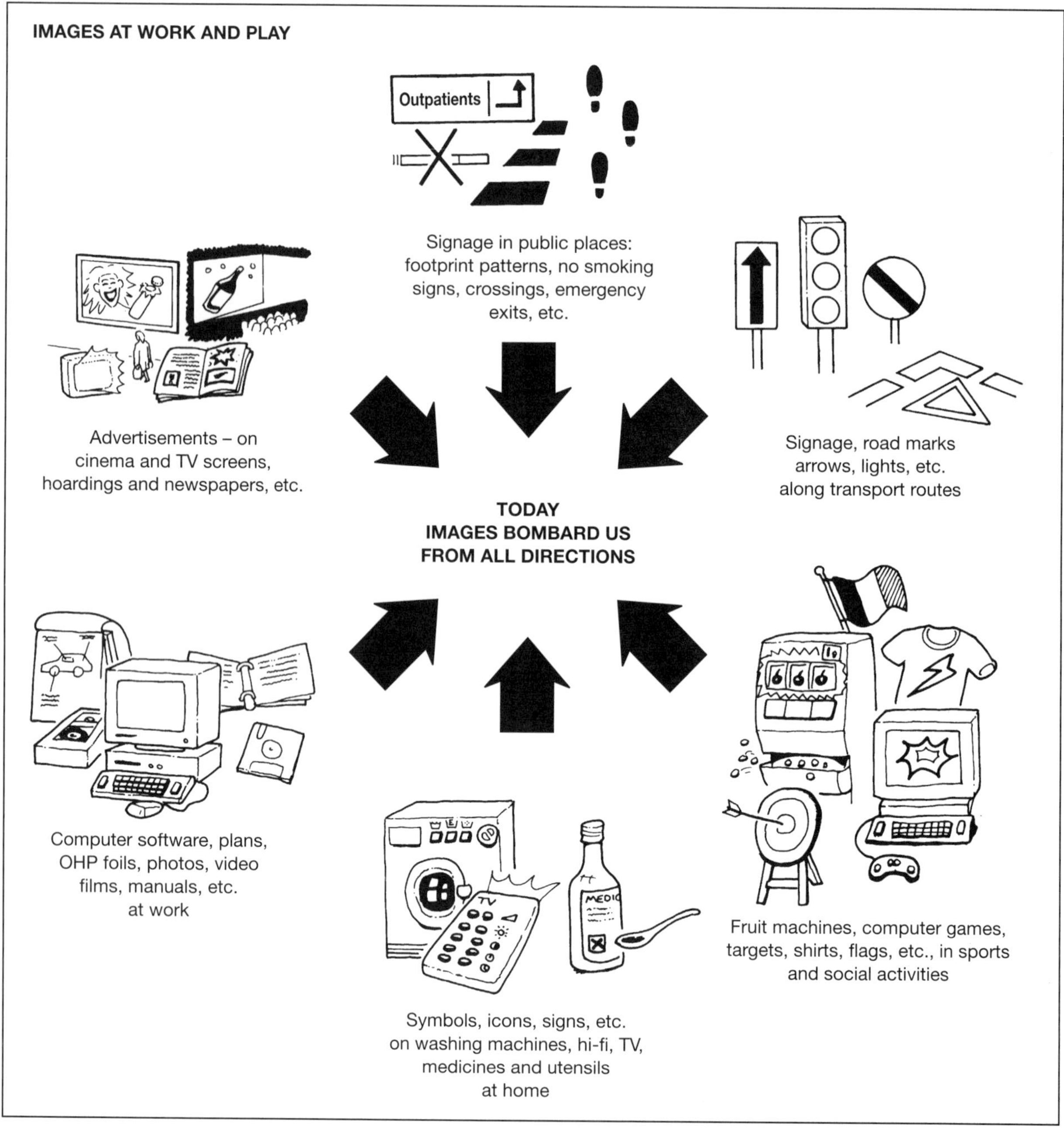
IMAGES AT WORK AND PLAY
Outpatients
Signage in public places: footprint patterns, no smoking signs, crossings, emergency exits, etc.
Advertisements – on cinema and TV screens, hoardings and newspapers, etc.
Signage, road marks arrows, lights, etc. along transport routes
TODAY IMAGES BOMBARD US FROM ALL DIRECTIONS
Computer software, plans, OHP foils, photos, video films, manuals, etc. at work
Fruit machines, computer games, targets, shirts, flags, etc., in sports and social activities
Symbols, icons, signs, etc. on washing machines, hi-fi, TV, medicines and utensils at home

Few people alive today can be unaware of the fact that we are living through an image-rich age. Images are continually being bounced at us, from television, cinema and video films; from bus, tube and billboard posters; from computer games and programs; as symbols and icons for traffic control and safety warnings; and from the millions of newspapers and magazines which people buy every day. Indeed, many young people today find it much easier to understand and respond to image communication than they do to the spoken or written word. Their skills of co-ordinating hand and eye in, say, playing a computer game are far more developed than those of their parents.

Also, an increasing number of people at work rely on images to do jobs which are sometimes life protecting and saving – such as doctors viewing X-ray films and using ultrasound scanners and air-traffic controllers monitoring radar screens. Sometimes they are routine – such as marketing managers analysing sales statistics or designers using 3-D software to create a new dress or car body shell. Thanks to the astounding developments in IT, many junior and middle-tier employees can access a range of computer programs in the course of their daily work, which require skills in handling images, such as spreadsheet, desk-top publishing, drawing and graphics software packages.

Moreover, images have not only become a widespread medium of communication at work, but we also use them increasingly in our home lives – whenever we toast a piece of bread, use a washing machine, drive a car, watch television, or reach for the medicine cabinet.

Because we are exposed to so many images today, in either still or moving form, we tend to take them for granted. Yet we should not, since there are as many, if not more, ugly and poorly designed images as good and pleasing ones which surround us daily. Thus Chapter 3 is concerned, not merely with explaining how a given image is put together, but also with the differences between good, effective design and its opposite.

The reasons why organisations make use of images

Human beings, unlike many other creatures, have well developed binocular vision – much better than that of the poor rhinoceros, which has to snuffle through life, yet not as powerful as the eagle's, which is some twelve times more powerful than human vision and enables it to spot its prey while circling high up on the wind. Although human brains react most strongly to smells (which have the power to remind us instantly of an experience unthought of for, say, over forty years) they take in information most rapidly with the eye. Visual information is also grasped and responded to much more readily than that heard or read – hence the ancient Chinese proverb:

> A picture is worth ten thousand words.

It is also why organisations selling goods and services spend most of their money producing advertisements which contain a powerful visual element, such as television commercials, full-page photographic, colour advertisements in magazines, display advertisements in newspapers and posters along roadsides.

Images are used in the workplace, not only as a means of persuading customers to buy, but also as a way of informing employees about a host of situations and events. For example, an accounts or marketing department will make extensive, daily use of numbers displayed on spreadsheets (a form of electronic table), which can be quickly changed to reflect various possible scenarios, such as the likely outcome in sales terms of increasing prices by 10%. On the factory floor, a skilled tool-maker may study a three-dimensional drawing screened on a computer of a new tool to be constructed, and in a multi-storey office block, a facilities manager (who is responsible for the upkeep of the building) may consult a computerised map of the water, electrical and telecommunications pipes and conduits before permitting a worker to knock a hole in a wall or floor.

The above examples represent only a tiny fraction of the millions of different uses of images which organisations employ daily, so it is more helpful to summarise the reasons for using images in organisations, than to try to account for each particular use in detail:

CHECKLIST

The main reasons why organisations make use of images

- in a selling context – **to persuade visually** (and powerfully)
- **to display number information** in a clear way
- **to communicate some information more clearly** than can be done using either the spoken or written word (e.g. maps, diagrams, photographs, etc.)
- **to provide a welcome change of communication medium,** say by switching on a slide photograph or overhead projection foil during a talk
- **to reinforce and to emphasise points made in writing** (say with a photograph in a report, brochure or magazine article)
- **to add an element of visual design which enriches printed information** (say in the form of a border around a notice, or a clip-art illustration on a leaflet)

During the second half of the twentieth century, we have all become so used to receiving information in a mix of text and image (or indeed as image only), that most of us would find it very difficult to maintain the patience and concentration needed to read the kind of books published in Victorian times. These used very small print, and were usually several hundred pages long, with their vast deserts of prose relieved only very occasionally by the odd oasis of a black and white drawing (before the introduction of photographs)!

By contrast, even a small business owner today is able to produce crisp advertisements with colour illustrations, using a desk-top publishing kit costing only a few hundred pounds. And the publishers of magazines which entertain and texts which educate can now produce materials to stimulate their readers and hold their interest, thanks to the amazing advances made in processing colour images cheaply using IT equipment.

WHAT DO YOU THINK?

1. Do you agree that people today are exposed to a welter of images? If so, what effect does this bombardment have upon them?
2. *Is* a picture 'worth ten thousand words'? If so, why? If not, why not?
3. Are young people today likely to grow up more able to handle information which is conveyed visually, but less able to handle the printed word? If so, should anything be done in the course of their education to counteract this trend? Or does it no longer matter?
4. Given that business organisations now have access to very powerful communications media, such as television, video films and computer software applications, are they now in a position to get at individuals unfairly through a continual broadcasting of advertisements which have a strong visual appeal?
5. One side effect of image communications is that information now tends to come in small bite-sized pieces, such as a large photograph and a small caption on the front page of a tabloid daily newspaper. Is there a danger of people losing their ability to digest information which extends over a number of pages in a book, magazine or newspaper? If they did, would it matter?

SUMMARY OF KEY POINTS

Why organisations use images

- At the end of the twentieth century, people in developed countries are surrounded by images – both at work and at home – as information to persuade and inform.
- Work organisations make very extensive use of images today – to advertise products or services, to provide specific information and to add visual interest to spoken and written word messages.
- Developments in IT over the past twenty years have enabled both small and large organisations to use computer-based techniques to include images in all kinds of printed documents – sales leaflets, bulletins, posters, manuals, instructions, etc.
- The wide-spread use of the image as a medium of communication has had a very great effect upon how people recognise and respond to information today, particularly when it is in the form of symbols, icons and signage designs which are used to communicate messages quickly.
- People at work today cover a lot of ground; they send messages to contacts all over the world via computer networks, drive many miles, use trains and planes regularly, and interact continually with computers; shorthand symbols are used frequently as a means of saving time and effort.
- Around tomorrow's corner is the all-singing, all-dancing pc/tv set, which will enable people at home and at work to press buttons, arrow icons and generally respond on a daily basis to an array of visual images; fortunately, today's toddlers and primary school children are finding no problems in growing up in this image-rich environment!

SELF-CHECK REVIEW TEST

The major uses of images in organisations

1 List four main reasons why organisations make use of images.

2 Explain briefly how the development of graphics software has made it possible within an organisation to make written documents more appealing to the eye.

3 List three types of document produced by organisations which are likely to use images, and explain why for each one.

Continues 

4 Explain briefly the difference between an icon and a piece of clip-art.

5 What is meant by the term *signage*? How is it used in large organisations?

When you have completed the above questions, turn to page 304 to check the answers provide against your own. Revise the appropriate section of Chapter 3, if you got the answer wrong.

STUDENT PAIR SKILLS-BUILDING ACTIVITIES

Researching the use of images in the workplace

Task 1 First, decide, with the help of your teacher, whether you will research into organisations in the public or the private sector. Then select *one* of the following research topics about the use of images at work:

1 The use of signage and symbols in large public buildings (e.g. hospitals, county council offices, education centres)

2 The use of images in publications produced by organisations (e.g. sales literature, Health and Safety at Work leaflets, induction booklets, annual reports)

3 The use of images in local transport systems (e.g. an airport, railway or road network, or in a port)

4 The use of images in computer software and operating systems used by organisations

5 The use of images in a manufacturing environment (e.g. computer CADCAM software, HASAW posters, operating instructions)

6 The use of images in either an accounts, manufacturing or personnel department

7 The use of images in either the leisure or entertainment industry

Use your initiative and your teacher's guidance to research into the use of images in your selected area. Your main aim is to collect examples of some ten major types of image, and to find out how and why they are used, as well as how they help people to do their jobs or to find their way, etc. Make notes on what you discover. If you are unable to obtain a sample of an image, seek to draw or photograph it.

Task 2 When you have completed your research, prepare a 3–5 minute talk to give to your class on what you discovered, and include the most interesting images in your talk as illustrations. Note: you may need to convert an image you found into an OHP foil or into a drawing on a handout. But remember, too, that an effective use of an image during a talk is to pass round an example of it.

Task 3 In a general class activity, produce a factsheet which summarises your findings, and which all class members can store as a revision aid.

Images with a number content

As you are now already aware, many employees in both private and public sector organisations use information in the form of numbers very extensively in the daily jobs they do – accounting and book-keeping staff, production personnel and the employees working in marketing or research. Even the most modest small trader has to keep a set of books which summarise the financial side of the business.

Over many years, many image structures have been designed which are able both to store and to display data visually. These structures are based upon the ways in which numbers and quantities relate to each other. The most important images of this type are:

- the table
- the line graph
- the pie chart
- the bar chart

In this section you will develop the ability to create each of the above images confidently, as well as to interpret and analyse correctly those which you meet in the future.

The table

The term 'table' is used to describe a method of displaying numbers in columns with totals and sub-totals. Once the table has been put together, it is possible for its reader to see how a list of ingredients combine into a total, and to react accordingly. A very simple table is the one which is produced in supermarkets to total goods purchased. The checkout operator passes each item over a scanner which reads its bar-code. The automated till picks up the details and enters them as a vertical table. When, for example, several tins of dog food are purchased at the same price, individual tins will be priced and the sub-total printed. When all items have been entered, a grand total is printed. If the shopper has selected more goods than he or she can pay for, the reaction to the grand total can be embarrassing! Figure 3.1 (below) shows how tables store and present number information.

Figure 3.1 displays a set of collected data for six types of operation at Midchester General, carried out in the first three months of the year. The table displays the data in two main ways:

- by type of operation
- by calendar month

It also classifies the data into three types of total:

- across: the same type of operation for the first quarter of the year
- down: the total of all operations carried out each month
- a grand total of all the operations carried out during the first quarter (407)

Some tables provide number information which displays numbers into three or four decimal points, say of a highly developed measurement of temperature: 17.332 degrees. In this way, tables are capable of storing very precise and detailed information. They are also good at showing clearly the sub-totals and grand totals of data collected under the same heading – cataract or heart-bypass operations, or Jan/Feb totals, etc.

What tables are not very good at displaying at all, however, are the general relationships between one set of figures and the next, nor the

BREAK-DOWN OF OPERATIONS CARRIED OUT AT MIDCHESTER GENERAL HOSPITAL FIRST QUARTER OF 199-

	JAN	FEB	MAR	TOTAL
Tonsils	24	13	32	69
Appendix	15	17	14	46
Cataract	25	34	47	106
Gall-stones	09	07	05	21
Hip replacement	12	17	27	56
Heart bypass	22	38	49	109
TOTAL	107	126	174	407

J. Jones Statistical Officer
31.3.199-

Figure 3.1

trends which may be occurring. For instance, in the table in Figure 3.1, which type of operation is growing at the fastest rate? While we can see that both cataract and heart bypass operations have occurred most frequently, our eye finds it difficult to pick out which has the fastest rate of growth, and we need a line-graph to do that for us.

The line graph

Line graphs are most usually constructed by using two axes, one going up vertically, and the other going along horizontally:

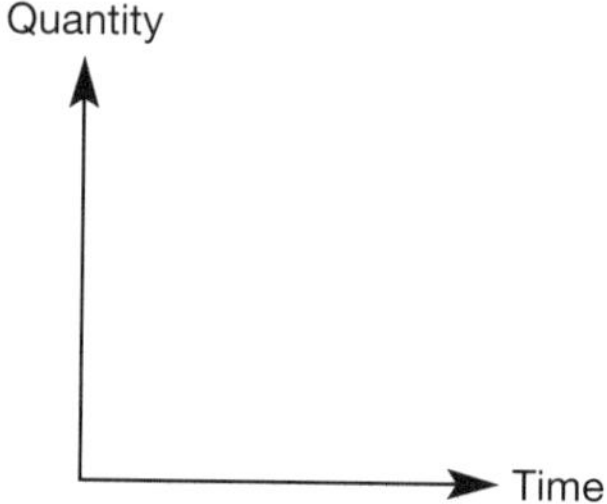

As you can see above, the vertical axis usually plots one or several items in terms of their quantity, (amount or size, etc.), while the other plots them against the elapse of time. If we plot the entries of the operations table in Figure 3.1 as a line graph, it would look like Figure 3.2.

Figure 3.2 shows us just how good line graphs are in displaying features like trends. We can now see quite clearly that the heart by-pass operation is not only the largest in terms of the number of operations carried out, but is also increasing (overall) at the fastest

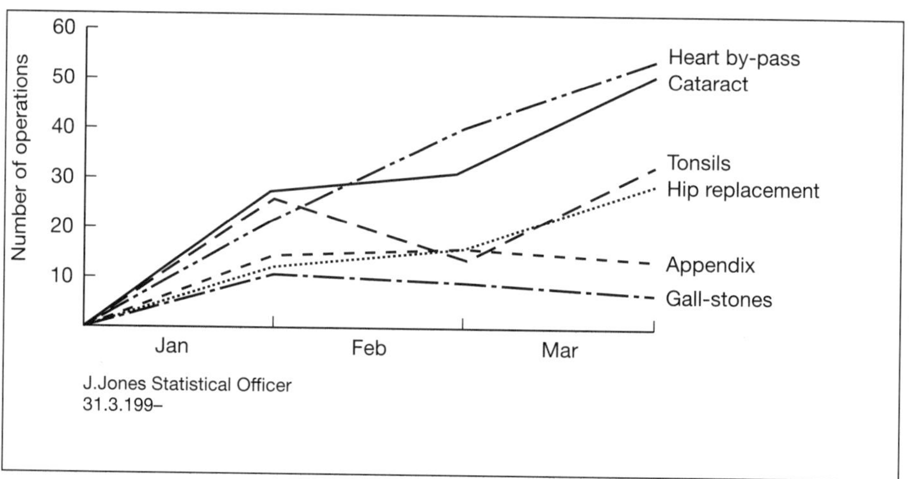

Figure 3.2

rate. The trend in cataract operations is also increasing, but flattened out noticeably during February. Similarly, we can see that the trend in gall-stone operations is downwards, as is that for appendix operations. Tonsils operations seem to fluctuate.

Thus line graphs can show overall trends and comparisons between items plotted much better than tables can. Moreover, they can also be used to forecast future likely developments. For instance, if you were a hospital manager charged with making beds available for patients coming in for operations, for which operations would you reserve more beds, heart by-pass and cataracts, or appendix and gall-stones? Why? How can you justify your decision?

As the above questions indicate, line graphs help their users to anticipate likely future trends, as well as showing actual outcomes.

However, as the above line-graph illustration also points out, they are not particularly good at showing the performances of five or more plotted items, if – as in the month of January – they all have to be plotted closely together. Further, if they have to be printed in black and white instead of in contrasting colours, a series of line patterns has to be devised to distinguish them. Thus line graphs cannot easily support more than four plotted items, are sometimes difficult to interpret in black and white, and also lack the ability to store data to several decimal points. Imagine, for example, trying to plot (and to obtain from the graph) an entry of 15.423.

On both the table and the graph it is essential to label entered or plotted items accurately:

- by name of item (tonsils, appendix)
- by quantity (number of operations)
- by time (Jan, Feb, Mar)

Also, notice how important it is to provide a key to identify each plotted item in the graph clearly.

Lastly, all graphs and charts should include:

- a clear title
- details of its author
- a date when produced

This enables users to decide whether or not the information displayed is useful and up-to-date, or likely to have been overtaken.

The pie chart

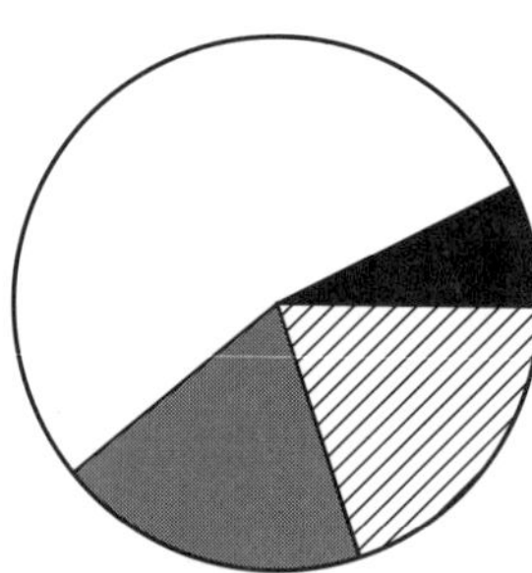

Figure 3.3

The pie chart gets its name from looking like a circular pie which has been cut into various segments, or slices of pie. As Figure 3.3 shows, the total area of the pie is that of a normal circle. As you will be aware, circles are divided into 360 degrees. Half the circle amounts to a 180 degree segment, and each quarter (of 90 degrees) is characterised by a right-angle (see Figure 3.4). So far, so good. One problem does arise, however, when creating the parts of a pie chart. It is not so difficult to recognise that a quarter of the circle's area, the 90 degree segment, stands for 25% of the total in percentage terms. What is more difficult is to work out how much of the circle's area should be allocated to, say, a value of 17% or 29%, etc. Fortunately, a simple sum enables the conversion from percentages to degrees to be made:

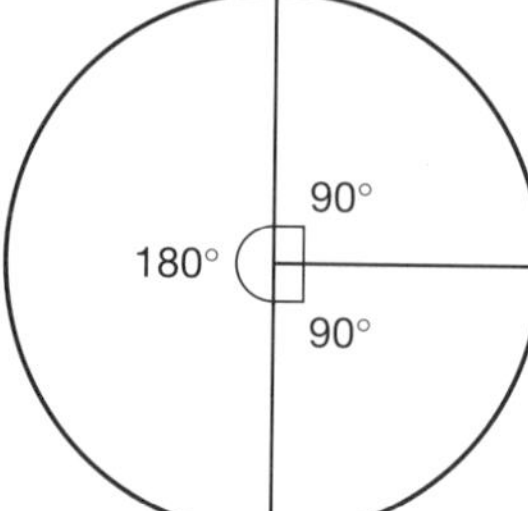

Figure 3.4

$$\frac{360}{100} \times \text{the percentage of the segment} = \text{slice of pie to be plotted}$$

Example

Task: plot a segment in a pie chart which is 34% of the total area of the circle:

$$\frac{360}{100} \times 34 = 3.6 \times 34 = 122.4 \text{ degrees}$$

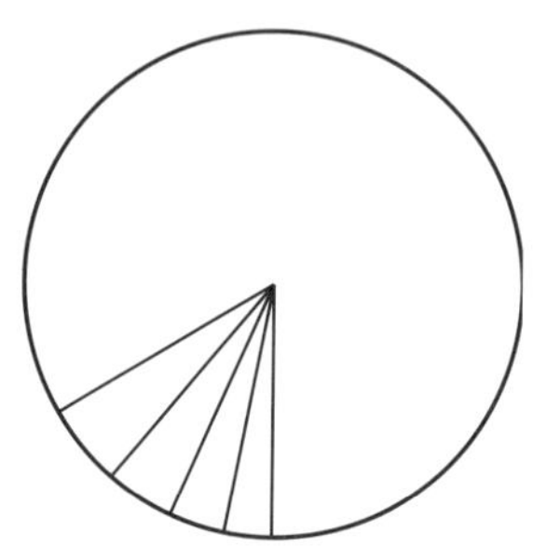

Figure 3.5

As a rough check, we know that 90 degrees represents a 'right angle' quarter of the circle, so this slice of pie must be some 32 degrees larger. However, in order to plot it accurately, we should, ideally, have each pie chart circle marked off in one degree notches, from 0 to 360 degrees. As you can now appreciate, without a protractor to hand, plotting a pie chart is not that simple. And indeed, like the line graph, pie charts are best suited to giving indications of the comparative sizes of pie slices, rather than dimensions for each, correct to three decimal points. And also like the line graph, pie charts are not that good at indicating comparisons between slices of similar sizes (see Figure 3.5).

KEY POINT

A pie chart is only suited to displaying data visually if:

- a total is known of all the slices, since this total makes up the 360 degree sweep of the circle
- the quantity for each slice can be converted into a percentage, using the above calculation, and plotted (with the help of a protractor).

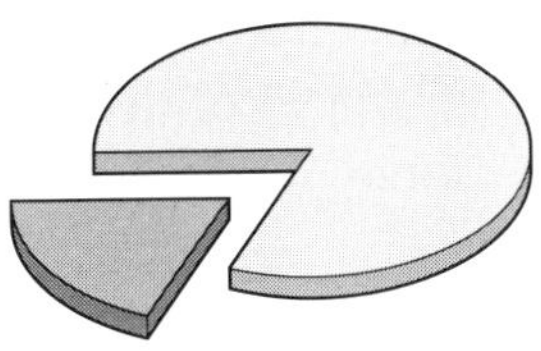

Figure 3.6

Sometimes, pie chart designers show the slices of the pie in what is called an exploded view, by separating them as seen in Figure 3.6.

Pie charts, just like other charts displaying number data, require a title, author and date of production as in Figure 3.7. To help the reader understand more easily what each pie slice stands for, they are almost always labelled with details of their amount or size and what they represent. So remember to include this important, explanatory detail whenever you devise a pie chart. Also, whenever possible, colour the pie slices to make them stand out. If you are limited to using the black to white span of tones, you may be able to access software which gives each slice of pie a contrasting tone.

Figure 3.7 provides a typical illustration of the pie chart's display abilities. As you can see, it communicates strongly how close Comfort Shoes Limited is to gaining half of the entire UK market for ladies' boots and shoes. It also shows quite distinctly the difference in product sales between court/fashion shoes and, say, evening dress shoes. However, we need the labels to enable us to see that knee-length boots have a single percentage point less market share than ladies'

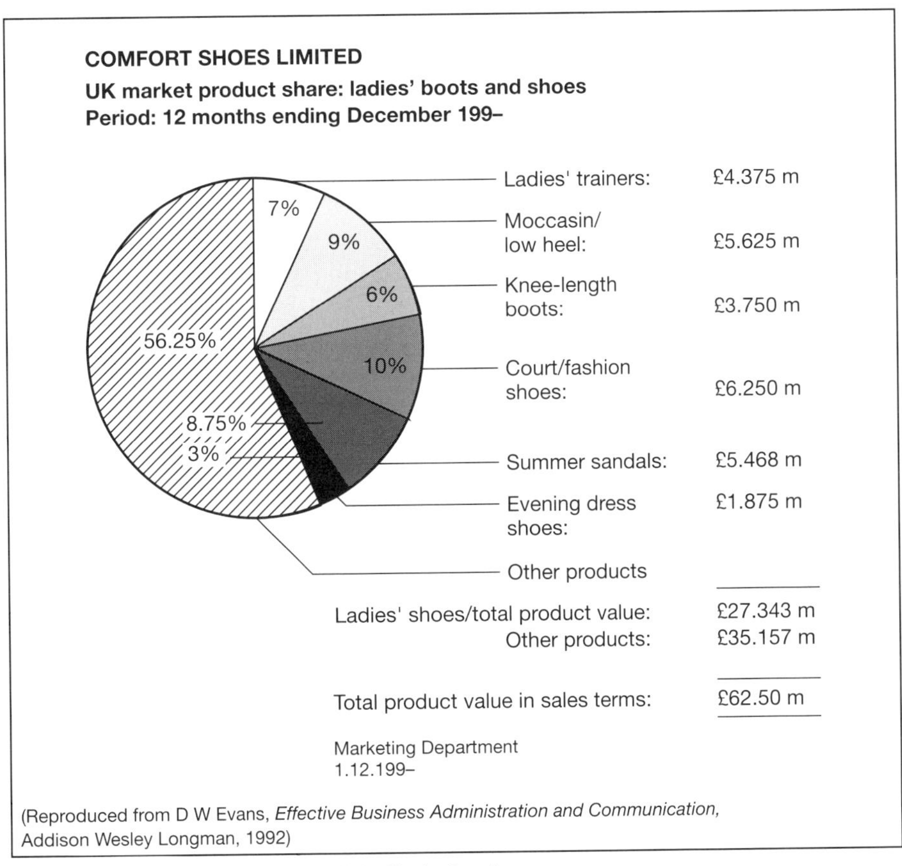

Figure 3.7 **Example of a fully labelled pie chart**

trainers (6% and 7% respectively). Note, too, that the pie chart designer has helpfully included not only the various percentage shares of the market, but also what each percentage stands for in money terms.

The bar chart

Bar charts are very similar to line graphs, in that they both make use of vertical and horizontal axes. Also, the bar chart's vertical axis displays quantity. However, a difference occurs in the use of the horizontal axis, which is used to place bars or columns of items next to each other in order to provide a ready visual comparison of their totals:

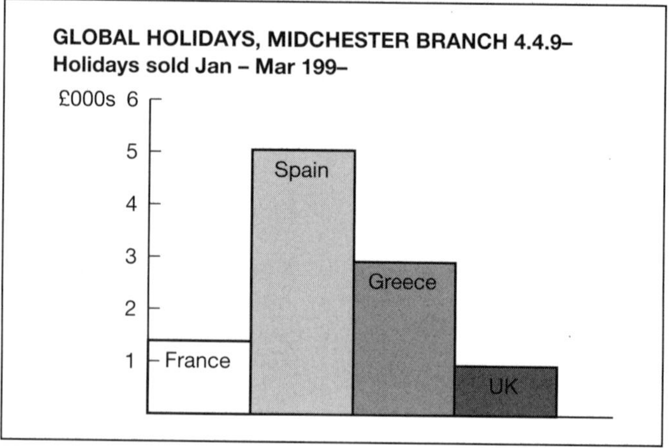

As the above example illustrates, bar charts are very good at displaying significant differences in the totals of the bars which make up the chart. However, they are not so good if the totals of the bars are almost the same:

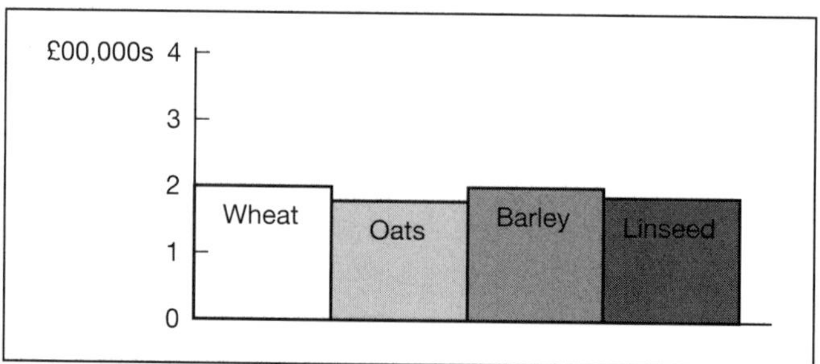

When faced with such a display problem, an effective answer may be to change the value of the vertical axis in this way:

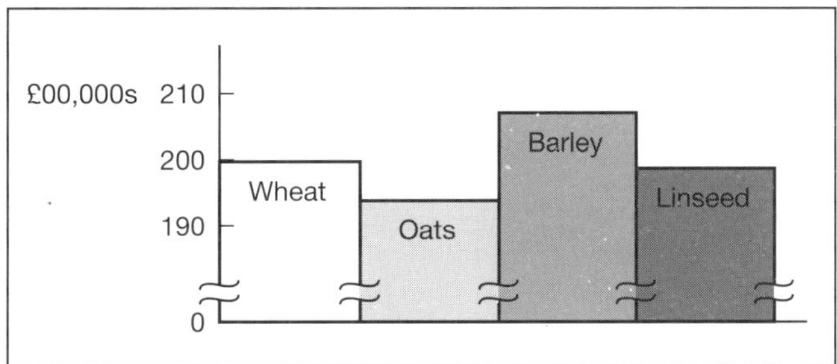

Notice that the broken line of the vertical axis is given a wavy line to indicate that a section has been omitted.

KEY POINT

Never mind the quality, check the widths

For a bar chart to display data so as to make comparisons of the bars valid, each bar must have an identical width. If one has a broader or narrower width, this will inevitably change its area and thus make any comparison worthless.

Stacked bar charts

Sometimes bar chart designers wish to compare several items common to each of several bars. For instance, four retail stores which form a small private limited company may have their sales products grouped into: newspapers, magazines, stationery and greetings cards. A stacked bar chart can be used not only to compare the total sales of each store, but also their sales of each of these four main product categories (see Figure 3.8 on page 186).

Sometimes bar charts are given a 3-D effect, which is used to make their bars stand out more interestingly. Graphics software packages are frequently used to achieve this effect, simply by entering the totals for each bar (see Figure 3.9 on page 186).

As the overleaf examples show, bar charts provide an effective means of comparing some three to five items whose totals vary sufficiently. Like the line graph and pie chart (and unlike the table), bar charts are not suited to storing and displaying data where the totals extend to several places behind a decimal point. Therefore only approximate totals can be obtained when reading data off them. This is why the totals they display are provided for us (e.g. *Comfort Ladies Shoes Limited, Ladies Trainers: £4.375 million*).

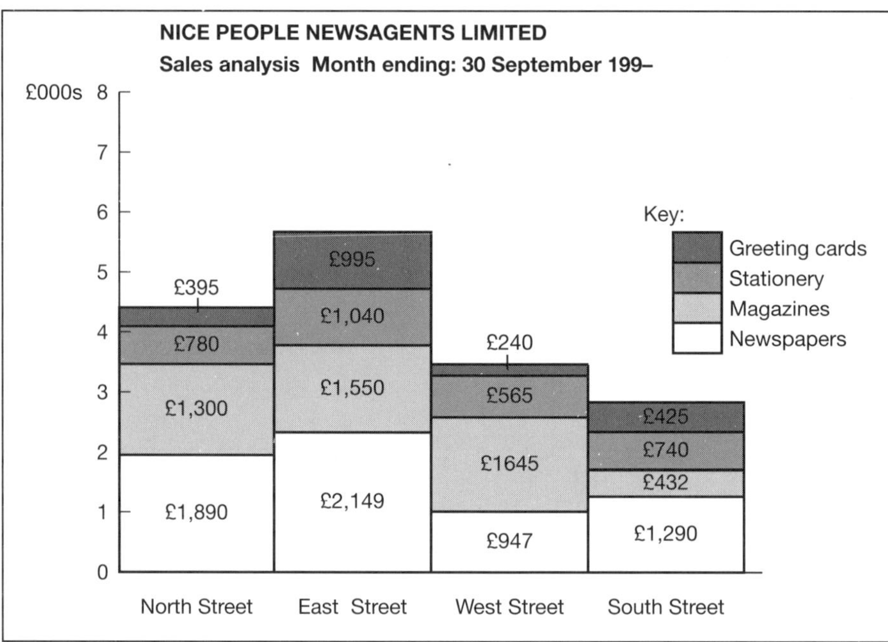

Figure 3.8 **Example of a stacked bar chart**

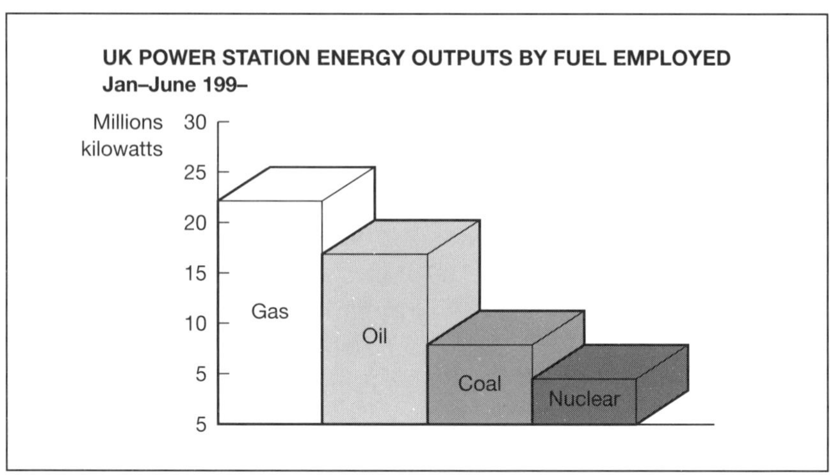

Figure 3.9 **Example of a 3-D bar chart**

WHAT DO YOU THINK?

1 What do you see as the advantages of communicating information by means of a chart, as opposed to using the printed word?

2 Some people say that when they meet numbers – in tables, graphs or charts – they get a kind of mental block, freeze and find themselves unable to make head or tail of the information. Has this ever happened to you? What actions could a person so affected carry out to overcome this problem?

3 Can you think of any communicating situations in which the use of number-based images is by far the best way of sending a message?

4 Can you see any dangers in feeding raw numbers into a computer software package which then converts them into a slick graph or chart, ready for printing out at the touch of a button?

5 Does a line graph communicate its data better than a table, or is it simply a matter of personal opinion and preference for one or the other?

SUMMARY OF KEY POINTS

Images with a number content

- Tables, graphs and charts are used in organisations to communicate information which is mainly number based. Such data is used in oral presentations in the form of OHP foils or slides, and in reports and briefing papers.
- The most frequently employed number-based images include tables, line graphs, pie charts and bar charts.
- Some of these images are best at storing number data in a highly precise and accurate way (such as the table), and others are best at providing a visual structure which enables its reader to compare movements up or down, and overall trends (such as the line graph).
- All number-based images benefit from the use of colour to contrast their parts. Graphs, pie charts and bar charts are not very suited to displaying more than four or five items as plotted lines or bars. Nor are they good at communicating differences between items of a similar amount.
- All number-based images should include these details: clear title, author, date of publication, a key (where needed) and labels to indicate the values given to vertical and horizontal axes in line graphs, and what pie slices or the bars in charts stand for.

SELF-CHECK REVIEW TEST

Images with a number content

1 List four images which are used to communicate number-based information.

2 Why is a table good at storing number information, but not so good at displaying it?

Continues 

3 What information can a line graph convey which is much more difficult to pick up from a table?

4 What items are normally plotted on a) the vertical and b) the horizontal axis of a line graph?

5 What sort of information is virtually impossible to obtain from examining the data of a line graph, pie chart or bar chart?

6 What is the calculation which converts the total of an item expressed as a percentage into degrees of a circle?

7 Explain simply what a bar chart is.

8 And also, what a stacked bar chart is.

9 What key information is needed to label an image with a number content effectively?

10 Explain briefly how the use of colour helps to make an image with a number content easier to grasp.

When you have completed the above questions, turn to page 305 to check the answers provided against your own. Revise the appropriate section of Chapter 3, if you got the answer wrong.

INDIVIDUAL SKILLS-BUILDING ACTIVITIES

Creating number-based charts

Task 1 Read carefully through the following extract, which provides an account of Katie Bailey, owner of Bella Boutique, reviewing with an assistant what stock she sold between 1 January and 31 March of this year:

> Now, let me see, in January we sold 65 skirts and 34 pairs of jeans, but funnily enough, we sold more skirts in March – 84, and only 48 pairs of jeans. Must have been the weather. In February we sold 47 tops, which was more than January's 31, thank goodness. Shoes haven't gone at all well, though, 16 pairs in January, 21 in February and 26 in March, despite the promotion we did of moccasins with jeans. Do you think our shoes are over-priced? Well, anyway, according to this, we sold 59 skirts in February, thanks to our twosome promotion. Ah, here it is, I've found the March tops total, 62, thanks to an early Easter this year. What total do you still need? Oh yes, jeans for February, here it is, 37.

Devise a table which provides totals by month, by product, and by overall total of product items sold. Make sure you label your table suitably.

Task 2 When you have produced your table, consult it to provide written answers to these questions:

1 Which product proved the best seller in the first quarter of the year?

2 Which was the worst?

3 How did Bella Boutique's business do in the first three months of the year? If you were Katie, would you be pleased or worried about how stock moved?

4 Assuming that Bella Boutique is holding some 82 pairs of shoes in stock at the beginning of April, what advice would you give to Katie, based on your reading of your table?

5 In December of the previous year, Bella Boutique was holding a skirt stock of 78. Consequently, Katie decided to hold a January skirt sale. She invested the proceeds of the sale in buying in some brightly coloured and patterned cotton skirts on the basis of a long-range weather forecast for a warm Easter. Did she do right or wrong?

Task 3 Construct a stacked bar chart of Bella Boutique's stock turnover for the months of January, February and March, and label it suitably.

Task 4 Global Holidays Limited has produced the following table of its holiday sales for the last financial year (the totals shown are in thousands of pounds sterling):

	April	May	June	July	Aug	Sept	Oct	Nov	Dec	Jan	Feb	Mar
UK	8	11	23	31	44	29	5	3	9	2	3	7
Mediterranean	6	13	46	74	98	65	33	12	15	9	7	5
USA/Canada	6	9	14	23	36	18	12	7	22	26	23	15
Australia/NZ	12	8	7	5	4	14	17	26	23	19	17	14
S.E. Asia	14	16	23	25	22	18	16	12	13	9	7	10

Construct a suitable line graph which shows the monthly sales of each holiday category clearly, and then answer the following questions:

1 Which is Global's best selling holiday category?

2 Which is the worst selling?

3 Can you think of a reason why holiday sales to Australia and New Zealand do not follow the same patterns as Mediterranean holiday sales?

4 Given the patterns of holiday sales shown in the graph, which type of holiday in your opinion should be advertised when, in order to give sales a boost?

5 The board of directors has made available some £20,000 to promote holidays in the slowest month of the year for sales. Which month would you advise Global to promote in with this money? Which type of holiday do you think the money should concentrate upon promoting, and why?

Task 5 Using the data in the table shown in Task 4 above, construct a pie chart to display the comparative yearly sales turnover of Global's holiday categories. Then produce two more for the months of a) August and b) April.

When you have completed the two pie charts, a) and b), write a brief statement which explains in your opinion the reasons for the changes in the share of Global's sales turnover of the holidays it sells in April and August.

STUDENT PAIR SKILLS-BUILDING ACTIVITY

Developing skills in interpreting number-based images

During the course of the next week, collect a set of examples of each of the following:

- tables
- line graphs
- pie charts
- bar charts

Use the facilities of your study centre and local reference libraries, as well as copies of broadsheet newspapers and magazines, etc., to comb through printed matter for likely examples. Remember that local councils publish many leaflets (such as break-downs of how council tax is spent) which use number-based images, and that public limited companies publish annual reports which are a rich hunting ground for such material.

When you have found two or three examples of each image, decide which is the most effective example and why. Then share your findings with your class students by explaining what each image is communicating, and pin the best examples to your base-room noticeboard.

Images using lines and spaces

Diagrams

Workplace organisations also make much use of images which communicate information through the use of space, rather than by number. For example, the monthly process of selling goods or services on credit and then obtaining payment from account customers, or of calling a monthly committee meeting and then sending out the minutes of the meeting, could be expressed in terms of a circular movement to denote a repeating cycle of activity (see Figures 3.10 and 3.11).

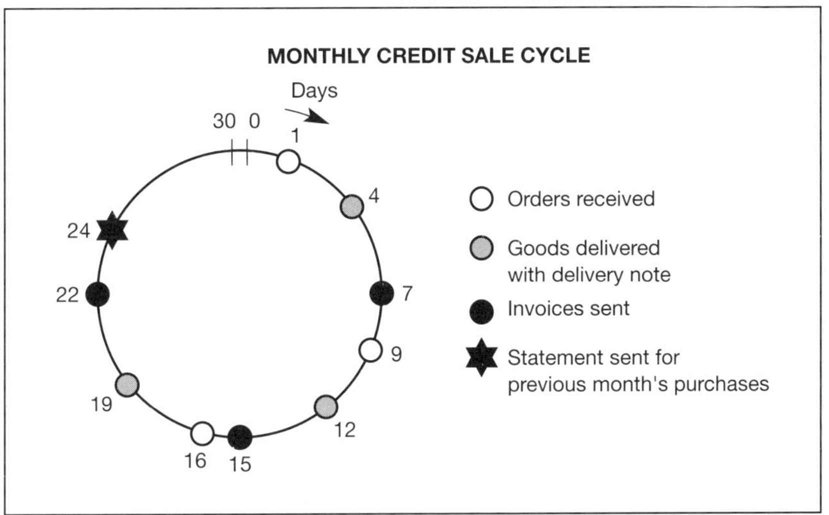

Figure 3.10

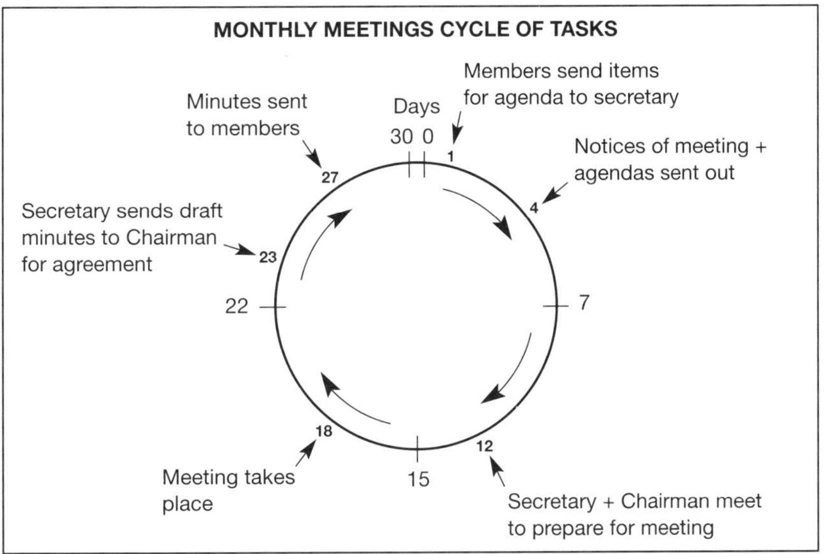

Figure 3.11

In another use of space, an organisational chart is used to show on the one hand who is more senior and who more junior in an organisation, and on the other who is on a par or equal in status with others (see Figure 3.12 on page 192).

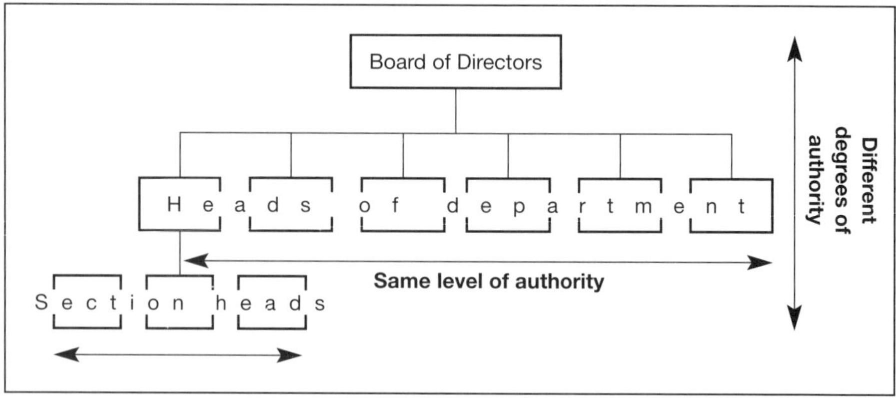

Figure 3.12

As the above examples show, arrowed lines may be used on a single dimension (the flat plane of a sheet of paper) to illustrate the passage of time: 7 –> 15 –> 22 –> 30 days, or the positioning of boxes on a similar sheet may indicate either an 'above–below' or 'same as' relationship, such as the job titles of employees in an organisation.

Another way in which space is used on paper to communicate a relationship occurs in flow charts and decision trees. A flow chart, uses space and arrows, plus numbers to communicate a process moving through a sequence of steps, while a decision tree indicates a route to specific information as a result of answering either 'yes' or 'no' to a series of questions (see Figure 3.13 on page 193).

In Figure 3.14 on page 194, a simplified drawing of a desk-top computer terminal is used to stand for all the company's installed network of terminals. Arrows also indicate either one-way or two-way routes of communication, and each step in the process is clearly explained. The use of icons – for the terminals and the incoming letter – help to give the diagram visual interest.

Another use of the shape-based image is to create what is basically a summary. Consider, for example, the design in Figure 3.15 on page 195 to introduce a section of a textbook on persuasive communication. Here, the designer has brought together a number of posters and advertisements which are seeking to persuade people to eat at a restaurant, see a show and make use of a certain car repair business or decorating firm. None of the sales information in the summary can be read entirely, but by grouping such advertisements together into what is called a **collage**, the designer manages to create an eye-catching image to summarise a chapter on persuasive communication.

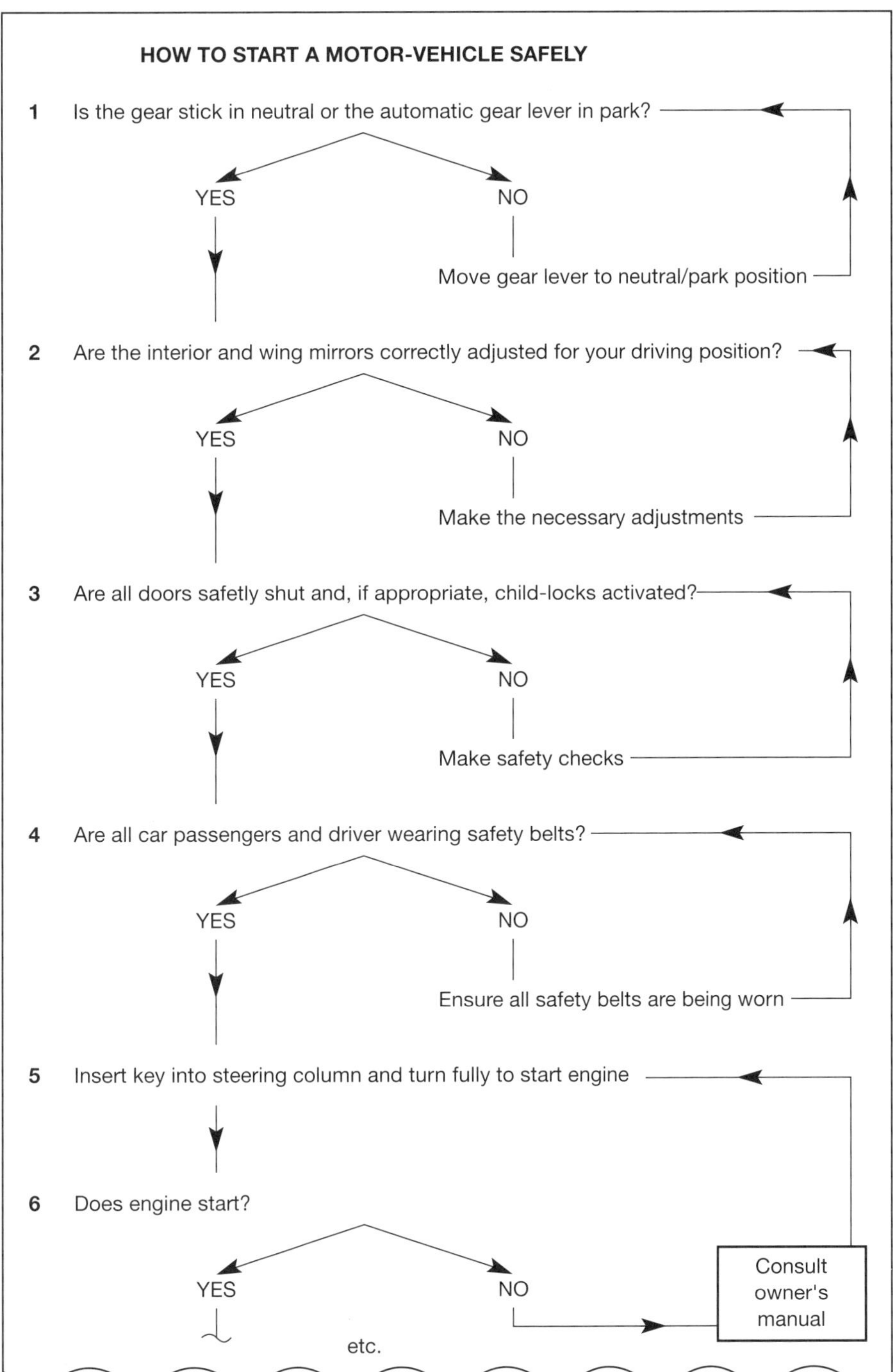

Figure 3.13 **Example of a decision tree**

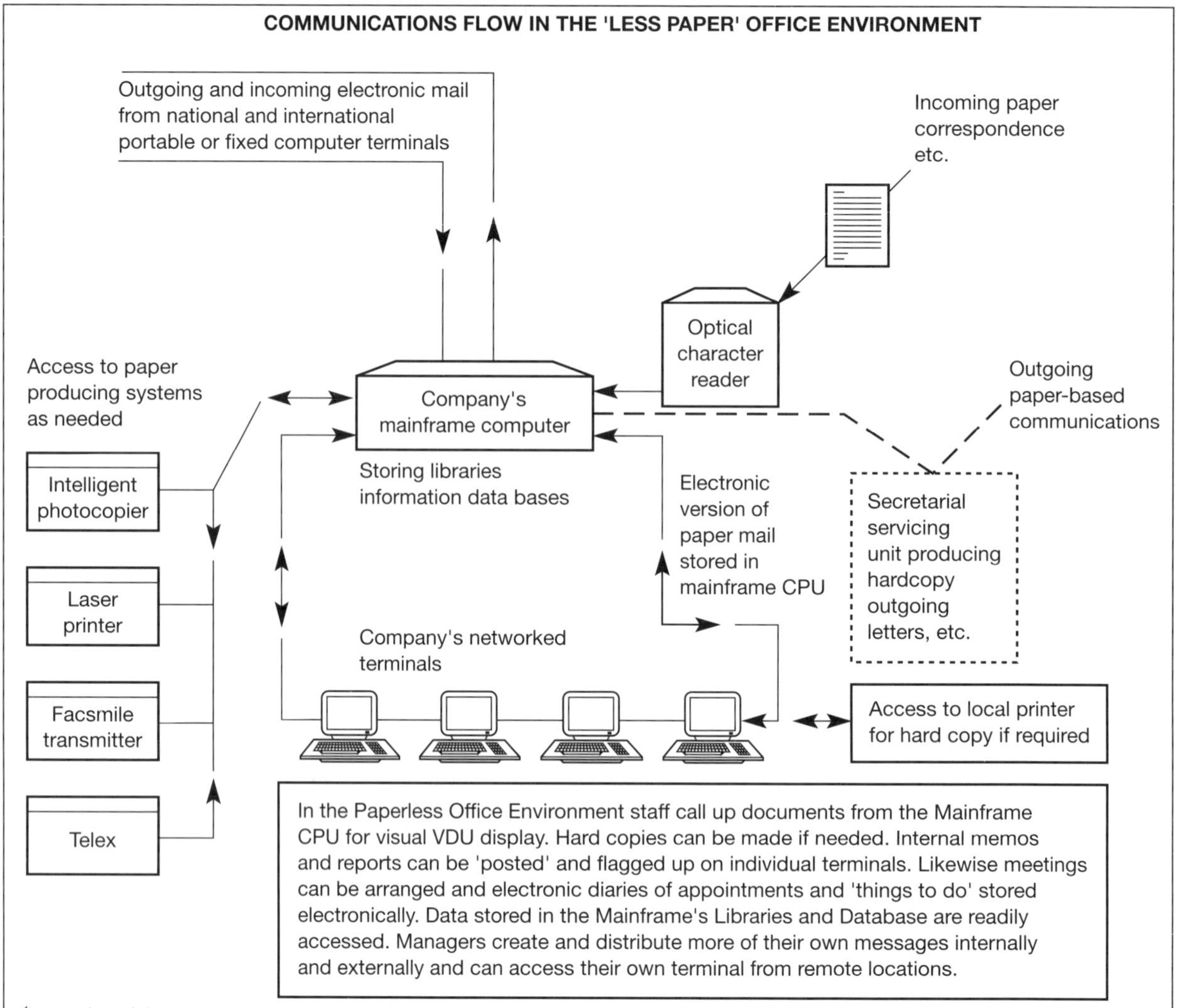

COMMUNICATIONS FLOW IN THE 'LESS PAPER' OFFICE ENVIRONMENT

Outgoing and incoming electronic mail from national and international portable or fixed computer terminals

Incoming paper correspondence etc.

Optical character reader

Access to paper producing systems as needed

Company's mainframe computer

Outgoing paper-based communications

Intelligent photocopier

Storing libraries information data bases

Electronic version of paper mail stored in mainframe CPU

Secretarial servicing unit producing hardcopy outgoing letters, etc.

Laser printer

Company's networked terminals

Facsmile transmitter

Access to local printer for hard copy if required

Telex

In the Paperless Office Environment staff call up documents from the Mainframe CPU for visual VDU display. Hard copies can be made if needed. Internal memos and reports can be 'posted' and flagged up on individual terminals. Likewise meetings can be arranged and electronic diaries of appointments and 'things to do' stored electronically. Data stored in the Mainframe's Libraries and Database are readily accessed. Managers create and distribute more of their own messages internally and externally and can access their own terminal from remote locations.

(Reproduced from D W Evans, *Secretarial Procedures in the Electronic Office*, Addison Wesley Longman, 1989)

Figure 3.14 **Example of a well designed diagram with a space and relationships content**

Symbols used in charts

People whose jobs involve designing charts and diagrams on a regular basis use a variety of pre-designed symbols (just like clip-art) to save time. These symbols include different types of box, arrow or frame, etc., which help to make a chart easier and more interesting to read:

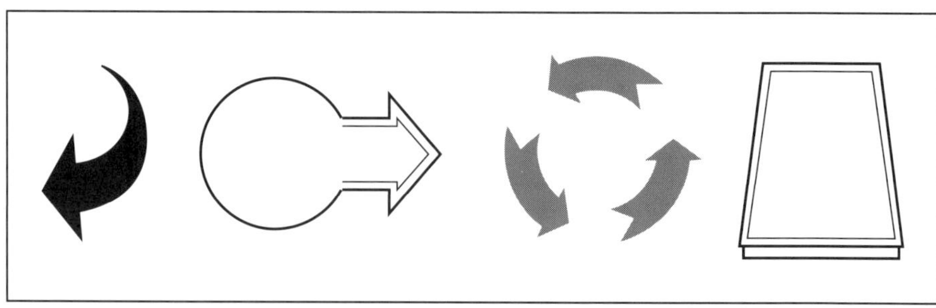

Figure 3.15 **Example of a collage effect** (reproduced from D W Evans, *Effective Business Administration and Communication,* Addison Wesley Longman, 1992)

Maps

Maps are used in organisations for a host of purposes, for example:

- to help visitors find their way in large buildings and sites
- to show the location of premises within a district, together with main road and rail access routes
- to enable sales representatives to reach their destinations (e.g. national road maps)
- to indicate the correct exit route from a room or location in case of fire or emergency.

As the above list indicates, organisations tend to use maps for specific purposes related to their activities. For this reason, they often have to produce them in-house, say as a map of a site or location of departments on the various floors of an office block.

In early mediaeval times, map-making was a haphazard affair. Such maps of, say, Europe were drawn without scales, and what could not be produced on the basis of factual knowledge was easily made up for by imagination, such as the vast expanses of Russia, which appeared with a warning for would-be travellers: 'Here be dragons!' with a fierce drawing of one thrown in for artistic good measure!

Today's maps are much more accurate, if not as exciting. The following checklist illustrates the features which an effective map should display:

CHECKLIST

Key features of an effective map

- **a scale** (shown in metres, feet, kilometres or miles, etc.), which is usually placed at the foot of the map
- **an orientation** (which means which part is placed at the top of the sheet); all geographical maps, by international agreement show north at the top of the map, and the other compass points where they then fall, with east to the right, etc.
- **a key** which makes clear what the signs and symbols mean which have been used on the map
- **word labels** to identify, for example, the names of places, buildings or streets
- **a title** for the map, its author/publisher and a date of its publication

SELF-CHECK REVIEW TEST

Images with a space content

1 Explain briefly what an organisation chart communicates.

2 Give an example of a diagram which displays a process.

3 What is a collage?

4 Give three examples of the uses of symbols from graphics packages like those illustrated on page 194.

5 List the main features which should be included in an effectively drawn map.

Continues ▶

When you have completed the above questions, turn to page 306 to check the answers provided against your own. Revise the appropriate section of Chapter 3, if you got the answer wrong.

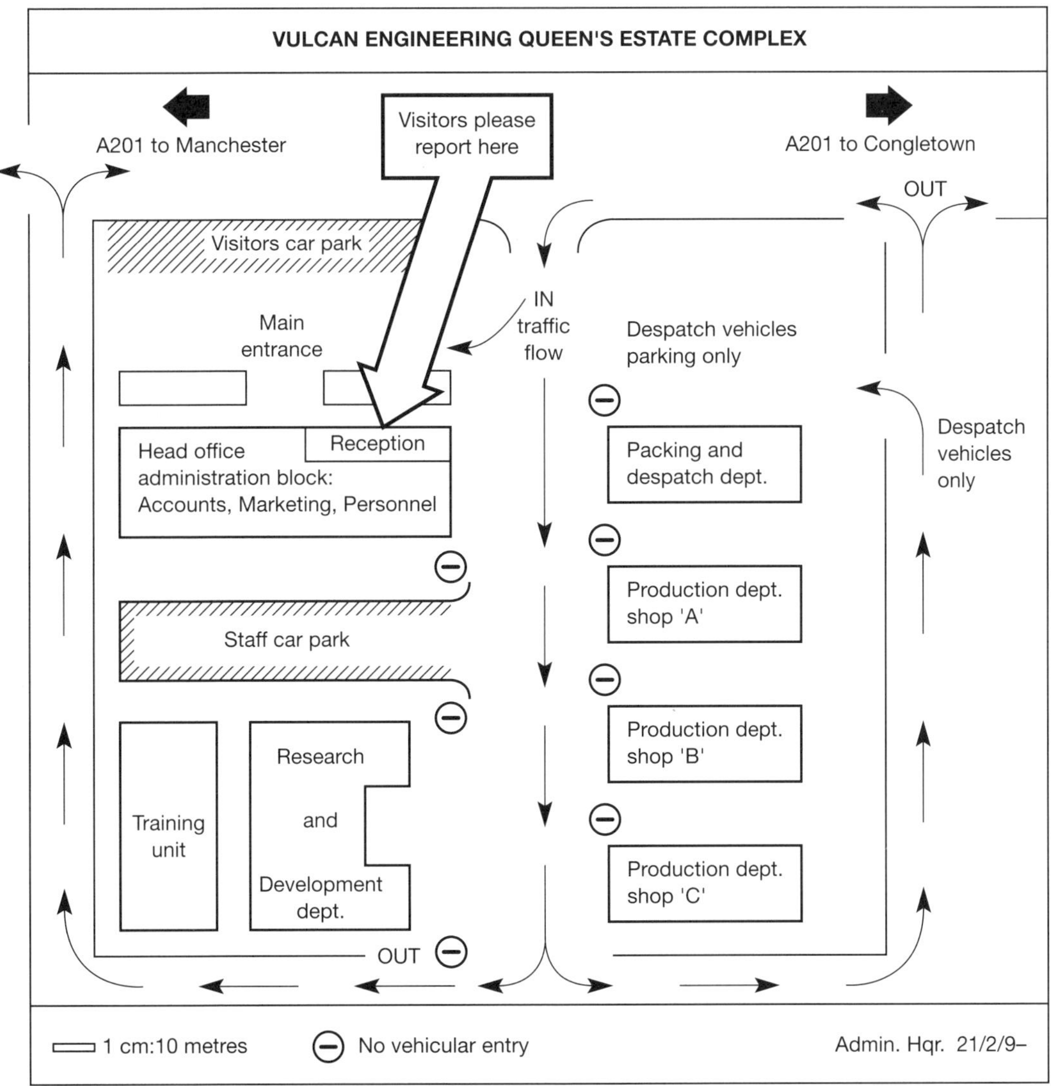

Figure 3.16 **Example of a map of an organisation's premises**

Organisations also use especially drawn maps to indicate major routes to offices or premises from road and rail links, and may highlight the best route for a visitor to whom such a map is sent in advance (see Figure 3.17 on page 198).

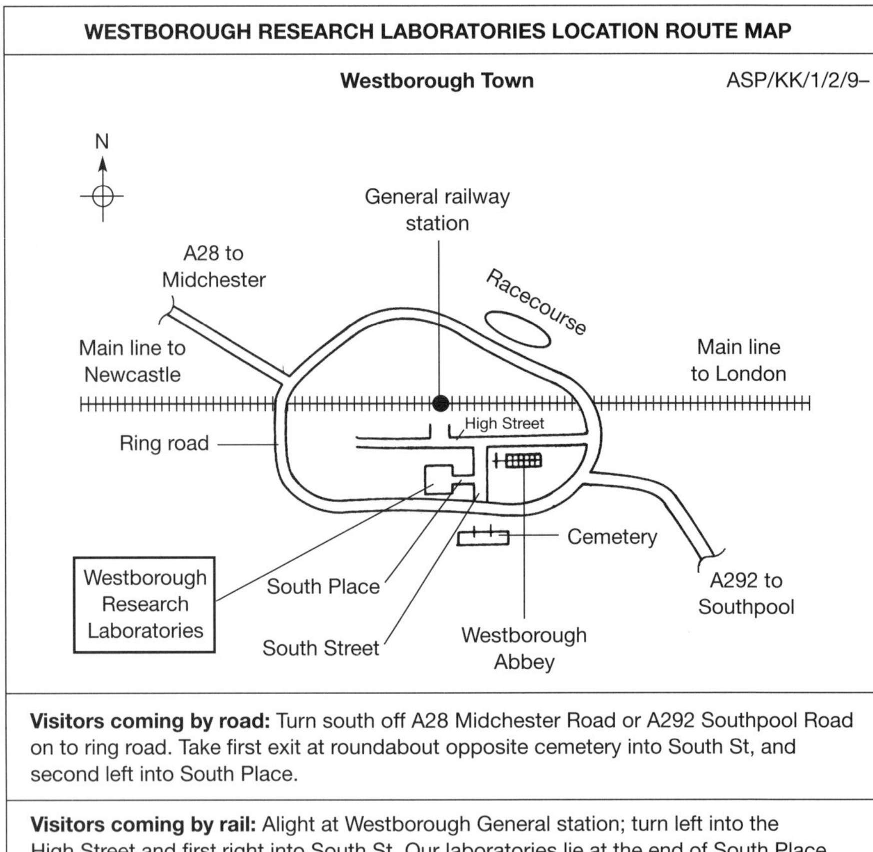

Figure 3.17 **Example of a local route map**

KEY POINT

Design maps which are clear and simple

Effective maps communicate clearly, simply and quickly. Avoid including unneeded small details in local or district maps, but label key sections precisely. Use arrows and other symbols to indicate flows of traffic, approaches, etc.

Remember to give your maps a relevant title, an orientation (e.g. north), date of publication and author reference. Always include a scale if appropriate.

INDIVIDUAL SKILLS-BUILDING ACTIVITIES

Developing skills in map designing

Task 1 During the coming week, hunt down a map of your locality especially designed to meet an organisation's requirements. Either bring the original or a photocopy of it to your class to display and form the basis of a general discussion of its effective and weak features. Pin up the best examples on a noticeboard in your classroom.

Task 2 The head of your department wishes to update the map of your study centre which is sent to visitors, etc. Design a suitable map which shows clearly the location of your department, and the HOD's office within it, as well as its position on the overall campus. Produce the map using black ink and white paper, and label it suitably, bearing in mind what a visitor will need to know.

Task 3 Having seen what a splendid job you did for Task 2, your headteacher/principal has now asked you to produce a similar map showing main routes to your study centre from road, rail, air and port links. Include as part of your map a brief set of instructions for visitors coming from both your nearest main-line railway station and main trunk roads to your study centre. In addition, provide your map with suitable titles.

Task 4 Not all route maps are drawn for the eye to follow. Blind and partially sighted people, for example, rely heavily on the medium of the spoken word. Practise your skill in composing an **aural** route map (a set of spoken word instructions) to help a blind person find your classroom from one of the following:

1 the main entrance

2 the refectory

3 the library

Test out your recorded set of instructions with your co-students and decide which aural map would be most effective. Remember that instructions like 'Turn left at the picture of the college/school' are not going to be of much help.

Photographs

Photographs – both colour and black and white – are used a great deal in many organisations. Sometimes, a company estates manager will take a Polaroid instant photograph of premises which his company is thinking of buying, or a marketing executive will ask an advertising agency to produce professional photographs of, say, new fashion wear for an advertisement in *Vogue* or *Elle*. Again, an accident inspector or an engineer may take close-up photographs of a particular joint or machine part in order to check it for defects.

In other words, photographs are used in all kinds of situations at work as a means of capturing, storing and presenting picture information. The following checklist illustrates some of the main uses of photography in the workplace.

CHECKLIST

Major uses of photography at work

- **to advertise products or services** in magazines, brochures, newspapers and point-of-sale merchandising materials
- **to publicise the faces of key staff** on noticeboards or in in-house newspapers, etc.
- **to make effective recordings of events or conditions**, say of a faulty piece of equipment, or the opening of a new store
- **to illustrate in-house publications**, such as company annual reports, or a brochure to introduce new councillors to a local community
- **to provide visual support** or explanations in presentations and talks, etc. in the form of slides
- **to illustrate training manuals or instruction booklets** used to develop staff

As a result of the widespread use of photographs in the mass media of magazines, newspapers and advertisements, we are all extremely used to seeing all kinds of photographs taken by highly skilled professional photographers. And for this reason, we tend to look down our noses at family snapshots which behead Auntie Gladys, or capture a blurred thumb in the foreground of the photo.

While, however, we may not wish to become a David Bailey or Lord Lichfield, the basic skills of photography are well worth mastering in the course of preparing for a full-time working career. This section of Chapter 3, therefore, concentrates on explaining in outline how a camera works, and what skills are needed to take photographs of a satisfactory standard. After all, you never know when you may be asked to produce some photographs at work which could do your career prospects no harm at all!

How a camera works

Since the early days of photography in the 1840s, camera technology has come a very long way. Nevertheless, the essentials of photography have remained the same. In order to take a photograph – then and now – the process in the following checklist has to be followed:

CHECKLIST

How a photograph is taken

- Simply, a camera is **a box which allows a certain amount of light to enter it through a lens** which picks up the images of people or things at which it is pointed.
- In order to produce a sharp and clear picture, **lenses in modern cameras can be adjusted to focus precisely on subjects at certain distances from the camera,** by the use of a mechanism called the f stop. Also, some cameras are fitted with zoom lenses which enable the photographer to use the camera like a pair of binoculars by bringing distant objects nearer and increasing their size on the film.
- **Behind the lens is an aperture mechanism,** which acts rather like a circular door (popular on some spaceships). The aperture can be set to allow more or less light into the camera as a shot is taken. As you can imagine, in poor lighting conditions, more light is needed than on very sunny days to ensure that a photograph's content is sufficiently bright.
- The camera's photographing mechanism can also be adjusted to **allow the light into the camera for more or less time,** measured in parts of a second (unless a prolonged exposure is being taken in very dark lighting conditions), for example, 1/60th to 1/1000th of a second. The adjustment affects the speed at which the camera's shutter is opened and closed, and therefore, how much light is allowed to hit the film.
- Also, **the choice of film installed in the camera affects the kinds of photographs taken**. Basically, films are coated with a chemical which reacts to light, so as to produce a precise image of the outside picture (being photographed) from the light flooding in through the lens and aperture on to the exposed section of film. Films are given international ratings which inform the user of their suitability for various inside and outside light conditions. An all-purpose film speed is rated as DIN 200.

Fortunately for most of us, many of today's cameras possess a wide range of automatic features – hence the rise of the term 'point and click' cameras. Such cameras take readings of available light, as well as the distance of the object to be photographed from the lens, and calculate automatically the settings for:

- focal length
- aperture setting
- shutter speed setting

In addition, many cameras today can recognise the speed of the film which has been loaded. Add to such automatic features the ability of many modern cameras to make similar automatic calculations when a flash-light photograph is taken, and you can readily appreciate the distance photography has travelled from those times when a photographer had to disappear under a black sheet, look at the subject upside down, and ask people to remain stock still for many seconds, while a loud flash of light was emitted from a hand-held, magnesium-powered torch!

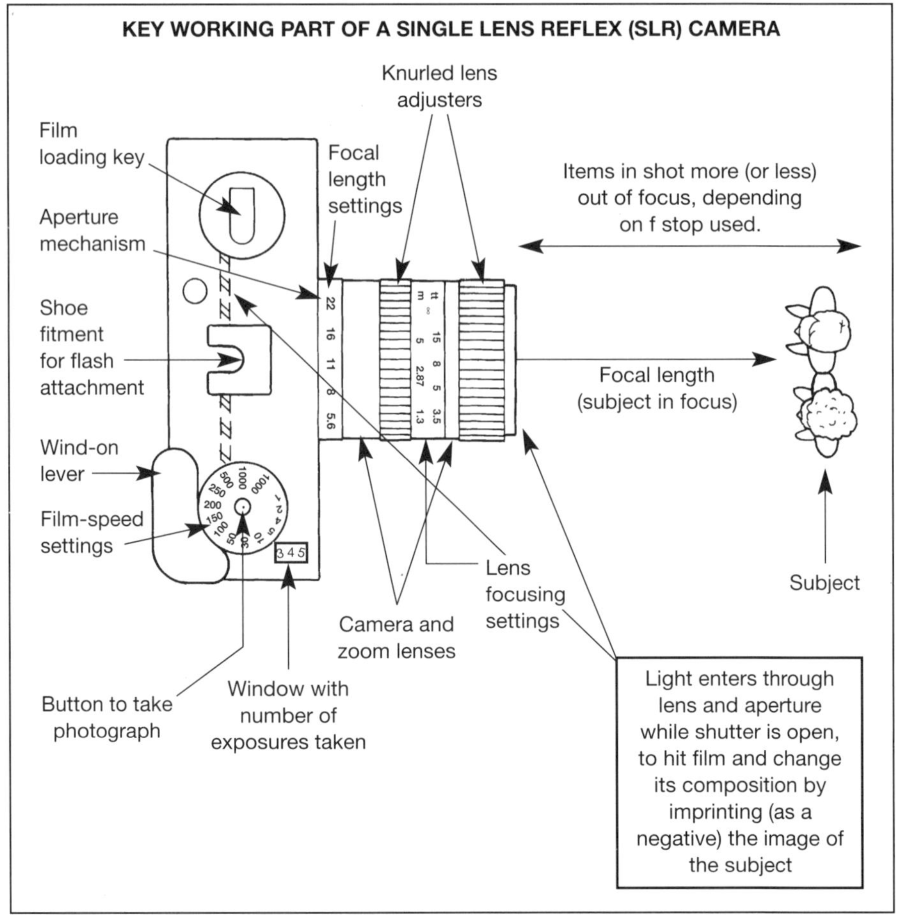

KEY POINT

Make notes when you take photographs

The best way of learning how to take successful photographs is to start taking photographs! But, to do so with a system. In order to check out the behaviour of the camera you will use, it really does pay to buy, say, a 24-exposure film, and to take some pictures using this approach:

- For each exposure taken, log in a notebook the focal length and shutter speed settings you use.
- Also, make a note of general light and weather conditions for each picture.

When your films are printed, you can refer to the numbers printed on each of their negatives and check your notes when examining them for clarity of focus, under- and over-exposure, etc. In this way, you will soon become expert with your camera and what settings to use in what conditions.

Composing effective photographs

It is one thing to be familiar with the basics of a camera's working parts, but quite another to become expert in composing interesting photographs! Again, practice makes perfect. For example, some viewfinders in modern cameras show more to the eye than will actually appear on the photograph. The users of such cameras need to be sure that their subjects are located in the centre of the viewfinder, surrounded by a reasonable margin of non-essential background. Also, the human eye is much keener than many camera lenses. Therefore, it is tempting to take a photograph of, say, three skiers some 150 metres from the camera. To the human eye they will appear quite distinct. But in many resulting photographs, they will appear as tiny and indistinct objects.

To develop your skills in composing interesting and effective photographs, keep the following guidelines in mind:

CHECKLIST

Guidelines on composing effective photographs

- **Take good care of your camera,** keep it protected in its case, and ensure that the lens is kept clean and free from finger marks, dust, etc.

Continues ▶

- **Take care when setting the f stop on your camera**, so as to ensure that all your chosen subject will be in focus.
- **Avoid asking people to hold poses too long** – especially in strong sunlight - they will end up looking unnatural or squinting; try to catch them unawares, with natural and unstressed expressions and poses.
- **Avoid placing your subjects smack, bang in the centre of your viewfinder**, since this makes for a dull composition; try to set the subject a little to one side, or to the top or bottom of the picture.
- **Keep your subjects simple**; avoid distractions, such as branches casting shadows across faces, or including an over busy background, with too many details in it.
- **Make effective use of light and shade**; shadows, for example, across water or on the sides of buildings often create different tones which add interest to the composition.
- **Look for the unusual angle or position from which to photograph**; even routine events or ordinary objects can be made to appear more interesting if seen from an unusual view.

Needless to say, there are also a number of dangerous pitfalls to avoid when taking photographs as a beginner, as this short checklist illustrates.

CHECKLIST

Pitfalls for the unwary photographer

- Whenever possible, use a tripod to hold your camera steady, or adopt one of the holding positions shown in most camera manuals, since moving the camera at the precise moment of taking the picture – camera shake – is one of the most common causes of blurred pictures.
- Take especial care when setting focal lengths and when focusing the lens manually.
- Watch out for unwanted camera straps or thumbs appearing in the viewfinder because they have strayed in front of the lens.
- Check that you are not going to clip part of your subject off and thus out of the photograph; remember that sometimes you will need to position groups of people closer together than they normally would stand.

Continues 

- Avoid pointing your camera into the sun, since this will destroy the settings you have made and result in a photograph with white, empty sections.
- Make sure that exposure is wound on fully, or you may take one photograph over another, with unexpected results!

Figure 3.18 **Example of a well composed photograph: this imposing Asian building is made more interesting by being photographed from an angle rather than head on, which can produce a flat effect.** (Reproduced with kind permission of Expert Software USA from the 3000 Images Photo Gallery © Expert Software Inc. and Media Graphics Int., Inc.)

Figure 3.19 **This well composed photograph centres upon a solitary boatman working amid a jumble of boats.** (Reproduced with kind permission of Expert Software USA from the 3000 Images Photo Gallery © Expert Software Inc. and Media Graphics Int., Inc.)

WHAT DO YOU THINK?

1 Why do *you* think photographs are used so much by organisations?

2 Does the widespread publication of top-class professional photographs in, say, hobby and general interest magazines set such high standards that most of us are put off taking photographs as amateurs?

3 Twenty or so years ago, SLR cameras with fully manual mechanisms were extremely popular. Today, most ordinary people buy point-and-click alternatives. Has a lot of personal satisfaction been taken away from them by reducing the art of taking a photograph to a completely automatic process?

4 What, in your opinion, makes a photograph a work of art?

5 What is it about photography that puts you off taking more pictures each week or month of your life?

SUMMARY OF KEY POINTS

Photographs

- Organisations make extensive use of photographs, from advertising products or services, to creating visual records of processes, equipment or buildings.
- Photographic technology has come a long way since its start in the 1840s and the slow but determined pace of developments from black and white films on glass to colour films able to reproduce faithfully all the colours of the spectrum.
- Today, many popular cameras are able to make the settings for a photograph fully automatically, including the setting of focal length and shutter speed.
- Great strides have also been made in developing films suited for widely varying indoor and outdoor lighting conditions and enlargement demands.
- A successful photographic composition is one which sets its subject in a clear focus and in a pleasing relationship with its background, making use of unusual viewpoints and effects of light and shade.

SELF-CHECK REVIEW TEST

Photographs

1 List four main uses of photographs in organisations

2 What is meant by the terms *aperture setting* and *shutter speed setting?*

Continues 

3 How does the speed of a loaded film affect the taking of a photograph?

4 List three useful tips to help the beginner photographer.

5 List three pitfalls to avoid when taking photographs.

6 What is meant by the term *camera shake?*

7 What is a point-and-click camera?

8 What does SLR stand for?

When you have completed the above questions, turn to page 306 to check the answers provided against your own. Revise the appropriate section of Chapter 3, if you got the answer wrong.

INDIVIDUAL AND STUDENT PAIR SKILLS-BUILDING ACTIVITIES

Developing photographic skills and appreciation

Task 1: whole class activity In the course of the coming week, collect some six photographs – three black and white, and three coloured, which you think particularly effective in terms of their composition and the communication they make. With the help of your teacher set up an exhibition of them in your classroom. You may, for example, choose a photograph in a newspaper, magazine, on a record album cover, from part of an advertisement, etc.

When your class had had an opportunity to view the exhibition, hold a general discussion on what you think makes the ones considered the best to be most effective.

Task 2: student pair activity With your teacher's guidance, select one of the following photographic tasks:

1 Your head/principal is looking for some unusual and interesting photographs of your study centre to go into the next edition of the prospectus. You have been asked to take about five photographs for consideration in either colour or black and white.

2 You work part-time for your local Tourist Board. The manager wishes to put together some photographs of well-known monuments, land-marks, historic buildings, etc., in a forthcoming advertising brochure to be sent to EU travel agents, and has asked you to produce about five possible subjects for inclusion.

3 Your local History Society is putting together a collection of photographs of current equipment in popular use – televisions, micro-wave ovens, computers, photocopiers, hi-fi stacks, etc. – to form part of an archive for future generations and has asked you to provide some five examples

Arrange to take some eight to ten photographs from which you and your partner will select what you believe to be the best five. In a classroom presentation, show your photographs to your co-students, and decide which pair produced the best set of photographs and why.

Sketches and cartoons

As you can imagine, it is no quick or simple thing to design and copy maps, or to take effective photographs (perhaps other than Polaroid ones, which develop and print themselves). Thus another form of visual image is used by people in organisations who need to communicate visually on the spot, and that is the sketch. A well-known story goes that in 1995 one of the Bosnian political leaders drew a sketch of the Bosnian Serb's strategic plan for Bosnia-Herzegovina on a menu of the Liberal Democrat leader Paddy Ashdown during a meal at a conference. Other less famous sketches occur during daily routines at work, on scribble pads or copy paper to assist in situations like these:

> This is how I see the new open-plan office layout John …
>
> To my mind, we need to put another outflow here, to cope with any cloudbursts or flooding …
>
> Wouldn't it look better if the sleeves were more bouffant, like this …

In such instances, employees quickly move to a visual medium in order to communicate more effectively, whether in terms of desks, partitions and cupboards, highway culvert design or women's high fashion wear. Thus the ability to produce a sketch which is easily recognisable and communicates well is another important imaging skill to acquire.

Plan, side elevation and perspective

A set of terms exists in the realms of professional draughtsmen to describe certain types of drawing. Figure 3.20 on page 209 illustrates what is meant by the terms **plan, side elevation** and **perspective**.

PLAN

A plan drawing or sketch is produced to give its viewers an impression of looking down on it from above:

Plan of ground floor of 3-bedroom, 2-storey residence

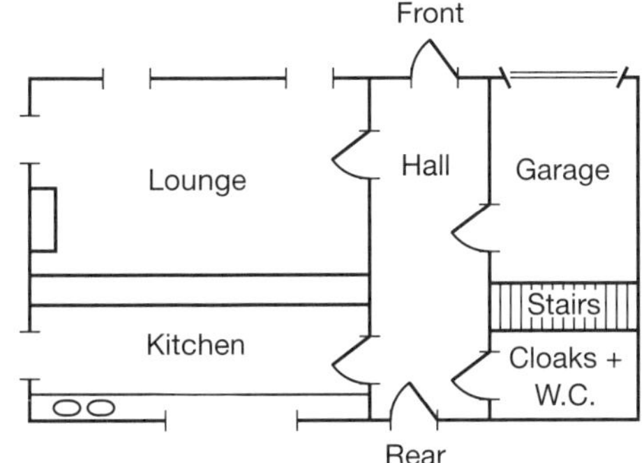

SIDE ELEVATION

A side elevation displays a drawing or sketch from one side only:

Note that both plan and side elevations are drawn in two dimensions only.

PERSPECTIVE

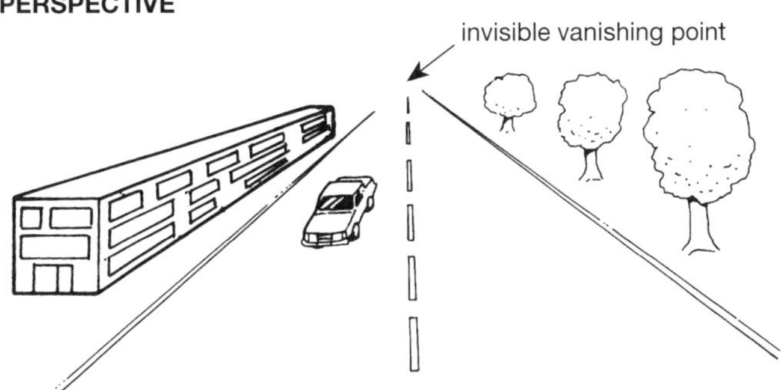

Perspective drawings are produced to give a three-dimensional effect, using the two dimensions of a flat paper sheet. Notice the lines of the left-hand building, road, pavement and trees all converge on a single distance vanishing point, which is a key feature of perspective drawing

Figure 3.20

CHECKLIST

Tips on producing effective sketches

Keep the following tips in mind when producing a sketch:

- Whenever possible, **prefer a pencil and eraser to biro or roller pen,** since they make revisions or corrections much easier without the sketch becoming confused by crossings out, etc.
- **Work out the rough dimensions** of a room, piece of equipment, etc., in outline, **before creating their detail,** since you may find that one item in a group is too big or small.
- **Work from the front to the back of your sketch**, since objects in the foreground may block out parts of ones which stand behind them, which will need their lines to be broken.
- **Concentrate on essentials only**, and use thicker line drawing and shading to make key features stand out clearly and boldly.
- **Remember to label main** features briefly and clearly, and to provide a title, author and date.

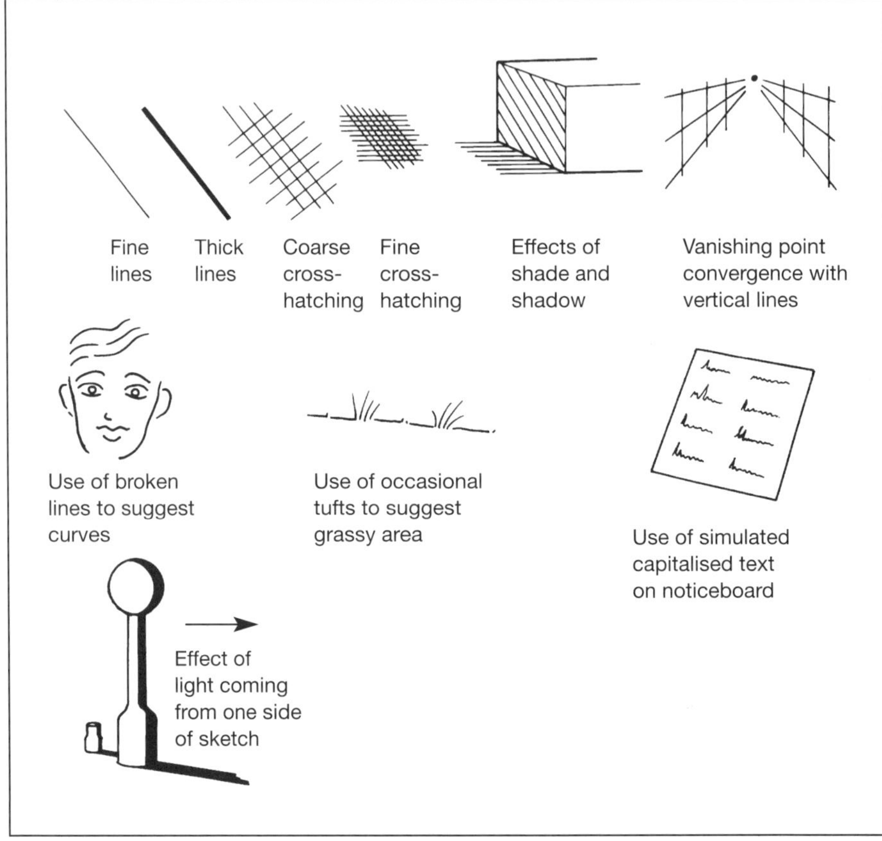

Figure 3.21 **Examples of techniques used in sketching**

Cartoons

Cartoons are used in organisations both to inform and to persuade. The modern idea of a cartoon is that of a simple sketch or drawing which is used to convey something funny. However, in earlier days, the term cartoon was also used by artists to describe a rough drawing from which a detailed painting would be created.

CHECKLIST

Major uses of cartoons in organisations

Organisations use cartoons for a variety of purposes:

- to communicate serious messages in a light-hearted way so that people will accept them more readily, such as the need to wear a hard hat on a building site
- to sell products or services (as an alternative to using a photograph)
- to provide some visual relief and to break up long passages of prose
- to capture readers' attention and to encourage them to read an accompanying message

Most modern cartoons share a common theme, which is to use humour as a tool of communication. We all laugh at the classic cartoon strip of the man carefully avoiding a banana skin on the pavement, when about to walk around the corner into the path of a hungry tiger! Such humour conveys the message that, no matter what precautions you take, the unexpected lies just around the corner. Another type of cartoon (of a serious nature) was the set devised some years ago by the Prudential Assurance Company showing the changes of expression in a man who had not taken out a pension. They range from total unconcern at twenty-something to worried dismay at sixty-something. The brewing firm Guinness produced a classic advertising campaign in the 1950s and 60s for its stout which showed a series of zoo animals interacting with a glass of Guinness. Not unexpectedly, the ostrich had the glass stuck halfway down its throat, while the toucan was balancing it on its technicolour beak.

In other words, cartoons provide organisations with a powerful way of putting a specific message across, whether about health and safety, a new product or a feature about a retiring manager in a house newspaper.

Devising an effective cartoon is not that easy, since creating a visually humorous situation requires some imagination and a natural flair. Some cartoons are funny, because they appear to take a ludicrous situation seriously, such as the business executive standing naked and dripping by his phone at home and saying into it:

> 'No, no, of course not boss, I was just reading the newspaper ...'

when he had clearly rushed out of the bath to take the call from his all-powerful boss. Other types of cartoon humour are created by devising a character and then producing a series of cartoons which display him or her in typical action, such as Peanuts of international fame, who is always receiving advice he finds hard to handle.

Figure 3.22 **Example of a cartoon used in the workplace to communicate a serious message**

WHAT DO YOU THINK?

1 'You can either draw, or you can't, and there's an end of it' True, or false?

2 What sort of situations can you think of occurring regularly in your vocational sector which would involve an employee in needing to draw a sketch?

3 Can you think of a topic in your GNVQ study area which could be effectively conveyed by producing a cartoon? Detail your topic and explain your thinking.

4 'The problem about using cartoons at work is that not everyone has the same sense of humour, and offence can easily be caused.' True or false? Can you think of any work-related scenarios which it would be unwise to use as

the subject-matter of a cartoon? If you can, provide details and your reasons for so thinking.

5 'The problem with the use of images at work – especially diagrams and sketches – is that they tend to oversimplify the information they communicate. Words, on the other hand, can convey lots of detail and fine argument.' Do you agree, or can you think of communications situations in your field for which an image is a much better communications tool than a page or two of words?

SUMMARY OF KEY POINTS

How to produce effective sketches and cartoons

- Sketches tend to be used in organisations at the drop of a hat because they are quick and easy to produce in the middle of a discussion, meeting, etc.
- Sketches at work tend to be drawn in either plan, side elevation or perspective views, and if they are to be used formally, require clear titles and labels, in the same way that graphs and charts do.
- Time and effort are saved by using pencil and eraser initially, and then going over a final draft in ink.
- Both sketches and cartoons should focus upon essential features, while providing only bare outlines of backgrounds.
- When sketches are produced in a technical context, then they should include details of measurements, specifications, etc.
- Cartoons tend to be used in organisations either to communicate sensitive information without causing offence, or to add a light touch to a document.

CHECKLIST

Tips on how to draw cartoons

- Consider, first, the caption for the cartoon you wish to draw; sometimes a proverbial saying can be illustrated in an unexpected way, or a straight conversational remark may be made to seem funny because of some absurd reaction to it by the figures in the cartoon.
- Keep the drawings of people very simple, and emphasise their expressions and gestures; all non-essential background should be drawn in the merest outline.

Continues ▶

- Do not crowd items into a cartoon, since they have to communicate instantly to work well.
- Only experienced, professional cartoonists are able to draw first and final drafts in one go, so be prepared to draw several versions until you are happy with the end product.

SELF-CHECK REVIEW TEST

Sketches and cartoons

1 What is meant by the terms *plan* and *side elevation* view in a drawing context?

2 What is different about a sketch drawn with a *perspective*?

3 What is a vanishing point in a sketch?

4 What techniques can a sketcher use to depict light coming from the right or left in a drawing?

5 List three uses of cartoons in organisations.

6 What tips can you supply for drawing effective cartoons?

When you have completed the above questions, turn to page 307 to check the answers provided against your own. Revise the appropriate section of Chapter 3, if you got an answer wrong.

INDIVIDUAL SKILLS-BUILDING ACTIVITIES

Developing sketching and drawing skills

Task 1 Your head of department is thinking of making some changes to the use of the rooms which make up the department, and has therefore asked you to produce a plan drawing of them – to scale and suitably labelled – to inform him/her of their current use. Draw a suitable plan (of some or all the rooms, depending upon your teacher's advice) on a sheet of A3 paper.

Task 2 The marketing team at your study centre are currently producing draft material for a new prospectus, and have invited students to submit perspective views of the centre for consideration. Select a suitable view, and then produce a perspective sketch which you think meets this aim.

Task 3 Your teacher is currently over-worked because of having to carry out a departmental project, and has therefore asked you to provide some assistance (in preparing material suited to GNVQ assessment). You have been asked to produce a sketch of one of the following items, which is intended to be converted into an overhead transparency foil to act as a teaching aid:

1 a desk-top personal computer and printer

2 a lathe

3 a wheel-chair with a seated occupant in it

4 a piece of equipment in a fitness centre

5 a piece of laboratory equipment

6 a tool used on a construction site

Your sketch should label principal moving parts and key features suitably, as well as provide an apt title. Your sketch may be in either black and white or colour and should be drawn on a sheet of A4, so that it could be converted into an OHP foil.

Task 4 In an effort to avoid injury, emotional upset or disappointment, as well as to create a lighter mood in your study centre department, you have been asked to design a cartoon to illustrate *one* of the following captions, which will be displayed on corridor noticeboards, etc.

1 'Accidents don't just happen. They are caused.'

2 'Don't tell me, you've just discovered that you've left your file with a year's work in it on the bus, and the depot says there's no trace of it!'

3 'S/he forgot to give his/her GNVQ portfolio activity in on time!'

4 'A GNVQ programme emphasises the development of the students' practical skills.'

5 'It's not *all* hard work, being a GNVQ student!'

Produce a suitable cartoon above one of these captions on a sheet of A3 paper. The colours you employ – of inks and paper – are entirely up to you.

Task 5 When your class has completed the above activities according to your teacher's briefing, display the results in a classroom exhibition, and carry out a survey to discover which drawing was generally considered to be most effective in each category and why.

PORTFOLIO-BUILDING ACTIVITIES

Introduce at least two pieces of written material in which an image has been used to illustrate a point on a straightforward matter.

Note that some of the following activities take the form of a presentation or discussion as required by the Foundation GNVQ specification.

1 Select one of the following topics, and then carry out the task detailed below:

(a) powering up a computer or terminal you use at your study centre and creating a file in which to enter data in either a word-processing or spreadsheet application.

(b) daily dental care

(c) safety precautions to be aware of when using a fitness centre, scientific laboratory or workshop

(d) making out a petty cash voucher

(e) setting up a work station for a painting or drawing activity

(f) making a holiday booking for a customer by on-line computer

First carry out your researches into one of the above topics, and then **compile a set of brief but clear instructions on how to carry out the activity.** A part of your instructions should be an image which illustrates suitably a key stage or which provides a helpful visual aid. Aim to produce your instructions on not more than one side of A4, suitably presented, and the image also on an A4 page.

2 Write a passage in about 150 words which describes one of the major tourist attractions in your locality. Hunt down and photocopy an image of the attraction which could be used to illustrate your paragraph. Give your paragraph a suitable title.

3 Design a pie chart which accurately reflects the favourite daily newspaper or leisure magazine read by students in your class. Label it suitably, and provide a short written explanation of your findings.

4 Design a bar chart which illustrates the totals of

a) full time, b) part-time day, and c) evening only students currently following courses in your department.

5 Design a line graph which shows clearly the following data:

Admissions to Midshire County Council's residential homes for the elderly

	JAN	FEB	MAR	APR	MAY	JUN	JLY	AUG	SEP	OCT	NOV	DEC
Yr A	181	167	155	143	128	110	94	83	101	133	173	201
Yr B	204	211	190	177	165	133	129	111	142	159	193	189
Yr C	122	135	169	186	175	189	167	155	133	126	159	171
Yr D	134	119	140	152	96	82	69	84	108	121	123	141

Answer the following questions beneath your line graph:

(a) If Year A plots the admissions for the past calendar year, and the rest for previous years, what can you determine with some degree of certainty about the trends of admissions to Midshire County Council's residential homes for the elderly?

(b) Can you think of any reasons for the peaks and troughs in the graph's plotted lines? Which months of which of the years A–D reveals the impact upon admissions of an unusual epidemic of flu in the district? How can you justify your answer?

(c) What justifications does the graph supply for the Social Services Chief Officer's request early this year for another residential home to be opened as soon as possible, given that the total number of available places in the county is some 190, and Year A is the past calendar year?

6 Your class is producing a scrap-book entitled: *People In The News*. Its aim is to provide a useful reference source about people in your locality who are active in your GNVQ vocational area (e.g. Business, Health & Social Care, Leisure & Tourism, etc). It is now your turn to organise the scrap-book for this week's entries. You are therefore tasked with the following:

Either a) take a photograph, or b) obtain a photocopy image of a person or a place relevant to your GNVQ study area who/which is in the news this week in your district. Then write a paragraph of about 100 words explaining the detail of the photograph and the news about the person, place or event.

7 Design a map of your town/city or immediate district which shows its major tourist attractions or areas of historic interest. Label your map suitably and use a sheet of A4 paper on which to draw it. Also, provide a suitable key for the items of interest you include on the map.

8 Design a sketch or cartoon to form a major image on a poster aimed at encouraging students in your study centre to do one of the following:

(a) stop dropping litter on the campus

(b) take an active interest in a local charitable cause

(c) join a study centre club

9 Research into one of the following topics, and then give a 1–2 minute talk to your class about it, using a suitable image to illustrate your talk:

(a) an analysis of the types of full-time job advertised this week in your local weekly newspaper.

(b) an IT-related development likely to happen in your GNVQ work sector over the next three years.

(c) a major impact upon your locality of the growing trend of residents to live much longer than they did 30–40 years ago

(d) an interesting trend in the use of a construction material today

(e) how CADCAM has changed an engineering/manufacturing technique

(f) an important current scientific development.

10 Take part in a group discussion on one of the following topics, and bring to the discussion a visual image which will suitably illustrate a main point you wish to make:

(a) There *is* a world of teenage fashion out there, beyond the forest of T-shirts and jeans!

(b) 'Unfortunately, good design died about 1968, and all attempts at mouth-to-mouth resuscitation of it seem to have failed since!'

(c) 'Young adults today just don't know how to spend their leisure time sensibly or usefully. In my day, there were plenty of organisations which gave service to the community – scouts, guides, cadets and so on. Today all this has been transformed into hanging out in pubs, discos and rave joints! Me, me, me, me and again me That's the youth culture of today!'

(d) 'It won't be over population, pollution or global warming that will see off the human race, Oh no, it will be their own endless greed, mark my words!'

(e) 'Women will never be the equal of men for the simple reason that they have always been their superiors!'

(f) 'Though they don't want to admit it, the vast majority of people today are much better off than their predecessors were thirty odd years ago!'

11 Provide a new design idea for one of the following, and illustrate it with a suitable sketch (on one side of A4). Describe your design in an accompanying paragraph of about 150 words.

(a) an office chair

(b) a day room in a care centre for the elderly

(c) a bench and shelves for a scientist's workstation

(d) a workstation for a computer technician

(e) a fitness room especially designed for paraplegics

(f) a sales area in a travel agency

(g) a shop front for a small general stores business

12 Deliver a 1–3 minute talk to your group about the main features you built into your design concept for the topic you chose in 11 above. Produce a suitable image visual aid to illustrate your talk (e.g. OHP foil, board-drawing or hand-out).

4 Read and respond to written material

Guttenberg made everybody a reader. Xerox makes everybody a publisher.

Marshall McLuhan, American expert on communication

What Chapter 4 covers

Chapter 4 explores the skills needed to read a wide range of written documents at work, so as to be able to respond and react to them appropriately. Here, the word appropriately means a whole manner of things, such as:

- reading a written message and telephoning someone immediately, because the matter is urgent
- reading a set of instructions very carefully – say on a health and safety matter – and building them into daily routines
- reading a memo from the boss asking all staff to make a particular effort to sell, because the firm is going through a bad patch – and deciding to make that extra effort
- reading through a source document, making notes on its key points, and relaying them in a shorter form
- reading a complicated document several times over, and perhaps consulting a dictionary at times, so as to ensure that its meaning is fully grasped.

As the above examples indicate, Chapter 4 will examine in detail the techniques of reading materials at work – not for simple enjoyment, but for a specific purpose directly related to doing the job well. It also deals with the skills needed to extract information from a document which has been asked for, or which is needed in order to carry out a task. Lastly, it supplies helpful guidelines on how to use sources of reference, like an English language dictionary, spelling dictionary or dictionary of abbreviations, to obtain information which helps to clarify your understanding about a subject. Also, Chapter 4 examines the skills needed to obtain information from written material which forms a mix of both text and image.

After working through Chapter 4, you will have acquired improved skills in reading and understanding written documents, how to extract key data from them and pass it on, and how to use a range of reference sources to support such tasks.

The main sections of Chapter 4

- Reading needs and expectations at work
- How to use reference sources
- How to take effective notes of reading material
- Extracting information from different types of document
- How to pass on information extracted from reading material

In addition, Chapter 4 includes:

- Sets of discussion topics
- Key tips on good practice
- Opportunities to practise newly acquired skills
- Sets of case studies for discussion and analysis
- Activities for assessment and portfolio building

Reading needs and expectations at work

How and why reading at work differs from 'normal' reading

After reading the above heading, you could be forgiven for thinking: 'Wait a minute, reading is reading is reading, isn't it?' And in many ways you would be right. But in some ways you would be wrong.

To explain, consider how we all read a novel or magazine article. We tend to float through it, letting its words flow over us. As we read them, our eyes take in their printed messages, and our brains interpret what they mean. But now and again, we come across a word or phrase that we have never met before, and therefore do not recognise or understand. Now when this happens in our casual and leisure reading, we simply skip over it, and read on. Of course, in the context of a 400 page romantic novel, or a football match report, the fact that some words or sections were not grasped does not really matter. Nothing is hanging on the outcome of our leisure reading.

At work, however, a failure to grasp fully the messages contained in a printed document could matter a very great deal. For instance, failure to understand completely a set of instructions for operating a newly installed piece of equipment could result in a nasty accident. Similarly, skipping over an unusual word like *courier*, as in *courier delivery*, could result in the reader failing to ensure that an urgently needed package gets to its destination in time.

Another aspect affecting reading at work is to be found in every employee's contract of employment. The employee, when starting a new job, undertakes to work conscientiously, to take active care in maintaining personal health and safety and that of co-employees, and to carry out any reasonable work request passed on by his or her superiors. Now, it is inevitable that some of the messages relating to doing the job are passed to employees in a written form. So this means that the employee has a legal duty to read all work-related documents conscientiously – however tedious or boring they may appear to be!

Key characteristics of materials to be read at work

At the start of a chapter on developing work-based reading skills, it is helpful to consider what makes up the key characteristics of organisational documents which have to be read in the course of doing a job.

CHECKLIST

Key features of workplace reading material

1 Materials produced in-house:

- **often tend to be part of an ongoing production of documents** – say letters or memos being exchanged, or sales/accounts delivery notes, invoices, etc., being sent out; this means that it is often necessary to check back through files to look up a specific point or reference
- **almost always form part of a process** in which a desired outcome is sought, and actions are being taken or requested to achieve this outcome
- **may frequently contain technical or jargon words and expressions** which no one outside of the profession or trade uses or understands, such as *feathering* in terms of abnormal tyre wear, or *cardio-vascular infarction* in terms of heart surgery; each vocation has its own particular set of such technical terms, which must be learned off by heart by each employee who cares about making progress
- **all contain internal reference names, numbers and codes** – of the employees who produce or receive them, of unique product references, of plan or map filing and reference numbers, etc; again each organisation tends to use its own, unique system for such referencing, which also has to be learned thoroughly if a filed document is to be located, or a precise and accurate reference is to be made to a set of design specifications, etc.
- **concentrate on supplying information as clearly and briefly** as possible (hence the use of technical terms which have very precise meanings); people at work today are kept very busy, and soon lose patience when having to read long-winded waffle.

2 Externally produced materials:

- **contain source, author and publication date references,** which always need to be jotted down and referred to when information is passed on; otherwise, the people receiving the relayed message may believe its content is highly current, when it may in fact have been produced over a year ago, etc.
- **may contain materials which have not been written with any particular organisation in mind;** this means that any information extracted may have to be explained in some detail in order for in-house readers to see its relevance or importance

Continues ▶

- **may also contain information which is either prejudiced,** tells only a part of a story, or lacks factual support; for such reasons, many people who summarise external information to turn it into briefing papers, etc., check other sources in order to cross-check an article's truth or factual honesty.
- **may contain information which is irrelevant to a given organisation's** needs; for this reason, its reader often needs to concentrate solely on one or two of a dozen pages, or to note down details relating to a single topic of several dealt with.

The formats of workplace reading materials

Just as it helps to become familiar with the key features of reading materials at work, so it pays to be fully aware of the formats they are likely to take, not only in overall layout, but in the ways in which the English language is used in them. The following checklist illustrates the major language forms used in the different formats you are likely to meet:

CHECKLIST

Major English language forms used in workplace documents

1 **Letters, memoranda, briefing and discussion papers:** In these documents, the English you are likely to meet will be set out as a series of prose paragraphs made up of strings of grammatical sentences. Sometimes a paragraph may include a set of bullet-point short phrases appearing as a kind of short statement shopping list, and the paragraphs may be given headings which summarise their key points. These documents tend either to seek action to secure desired outcomes, or to present arguments or discussions by balancing one viewpoint with another.

2 **Reports, factsheets and schedules:** Here there is likely to be a mix of paragraphs which explain points in detail, and sets of checklists which may not be written as sentences, but in a kind of abbreviated English form which simply conveys main points. Keep in mind that such lists may either contain important, key data, or simply provide a list of examples for a previous main point. This category is also likely to make extensive use of headings, sub-headings and number

Continues ▶

references (see Chapter 2, pages 140–141, on the short report). Such documents tend to convey factual details and to analyse problems and options in order to arrive at a reasoned conclusion.

3 **Product specifications, estimates, operating manuals, financial reports:** These documents focus almost entirely on setting down technical and complex information clearly and logically. They also tend to make much use of number information. Thus they are unlikely to contain extended paragraphs of English, but to compact and compress data into tables, lists, columns and diagrams. Such documents generally require several careful readings in order to understand them. Since they are mostly used as reference documents, they focus on accuracy and reliability, and make few concessions to a person's English language abilities. They, too, contain factual and sometimes highly technical information which cannot be skimmed over if it is to be understood.

4 **Sales brochures, advertisements, packaging, posters, in-house newspapers and magazines:** This category of reading material contrasts distinctly with those of **1**,**2** and **3**, which aim for the most part to inform factually. Here, writers seek to sway the opinions of customers, staff, the general public, etc. The writing, therefore, is likely to consist of short headings or slogans followed by brief bullet-point lists or short, connected sentences. The English used will not always be factual, and so the reader needs to be constantly on guard to check whether a point is a fact, or merely an assertion or view. Such documents are likely to contain images which also seek to persuade, and to communicate through examples which seek to influence heart before head.

Developing skills in reading written material

Various ways of teaching primary school children to read have been tried since the 1950s. These include the teaching of an initial alphabet, which spelled words in a phonetic system. This enabled children to make fast initial progress, but sooner or later they had to tackle the awfulness of English words like: *through, thorough, plough* and *rough*, not to mention *crescent* and *pharmacy*! Other early reading systems involved youngsters in learning monosyllabic words to start with, like *Jack, cat, pot, Tom,* and then learning how monosyllables can be joined together to form different words: *jackpot, tomcat.* Yet other systems relied on a look and say method, in which

MAJOR WORKPLACE ENGLISH LANGUAGE FORMS

Letters, memoranda, briefing and discussion papers

- series of prose paragraphs
- full, grammatically correct sentences
- facts, arguments, views, outcomes

Reports, factsheets, schedules

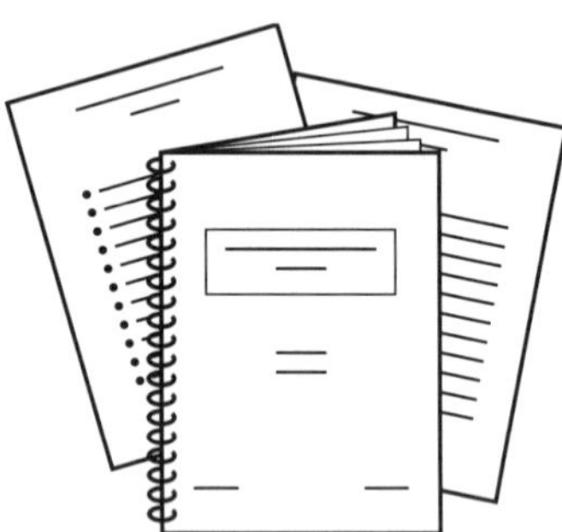

- series of headed sections
- schematic layout
- mix of sentences and lists (abbreviated English)
- factual, analytical, including number-based data
- may require several readings to grasp content fully

Product specifications estimates, operating manuals, financial reports

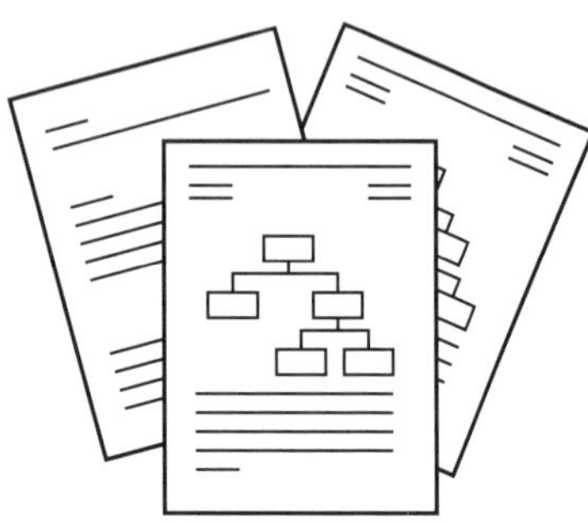

- technical English with jargon, specialist terms
- mix of paragraphs, tables, diagrams, images, etc
- closely written: several readings needed to absorb meaning
- factual, logical, analytical English

Sales brochures, advertisements, packaging, posters, in-house newspapers and magazines

- persuasively written
- mix of short textual points, slogans, headings and images
- relies on selective examples and assertions to make points
- may need to be read several times to separate facts from opinions

It pays to become familiar with the various forms of English typically used in workplace documents.

entire words were held up on cards, and children were taught taught to pronounce them and then to recognise them later from a mental picture of them retained in the brain.

Whatever system you were taught, it is likely that you started with single words and worked your way up to longer expressions and phrases, until you could read and understand the meaning of entire sentences. Yet, on reflection, this technique – though it works well with young pupils – is in some ways ineffective when it comes to developing advanced reading skills, since it does not reflect the way in which we all learned to *speak* English. Certainly, a baby in its first year starts to utter single words first such as Mama and Dadda, much to the delight of its parents. But as it develops, its hard-working, listening ear picks up not single words, but word clusters which are frequently used to communicate a simple (or complex idea):

> Open wide! Let go pussy's tail! Oh, do stop pestering!

Thus young children often act like parrots, and mimic their parents' utterances, especially those which are often made:

> Not another ruddy bill! Not one of Mummy's best efforts!

Initially, toddlers repeat such learned remarks without really knowing what they mean, or when to use them. By the time they reach three years, however, they have acquired, parrot-fashion, a whole string of expressions which they can use correctly, and which consist of several words. Importantly, such expressions were never learned word by single word until they knew the whole phrase, but all in one go, from the very beginning.

Now this kind of learning development is very important to keep in mind when developing your reading skills. This section explores the ways in which English is put together in various ways in workplace documents, and how its meaning can be more easily extracted by focusing on basic English language structures which involve what may be called word clusters – the same kind of clusters which we use when speaking, and which children pick up and eventually use as they develop their own speaking skills.

How the English language works

Consider this written message:

> The hard-working, young sales assistant greeted the elderly customer politely.

This particular message (expressed as a sentence) is made up of two main sections:

The hard-working, young sales assistant

greeted the elderly customer politely

The first section identifies the doer of the sentence – the one who is controlling its action. The second section identifies an action word – *greeted*, used to express an action (or thought), and also links it to an action receiver, *the elderly customer,* who is receiving the action.

The above example illustrates the most common way in which we write English word clusters down to form sentences. Whenever we write simple sentences, we compose word structures like this:

DOER OF THE ACTION → ACTION WORD → RECEIVER OF THE ACTION

KEY POINT

Doer – action word – receiver

Always remember that this is the natural structure in which we express ideas in written English. This will always help you to grasp the meaning of sometimes quite complicated written messages.

In grammar terms, the doer of the action is called the **subject**, the action word is called the **verb**, and the receiver of the action is called the **object**. Though it is useful to be aware of these technical terms, it is more important that you become familiar with the jobs they do in conveying written messages. It is necessary to recognise that doer words/subjects may occur as single words, or as word clusters:

John

The outdated computer

The hard-working, young sales assistant

As you can see, subjects can take the form of the names of people or of things. Moreover, they can also be preceded by describing words:

outdated   hard-working, young sales

Words which are used to describe subjects and thus to give them more meaning are called **adjectives**. As the above examples show, some adjectives, like *sales*, become so closely associated with the subject words they describe, as to be, in effect, part of them:

personal computer estate car waste paper bin

This being the case, like the young child, we tend to read them all as a single word cluster. But it is the naming word, *John, computer, assistant,* which is most important, since it alone controls the action of the verb. These naming words are called **nouns**, and naming words cover both people or unique things (Donna, St Paul's Cathedral, the Thames). When they are used in this way, they are called **proper nouns**, which *always take initial capital letters*. When they refer to everyday things – grass, car, mat, etc. – they are called **common nouns**. Remember, too, that the doer word of a sentence may take the form of: *I, you, he, she, it, we, you, they.* These words are called **pronouns** and are used to stand in place of nouns (to save repeating them):

John awoke late, and immediately, *he* knew *he* would be late for work.

Jennie......................................, *she.......she*...............................

Jennie and John.........................., *they.....they*..........................

Another type of word is used frequently in composing written English to add more meaning to verbs:

John awoke *early.*

Jennie dressed *hurriedly* and drank a cup of coffee *quickly.*

We can say that such words extend the meaning of the verb, and refer to them as verb extensions. More simply, in grammar, they are known as **adverbs**.

Now, in a short space of time, you have become familiar with all the components of written English which will help you directly to develop your reading skills.

CHECKLIST

Summary of English language structures and terms

1 The natural structure of ideas in written English is:

DOER/SUBJECT → ACTION WORD/VERB →
ACTION RECEIVER/VERB EXTENSION

2 Grammar terms for the above are:

- Doer word(s) = **subject**
- Action word(s) = **verb** (called technically **finite verb**, see below)

Continues ▶

- Action receiver word(s) = **object**
- Word(s) which extend the meaning of a noun = **adjective**
- Word(s) which extend the meaning of a verb = **adverb**

3
- Naming words (doer/subject words) are called **nouns.**
- Words which stand in place of nouns are called **pronouns**.
- Names of unique people or things are called **proper nouns** and are always given initial capital letters.
- Names of everyday things are called **common nouns**, and do not, generally, take initial capital letters.

KEY POINT

How to identify adverbs quickLY

Most, but not all adverbs end in *-ly.*

INDIVIDUAL SKILLS-BUILDING ACTIVITY

Practice in identifying parts of speech and grammar terms

Read through the following sentences carefully, and answer the questions which follow:

1 The weary tourist rose slowly.

(a) Identify the doer/subject.
(b) Identify the action word/verb.
(c) Identify the verb's extension.
(d) Say what parts of speech (a), (b) and (c) are.

2 A lovely young woman was singing beautifully.

(a) Write down the word cluster which is the subject of the sentence.
(b) Write down the words which are the finite verb.
(c) Write down the adverb which is the verb extension.

3 I shall write the letter immediately.

(a) What is the subject of this sentence? What part of speech is it?

(b) What is the technical, grammar term for *the letter?* (Clue: is it making or receiving the action?)

4 William Shakespeare wrote many famous plays.

(a) Identify the subject and say what part of speech it is.

(b) What is the technical term for the describing word *famous*?

(c) What job is the word *plays* doing in the sentence? What part of speech is it?

With your teacher's help, compare your written answers with those of your co-students, and be sure to correct any mistakes you may have made.

Adjectives and adverbs as word clusters

Just as the subject of a sentence can take the form of a cluster of words *(The young, hard-working sales assistant),* so can adjectives and adverbs describing nouns or verbs do the same:

The man *in the red hat* is called Santa Claus.

He drank the water *all in one gulp.*

It is not difficult to spot such word clusters – simply ask yourself to whom, or to what do they refer, and the answer becomes clear as to what job they are doing and therefore what part of speech they are.

Finite verbs and sentences

An important piece of grammar to learn concerns the label given to verbs in sentences. Action words in sentences are called **finite** (don't worry about this label, just about the form the verb takes) if they are written with these in-built features:

1 They must be either singular or plural: *it works, they work*, etc.

2 They must be written in the first, second or third person singular or plural:

Singular	**First**	**Second**	**Third**
	I work	you work	he, she, it works
Plural	**First**	**Second**	**Third**
	we work	you work	they work

3 They must be written in a tense (present, past, future, conditional, etc.):

- **present**: I work
- **past**: I worked, I was working, I have worked, I had worked
- **future**: I shall work, I shall be working
- **conditional**: I should work (if I wasn't injured)
  She would work (ditto)

Note that sometimes verb words ending in *-ed*, *-ing* (or occasionally -*en*) are used in sentences as follows:

The broken wheel fell off.

The dying day cast long shadows.

His speech was converted into printed word.

Verb words ending in *-ed* and *-ing* may sometimes be adjectives used to describe nouns.

KEY POINT

Spot the grammatically correct sentence!

Whenever a sentence contains:

1 a noun or pronoun acting as the subject of a sentence, and

2 a finite verb (with a number, person and tense)

then however short or long, the sentence is fully complete and grammatically correct! It should start with a capital letter and end with a full-stop:

Night fell.

The veil of night moved slowly across the copper-coloured sky.

English structures and reading skills

You may already have asked yourself: 'What on earth have English structures and grammar got to do with developing reading skills?' And the answer is, a very great deal indeed. Consider the following extract from a piece of work-based writing:

The stained and damaged kitchen fittings need to be replaced as a matter of urgency. The old sink is badly cracked and large amounts of water leak every day into a dirty bucket underneath, which amounts to a serious health hazard. Torn and slippery linoleum covers an uneven floor, with numerous loose planks which are also a danger to refectory staff moving quickly around the kitchen. The whole kitchen area needs to be refitted and redecorated as a matter of extreme urgency.

As it stands the above extract consists of four sentences and 82 words. A first reading tells us that the kitchen, wherever it is, is in a sorry state and urgently needs attention.

Now, if we apply the knowledge detailed above, which enables us to pick out key words and word clusters according to the jobs they do, we shall quickly realise how easy it is to strip away words which have a minor meaning and get to the ones which express key ideas. For example, in the first sentence:

- *stained and damaged* are describing adjectives
- *as a matter of urgency* is another (long-winded) way of saying urgently, and supplies additional, verb-extending adverb meaning

Neither word cluster is essential. The essential meaning is (ALMOST ALWAYS!) to be found in the doer/subject word, which here is *fittings* (or *kitchen fittings*). The action word cluster/verb is *need to be replaced.*

Thus the key meaning of this first sentence (of some 15 words) is:

The (kitchen) fittings need replacing (urgently).

In a similar way, a careful reading of the second sentence enables *old, badly, large amounts, every day, dirty, underneath* and *serious* to be glossed over, so as to reveal the subject and verb-based key meaning:

The sink is cracked, leaking water (daily), which amounts to a health hazard.

KEY POINT

Go first for subjects and verbs!

Whenever reading a document at work to extract key information, always look first for the meaning expressed through subjects and finite verbs. Remember that additional, descriptive meaning, provided by adjectives and adverbs, can often be disregarded, or shortened (as with urgently).

Remember, too, that a knowledge of sentence structures and grammar can be a very useful tool in all sorts of communication situations.

WHAT DO YOU THINK?

1 Do you agree that people adopt different ways of reading documents in different circumstances?

2 Can you still remember how you learned to read? Do you accept the idea of adults reading not single words at a time, but word clusters?

3 What do you make of the reading approach which enables you to identify and focus upon nouns and verbs as subjects, objects or action words?

4 Have you any tips to share with your co-students on how to make reading easier?

5 Can you think of any other ways, besides starting a vocabulary notebook, which you and your co-students could develop and use during your course to help you learn the meanings of unfamiliar words quickly but effectively?

SUMMARY OF KEY POINTS

Reading for a purpose

- Documents to be read at work contain features which link them to other documents produced either in-house or externally.
- Documents produced externally may have to be read carefully in order to see what their connection is with the organisation.
- Various types of document are written typically in an English which suits their aims: letters seek actions and outcomes and are almost always written in full sentences; reports and factsheets are bound to be written in a factual English, but may include short bullet-point phrases, etc.
- The English language normally follows a simple construction in sentences: DOER WORD/SUBJECT → ACTION WORD/FINITE VERB → VERB EXTENSION OR OBJECT.
- Subjects and objects are made up of single words or word clusters which are called either nouns or pronouns (pronouns stand in place of nouns).
- Two kinds of describing words exist in English: adjectives describe nouns or pronouns and adverbs describe verbs.
- A grammatically correct, complete sentence is one containing a subject which controls a finite verb.
- Documents can be read for their key meaning by focusing on their subjects (nouns or pronouns) and their finite verbs (and extensions or objects) and by skimming over adjectives and adverbs.

SELF-CHECK REVIEW TEST

Reading needs and expectations at work and developing skills in reading material

1 List three common features which documents created in-house display.

2 What sort of language are you most likely to find in reports and factsheets–persuasive or factual?

3 Are letters and memoranda most likely to be written in prose paragraphs or in a schematic layout?

4 List three types of document likely to use numbers extensively.

5 Explain briefly why adults tend to read in word clusters and not in single words at a time.

6 Explain briefly how knowing how to pick out a subject and its finite verb helps a person to extract information from written materials.

7 Explain briefly what adjectives and adverbs do.

8 What two key features must a sentence possess for it to be a full and grammatically correct one?

When you have completed your answers to the above questions, turn to page 307 and check them against the answers provided. Re-read the relevant section of Chapter 4 for any question you got wrong.

INDIVIDUAL SKILLS-BUILDING ACTIVITIES

Developing reading skills

Task 1 Read carefully through the third and fourth sentences of the extract about the kitchen on page 232, strip away word clusters of a secondary importance and write down the key point for each sentence.

Task 2 Read the following passages carefully, and then note down the words which convey their key points. Rewrite your notes into a shortened version of each passage as a grammatically complete sentence:

1 The battered, old lorry lumbered slowly across the bridge. Its flaking side panels bulged outwards from the incredibly heavy and bulky load which it was carrying slowly and laboriously towards the crowded and busy market of Karachi.

2 Why not take this year's summer holiday beneath the tanning sun and dazzling blue skies of our idyllic Campmed Resort of Ipsos? Your days will be full of fabulous fun and relaxation along miles of sunny, clean beaches, where the clear, warm Adriatic sea cools and revitalises. Your nights will be spent wandering along the famous and thrilling promenade, and its hundreds of bars, discos and rave spots will eventually exhaust even the most determined holiday-goer!

3 When you give medication to a resident, be sure to follow these guidelines. Firstly, check carefully to ensure that you are fully confident about the correct dosage to administer. Always consult the medication Day Book, and never be tempted to guess what the dosage might be. In any case, it may have been changed.

Next, make sure that the resident is comfortable and knows what the medication is for. Take pains to reassure the resident and never force medication upon him or her. In case of all refusals to take medication, consult with the duty senior care officer. Always count out tablets, or measure liquids in the presence of a fellow care officer, and ensure you both check that the dosage is correct according to the Day Book entry. Assist the resident by offering a drink of water (unless not permitted), and ensure that the medication has been taken, and not held in the mouth or hand.

Make sure that you record the delivery of the medication in the Day Book as indicated. Lastly, do not leave the medication trolley unsupervised at any time.

4 Have you tried the scrumptiously gorgeous taste of a *Yippee!* snack bar yet? If not, then you are missing out on a marvellously mouth-watering, taste-bud exploding experience! Just think, it's got a fat layer of toffee inside, which is first covered by loads and loads of crunchy hazel nuts and then by our own original cherry nougat! And if that's not enough to send you racing to your nearest *Yippee!* supplier – wait for it – you've guessed, its coated with deep, dark, tangy chocolate, covered in tongue-teasing ripples! *Yippee!*

5 Dear Sir

I am writing to complain about the Mark III Sinyo personal CD-player – the one with the built-in sound balancer and signal adjuster – which I bought last Saturday 17 July 1996 from your Brighton store, the one near to Marks & Spencers. The player was on special offer, and I managed to get it with £12.50 knocked of the normal selling price of £86.99. But what is the good of the discount, if it does not work properly?

When I got it home and put one of my favourite Oasis CDs in, it was OK for the first two tracks, but then it started to develop a wailing sort of whistle that nearly blew my head off! I mean, you don't expect that sort of thing to happen when you buy quality Sinyo gear. Also, I think the problem is all to do with the plug-holder for the ear-phones, which seems very loose when you plug in the little jack-plug thing.

I should be glad to hear from you before next Wednesday (when I take my summer holidays) about what you intend to do about it.

Yours faithfully

Task 3 When you have finished writing out your shortened versions of the above passages, take part in a general class discussion to identify which parts of them contain key points, and which contain information of minor importance. Identify for each passage the major and minor word clusters.

KEY POINT

Learning specialist terms is essential!

All types of organisation constantly use specialist terms and expressions developed in their sector of industry, commerce or public service. Make a habit, therefore, of jotting down such words in a pocket-sized notebook, so that you can check their meanings out accurately in your dictionary (see Figure 4.1). Do the same for any word you meet whose meaning you are unsure of. While this technique takes a little time and effort, you will soon be surprised at the difference it makes to your personal word power and ability to read all kinds of documents confidently.

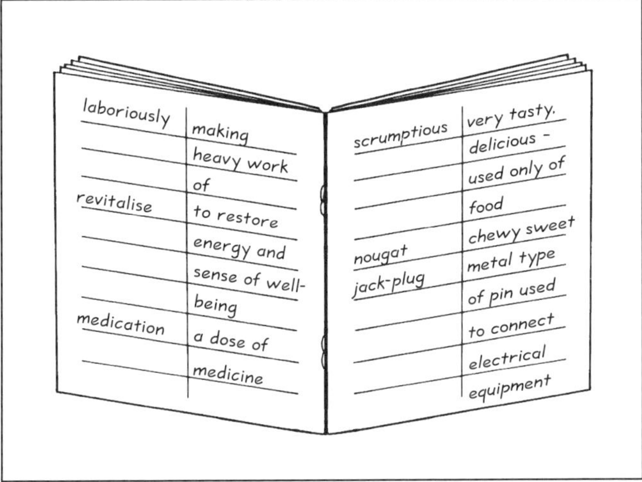

Figure 4.1 **Example of a vocabulary notebook**

How to use reference resources

If we were to ask a carpenter to show us what he carried in his toolbag, and to empty it for us to see, we should find a host of tools which are essential to his job – planes, chisels, clamps, hammers and so on. We would not expect such a carpenter to leave home for work without his trusty toolbag, which contains the tool he needs to do his job.

Yet for some peculiar reason, many employees who use words every day stream into offices, bureaux and council departments with only what they carry in their heads to help them to do their daily work. Like a golfer playing a round of golf with a putter only, such people work under a mighty handicap!

This section, then, guides you on what word-based reference tools to put into your personal toolbag, and how to use them. No one today can be expected to know what all the words and expressions mean which they meet, especially if they are technical and specialist words. So make up your mind not to cut corners when it comes to knowing how to use reference resources, and just think of the problems a carpenter would encounter, trying to plane a piece of wood with his bare hands!

The English language dictionary

English language dictionaries have been around for at least four hundred years, ever since English began to settle down into a single language during Elizabethan times in England. One of the first main supports they gave was in starting to standardise English spelling. William Shakespeare's name, for instance, was variously spelled as *Shakspere,* or *Shakspear*, and the blackbird was still known then as a *blakke berd.*

Also, because of the many dialects which abounded then in England, the same word could have different meanings in different parts of the country, so the development of English language dictionaries also helped to provide words with a meaning (or set of meanings) which everyone agreed to adopt and use, over a period of time.

Eventually the English language dictionary settled into providing these features for its users:

CHECKLIST

The main features of an English language dictionary

- Words are entered alphabetically from A to Z. Each entry follows this system. For instance, *access* comes before account, because, after the identical acc- which each word possesses, *e* comes before *o*.
- Each entry in the dictionary follows the same pattern of listing the word's specific features:

(a) **how it should be pronounced**; this is shown in the form of a phonetic version of the word: **conscious** (kon-shuss) **bureaux** (byur-ows)

(b) **on which syllable(s) the main stress should be placed** when saying the word; a ′ sign is placed after the stressed syllable: *acc′ ident, disgrace′ ful* etc.

(c) **what part or parts of speech it is**; this is shown as an abbreviation such as *n* (= noun), *v* (= verb), *adj* (= adjective)

(d) **which syllables are to be pronounced long and which short**; this is shown by using this symbol for short ∪, and this for long — :

∪ —   — — ∪ — ∪
extreme spoonful unlikely.

(e) **information on how the plural of the word is formed:**

fox (-es) **stadium** (-iums or -ia both accepted)

(f) **a brief explanation of the meaning** (or various meanings) which the word is given; some large dictionaries provide not only current meanings but earlier (and now obsolete) meanings:

clear (*adj*) (*kleer*) distinct, not obscured, visible; evident, obvious, understood
to clear (*v*) to make a space, move, get rid of, to sell as in clearance sale

(g) **larger dictionaries also provide examples of the use of the word in common expressions,** and to save space use this symbol to stand for the word ~ :

it's as ~ as mud! Have I made myself ~ ?
he enjoyed a ~ view of the game

(h) **lastly, some dictionaries provide details of the word's origins,** whether from Latin (L), old English (OE), or Anglo-Saxon (AS) etc:

starve (see sterven (OE) etc.)

As the above checklist illustrates, an English language dictionary provides a wealth of information about words and expressions, if only a little trouble is taken to learn the meanings of the abbreviations and symbols used.

The spelling dictionary

While English language dictionaries provide a great deal of information about individual entries, they are not much help when it comes to finding out how to spell a word correctly. For precisely these reasons, spelling dictionaries were introduced, not to reproduce the content of the English language dictionary, but to enable people with spelling difficulties to find out how to spell a given word correctly (see Chapter 1, pages 25–26).

Computer spellchecker software

When computer word-processing packages began to include a spellchecker facility, many people with a spelling problem breathed huge sighs of relief. At last, they thought, my worries are over; clever old PC will do it for me! However, they reckoned unfortunately

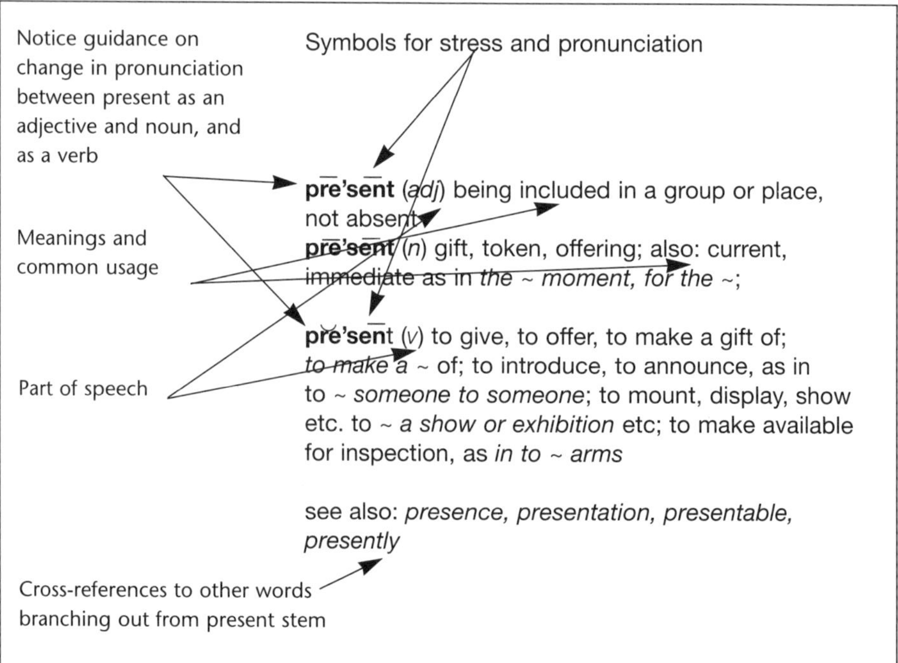

Figure 4.2 **Example of a typical dictionary entry**

without the limitation of clever – but stupid – old PC! For while computers can process data at a speed which we humans can only marvel at, they cannot, so far, distinguish between a correct and incorrect use of a given word in a given situation.

For instance, English abounds in words which sound the same (called homophones), but which have entirely different meanings. Here are just a few of these difficult duos:

load	lode	straight	strait
might	mite	site	cite
thyme	time	principle	principal
right	rite	weight	wait

Now, as long as either alternative is spelled correctly, poor old PC just cannot tell you which is correctly or which incorrectly used in a given sentence. As a result, you could write the following nonsense, which PC would approve instantly:

> Weight a minute! I want you to lode the wagon rite now. We don't have the thyme to delay. Drive rite away to the collage cite, and ask the principle wear he wants it putt.

KEY POINT

Be your *own* proof-reader!

Do not rely on spellchecker to solve your spelling problems! As the above example illustrates, only you can decide which spelling of which word is correct in the context in which you use it. If you know that spelling is not one of your strongest points, it is much better to buy a spelling dictionary and to use it to improve your own confidence in spotting incorrect spellings and putting them right. So, determine to be your own proof-reader!

However, it would not be entirely fair to PC or to spellchecker to move on, without mentioning that this spell checking service is an absolute boon, when it comes to spotting text-processing mistakes and drawing them to our attention. Indeed, some modern software, such as Word For Windows 95, corrects certain typos automatically, such as: becuase, nad, etc., by operating an autocorrect feature, as the word is keyed in.

Other helpful reference sources

The above two kinds of dictionary are likely to prove the ones you will make most use of when reading for meaning at work. However, you should become aware of and familiar with some other important reference sources which help when reading work-related documents.

The English language thesaurus

This is a reference book which groups together words and expressions which are similar in meaning (see Chapter 1 page 26).

A dictionary of abbreviations

Today, we are all plagued by the widespread use of abbreviations: OTT, GSOH, AIDS, WYSIWYG and so on. The problem is made even worse in specialised trades and professions, which employ all kinds of abbreviations as a kind of time- and space-saving shorthand: NCVQ, NVQ, GNVQ, BTEC, RSA, CGLI, LCCI, PC, VDU, CD-ROM, IT, etc.

To our rescue comes the dictionary of abbreviations, which lists such abbreviations alphabetically and explains what they stand for. They deal not only with the above kinds of abbreviation, called acronyms, where the first letters of individual words are set together, but also with, for example, Latin abbreviations used in meetings: *nem con, ad hoc, ultra vires,* etc., as well as other kinds of abbreviation such as *abs.* (absolutely), *p.a.* (*per annum* = yearly), etc. Such a dictionary is invaluable to the regular reader at work.

A dictionary of technical terms

Given the pace at which knowledge and technology have expanded during this century, it is no wonder that a host of technical dictionaries have been published in many specialist areas, such as electrical engineering, medicine, politics, science, the built environment and so on. Naturally enough, a general, English language dictionary cannot give that much room to each entry, nor can it provide in-depth details, which only an expert may need to browse through.

Example of an entry in a dictionary of specialist terms

local area network referred to frequently as an LAN, acts as a description for groups of terminals (and/or intelligent personal computers), linked to a central file-server or mainframe computer; the link is provided either by a form of cabling (coaxial or fibre-optic) or by radio signal; electronic messages are routed around the network in a form of topology (e.g. token ring) to individual terminals; increasingly installed in businesses for exchanging email messages and files; (see also: wide area networks, groupware, file-sharing, Internet and World Wide Web)

Access to a technical dictionary is an absolute must for anyone working in a field which makes extensive use of a technology or which uses specialist terms a great deal.

Each industrial, commercial or public sector field of work has its particular sets of references which have been developed to meet a need for access to highly specialist information which is kept up to date, as the following list illustrates:

CHECKLIST

Important reference sources in a selection of work sectors

- Business: Croner's manuals on *Employment Law* and *Office Administration*
- Public service: *The Municipal Yearbook*
- Leisure & tourism: *The British Leisure Centre Directory*
- Engineering: *British Standards Specifications*

WHAT DO YOU THINK?

1 Are *you* prepared to make the effort to look up words when you don't know their meaning? What advantages can you see for you personally stemming from doing so regularly?

2 How much of what a dictionary supplies in information did you already know about? What was new to you?

3 Had you heard about spelling dictionaries before? Would you be prepared to obtain one and use one? Or do you think it might damage your image among your co-students?

4 Do you agree that relying on a computer's spellchecker is dangerous?

5 Have you come across any other useful reference sources which help to make reading documents easier?

SUMMARY OF KEY POINTS

Using reference sources

- A good English language dictionary supplies information for each entry on: its correct spelling (singular and plural); how to pronounce it (stressed, long and short syllables); its part(s) of speech; common meanings, its use in common expressions; the original language(s) it came from.
- A spelling dictionary provides help for those with spelling difficulties by listing words phonetically (how they sound) and then their accepted English spelling(s).
- An English language thesaurus supplies entries of groups of words and expressions which are similar in meaning; it also provides cross-references from one group to another; this reference source is used mainly by writers to find alternatives to use, but may also help a reader explore word meanings.
- Other specialist dictionaries exist, such as dictionaries of abbreviations, technical terms, and on topics related to specific industry/commercial/public service sectors.

How to take effective notes of reading material

Most of the time when we read something, we simply read it once and the points in the document either stick in our minds for some reason, or they don't. When, for example, we read a newspaper report on our football team's performance last Saturday, or on what the latest fashions are coming out of Paris, a good deal of what we read does stick – because we may take an ongoing interest in the subject. However, much of what we have to read at work may not interest us at all, *but we do have to take it in and remember it*, simply because it is part of our job to do so.

This section, therefore, concentrates on explaining the techniques you will need to use in order to extract the key points from any given piece of reading material, so as to be able to relay a message to someone else, or to use it yourself.

Reading to extract meaning

Very many documents which people read are not really important; they exist only to provide a brief and passing interest. For example, the rail commuter buys an evening newspaper to read on the train to pass the time until he or she arrives at the home station. Then, either the paper is left on the seat, or it is binned in a waste-paper bin on the way out. Each article – in fact only the ones with eye-catching headlines – is read only once, and many are either left half-read or skimmed over.

Now such time-passing reading habits are no good at all when it comes to reading a document to extract its key meaning. On the contrary, a carefully planned and sequenced approach is needed, as the checklist below indicates.

CHECKLIST

Key steps in reading a document to extracts its meaning

1 **Checking on the document's key theme**: Read its title very carefully; it should provide you with a clear idea of what the document's main thrust and theme are about.

2 **Obtaining a first impression of the document**: Read the whole of the document through in one go taking your time, simply to let it 'wash over you', so that you obtain an idea of what information it contains; at this stage, do not stop to consider the meaning of any words or phrases you do not follow.

3 **Extracting the meaning of each and every word**: Go back to the beginning, and set out by your elbow: a) your English language dictionary and b) your vocabulary notebook. Now read the document through again, section by section; this time, stop at every word or expression you do not understand, and look up any word(s) you need to; write them down in your notebook together with a note of what they mean; carry on in this way until you finish the document.

4 **Viewing the structure of the document**: Now go back once more to the beginning of the document; this time, scan down each section or paragraph and note down what its main theme or key point is; when you have done this for the whole document, you will have set down – in their running order – a series of key points which will form the basis of your notes; also, in reading the document three times, for three different reasons:

   (a) general gist

   (b) meaning of individual words

   (c) sequence of main points

you will have become very familiar with it, and well be able to extract from it the notes you need.

Where key information is likely to be found in documents

Most documents share a common structure when it comes to setting out their meaning. For instance, we already know that a good title of a document will convey an outline of its main theme or content. Similarly, as Figure 4.3 illustrates, key points are likely to be found in certain locations within all documents.

Making notes from carefully read documents

Reading a document carefully, so as to understand fully what it is about, is the first of the two main steps needed to make useful notes of a document. The second is, of course, to make the notes themselves.

And, this is where the grammar you learned earlier in Chapter 4 (see pages 227–232) is going to come in particularly handy!

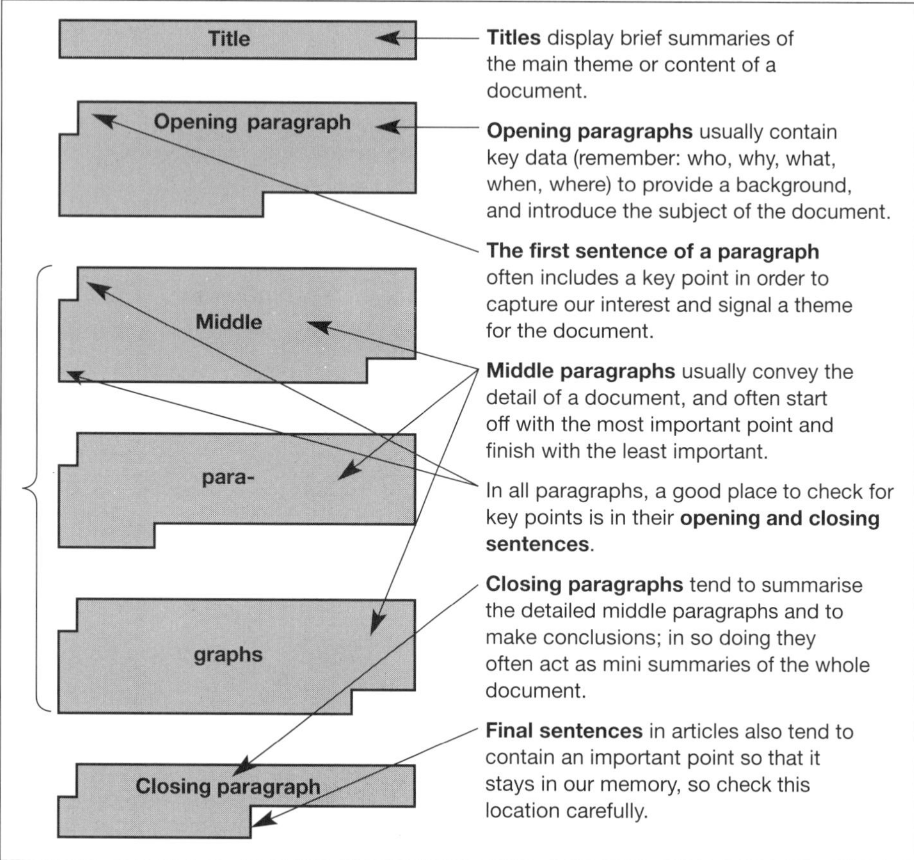

Figure 4.3 **Where to look for key points**

Making notes of a document is, essentially, a process which reverses what the document's author did when writing it. Most authors go through these three main stages when writing a document:

1 Rough ideas

2 Structured into an outline series of points

3 Written out in prose paragraphs

When a reader wishes to make notes of the same document, he or she needs to retrace the author's steps, by going back from the final stage three to the outline skeleton stage two.

To do so involves the note-maker in stripping away the words which are needed to express ideas in full sentences until the key, outline points are uncovered.

As we have already discovered, key meaning tends to lie in subjects, finite verbs and their extensions or objects. We also know where to focus an initial search for key data within the paragraphs or sections of any document. Much like the zoom feature in a word-processing package, we now need to zoom into a sentence or passage which contains, say, two or three key points, in order to see how the process of identifying them using the parts of speech approach actually works:

Study this passage carefully, reading it so as to extract its key meaning using the parts of speech approach:

How to make notes

In spite of a temptation to leap straight into the task, it pays to follow a careful series of steps in order to extract the key points from any article. Firstly, and very importantly, study the title of the document. It will provide a brief summary of the document's main theme. Then read the whole document through slowly and carefully, in order to obtain understanding of its overall content. Secondly, go back to the beginning and read the document again for the meaning of its individual words and phrases. Consult your dictionary when you meet an unfamiliar word and jot its meaning down in your notebook. Do this for each section or paragraph of the document. Thirdly, read the document again in order to pick out the main point of each section or paragraph. You can do this by scanning over the document, since by now, you will have obtained a clear idea of what it is all about. Write down the points in note form as you identify them. When you have completed this three-stage process of reading a document to extract its meaning, you will be in an ideal position to write down a set of its key points.

Analysing the reading for key meaning task:

How to make notes

In spite of a temptation to leap straight into the task, it pays to follow a careful series of steps, so that you can extract the key points from any article. Firstly, and very importantly, study the title of the document. It provides a brief summary of the main theme. Then read the whole document through slowly and carefully, in order to obtain understanding of its overall content. Secondly, go back to the beginning and read the document again for the meaning of its individual words and phrases.

Do not forget to consult your dictionary whenever you meet an unfamiliar word and remember to jot down its meaning in your notebook. Do this for each section or paragraph of the document. Thirdly, read the document again in order to pick out the main point of each section or paragraph, such as a point made in the first sentence. You can do this by scanning over the document, since by now, you will have obtained a clear idea of what it is all about. Write down the points in note form as you identify them. When you have completed this three-stage process of reading a document to extract its meaning, you will be in an ideal position to write down a set of its key points.

An analysis of the first paragraph shows how it helps to go first for the subjects, their finite verbs and either objects or extensions:

> it pays to follow … a series of steps; … you can extract … the key points; … (you) study the title of the document; It provides ... a summary of the main theme; … read the document through to obtain understanding of its content; … read the document (again) for the meaning of words and phrases.

In the same way, the key word clusters of the second paragraph can be extracted:

> … consult your dictionary; … when you meet an unfamiliar word ... jot down its meaning; … read the document again; … etc.

A glance at the following descriptive words (adjectives and adverbs) illustrates how much can be stripped out, without losing the passage's essential meaning:

> careful ... firstly and very importantly … brief … whole … slowly and carefully … overall … Secondly ... individual … in your notebook … Thirdly … etc.

Word clusters to skim over

As well as skimming over word clusters which provide additional, but not essential descriptive information, it helps to leave out of consideration the following kinds of word clusters:

- word clusters used to introduce or to link ideas together, which contain no important point:

  In spite of a temptation to leap straight into the task,

  Firstly, and very importantly

  Secondly, go back to the beginning and

- words or phrases which are repetitions or restatements of points already made:

  Do this for each section or paragraph of the document.

  of reading a document to extract its meaning,

- words or phrases which are examples or illustrations of a main point:

  such as a point made in the first sentence

In point of fact, the above worked example is fairly closely written, in that there are not very many word clusters which are of secondary importance. As you will discover when working through the individual skills building activities on pages 250–251, other kinds of writing include a far higher percentage of descriptive word clusters, unimportant linking pieces, repetitions and examples.

Example of the notes made on the above passage

How to make notes

1. It pays to follow – a series of steps – to extract key points – from articles
2. Study title of document first – for brief summary of main theme
3. Then: read through all document – for understanding of overall content
4. Consult dictionary on unfamiliar words – jot down meanings
5. Read document again for main points – scan over paragraphs
6. Write down identified main points in note form
7. Three-stage process – ideal preparation for note-making

KEY POINT

Good notes summarise information clearly and smoothly

As the above example shows, effective notes link main points together clearly, but in a format which saves time by not writing them out as complete, grammatical sentences.

SUMMARY OF KEY POINTS

How to take effective notes of reading material

- When reading a document for a purpose, read it three times: firstly to get a general idea of its main theme and content, secondly to find out what any unfamiliar word or expression means, and thirdly to see how the main points are structured.
- Remember where to look for likely key points: the title, the first and last sentences of the piece, and the first and last sentences of each paragraph.
- Use the parts of speech and grammar functions of word clusters to identify the most important words and ideas in sentences, and disregard the descriptive words (for the most part – but not entirely).
- Make notes of the important word clusters you identify in brief bullet points – not as full as complete sentences but not so abbreviated that even you can't understand them at a later date!

INDIVIDUAL SKILLS-BUILDING ACTIVITIES

Developing skills in making notes of documents

Read the following passages carefully, as explained above, and then write a set of notes of the main points of each using the techniques shown above:

1 The Bellavista rest home is most delightfully situated in the heart of the soft hills and valleys of the South Downs, midway between Petersfield and Midhurst, in the very heart of the Sussex countryside. Its welcoming gardens are full of sweet-scented blossoms and flowers through most months of the year, and particularly from May to October. Our residents enjoy walking out in our gardens or simply sitting in them to soak up the warm south-coast sun which, as our weather records show, shines on a higher than average basis on Bellavista than practically anywhere else in the UK!

2 The new and highly successful computer operating system – called Workstation Control System, or WSC for short – has been developed by a team of highly dedicated and expert programmers working out of what has become known as Silicon Glen, in the heart of the Scottish Highlands. WCS works by displaying a series of icons or symbols on the user's computer screen, which activate a series of commands relating to whatever activity the user wishes to carry out. For example, the file management icon, shown as an icon of a ring-binder, takes the user into a section of WCS which enables him to create a directory (in which to set up a series of new files all relating to a particular topic) or in which to scan all his created files – say in

order to find a document which was created some time ago). The beauty of the WCS operating system is that old files can be found – almost immediately – simply by keying in a key word or phrase which was used in the file, such as a person's name, a number reference or a specialist term. WSC is sure to sell like hot cakes, since it makes the whole business of running typical software packages – like word-processing, spreadsheet or database applications – so much faster and simpler!

3 Despite all the glamour and sense of freedom which people connect with it, starting up a small business is not a quick fix for those fed up with working for an employer! For a start, beginning a small business usually requires a lump sum of money – start-up capital as it is known – to buy or rent premises and to purchase stock. Moreover, given the high numbers of new businesses which have failed over the past five or so years, the High Street banks are very reluctant to lend anyone money without some form of security for such a loan, such as the deeds of the house they live in, if it has been paid for. Such an action is full of danger. For example, if the business should fail, and if it has not been set up as a limited company, then the owner will almost certainly lose his house, as the lending bank moves in to recover the value of the money it lent out, by selling the house over its owner's head. As this example alone well illustrates, the difficulties of obtaining a safe loan with which to fund the start-up of a small business is enough to put off most would-be small business owners.

GENERAL GROUP SKILLS-BUILDING ACTIVITY

Extracting and relaying information from written material

Read the following extract on your own, and make notes of what you believe to be the main problems facing Arun and Lata Patel in their business, and how they might best be solved. Then in liaison with your teacher, join a group to discuss and share your findings, and to agree on what the best course of action would be, once Arun has got his new computer home. Your discussion should last about 15 minutes.

'OPEN ALL HOURS!'

Arun and Lata Patel's lives had been 'open all hours', ever since they first bought their business – a minimarket in a suburban shopping precinct – some five years ago. Then, the 150 houses on the Westbury Park development had been only half completed and business had been slow and hard to build. Thanks to the Patels' relentless hard work and willingness to rise at the crack of dawn and retire well after midnight, the minimarket had prospered, as the Westbury suburb of Grafton, a busy industrial town, had rapidly expanded. The store, called the Minimax Grocers & Newsagents, was in the middle of five shops in a parade lying back from a busy through-route to the A6. The Patels, with their

Continues 

16-year-old daughter, Sonal, and 10-year-old son, Naresh, occupied a flat over the store.

Minimax had started out as a run-of-the-mill general store, specialising in those small order items which local shoppers had forgotten to buy at the supermarket or did not want to make a special journey for. With a bus service into town stopping just opposite, and room for parking out front, Arun quickly realised, however, that there was ample scope for selling newspapers, magazines and sweets, etc. Before much longer, he was employing six newspaper delivery youngsters. They also picked up orders for home-delivered groceries, which Arun delivered mid-mornings around the adjacent estates in his elderly but trusty van. The delivery side of the business expanded rapidly to a point where Arun had to stop taking on new customers – much against his will.

About a year ago, with the completion of the upmarket Westbury Park development, customers who had acquired a taste for exotic micro-oven ready meals gave Arun and Lata the idea of making room for another open freezer which would stock the spicy and different dishes which innovative food manufacturers were marketing under Chinese, Indian, Mexican and Indonesian brand names.

By this time, the Patels badly needed more helping hands. As luck would have it, two of Arun's nephews moved into the district looking for work in Grafton's textile industry. Both in their early twenties, they were just the trustworthy help that the shop urgently needed. Nor did they need much persuading, when Arun outlined his longer term plans for acquiring additional outlets. Ramesh, the elder brother, took over the newsagency and confectionery side, while his brother Raj delivered the grocery orders and with his easy humour and persuasive ways quickly extended business.

Soon after, an incredible stroke of luck occurred – the butcher's shop next door came on to the market. The sitting tenant had been content to provide a mediocre service, and as a consequence could not afford the new lease's increased rents. Arun was quick to see his chance and had clinched the deal before the local estate agent had even displayed the particulars in his front window!

This time it was Mrs Patel who had her say. 'You know,' she had said, 'what Westbury needs is a really good fast-food takeaway!' Always with an eye to market trends, she had overheard snippets of conversation among teenagers and young married couples about the nearest fast-food outlet some two miles away which had a good reputation for ample portions and really tasty dishes, 'If they'll drive over there, they'll walk in here,' she observed shrewdly. 'We could also fit in a few tables for people who want to eat here, too,' she added. After meeting some demanding requirements, Arun obtained planning permission for the change of use and early in November, the grand opening of Arun's 'Tandoori Takeaway' took place, with Mrs Patel in charge!

* * *

Some eight weeks earlier, Sonal had started a Foundation GNVQ course in Information Technology at Grafton College of Technology. From day one, with business in her bones, she had never looked back. She seemed to devour the course material – especially those parts dealing with business information processing. She had a natural flair with software and was achieving good grades.

One evening, having just finished an assignment, she poked her head around the door of her father's upstairs office in the flat. He was almost buried under paper! It bulged out of cardboard wallets, ring-binders and box files; it was festooned around the walls, suspended from rows of bull-dog clips; it littered his desk and window sills. Advice notes, invoices, handwritten orders, catalogues, price-lists, special offers and bank statements! It seemed as thought Arun had kept every single piece of paper since the first day's trading. Sonal scooped up a handful and let it drop back on to the desk.

'Stop that you silly girl!' shouted Arun. Now look what you've done. I'd just sorted those invoices into sequence!'

'Daddy, look at you! You're drowning in a sea of bumf!'

'What do you mean, bumf – I know exactly where everything is kept – or did until you interfered – now go away and let me finish!'

'Not until you make me a promise you'll keep.' Sonal paused dramatically, for she well knew she was the apple of her father's eye.

'Certainly not! What promise?'

'That first thing tomorrow you go down to Computerama and get fixed up with a decent PC set-up and some suitable software – before you go down for the third time and all your past flashes before your eyes! I don't know how you've managed up till now, but with the new shop and the deliveries expanding, soon you won't need to stop for sleep – you won't have time!'

* * *

For several days Sonal's words echoed around Arun's brain like an advertising jingle that wouldn't go away. Eventually he brought the matter up with Lata. 'I think she's probably right. You should move with the times,' Lata responded. 'How can you even think of new outlets when you're drowning in the paper from just two!'

Outnumbered and out-argued, Arun was waiting the next morning outside the front door as they opened up Computerama for business!

(Reproduced from D W Evans, *Effective Business Administration and Communication*, Addison Wesley Longman, 1992)

Extracting information from different types of document

So far, this section of Chapter 4 has concentrated upon making notes from a series of prose paragraphs, such as are found most often in letters, articles or memoranda at work. However, it is important to develop similar skills in extracting information from other types of document, such as a short report or factsheet, which often display information in schematic layouts (see Chapter 2 pages 137–142) and which may use abbreviated English forms to express ideas. Consider, for example, the section of a schematically laid out short report in Figure 4.4.

Background to the report extract

The report extract in Figure 4.4 on page 254 is in fact its whole middle section where its detailed information is set out. In this particular report, this is called the *FINDINGS* section. The task of the report's author was to investigate into how a flexible working hours system works, and to consult with a firm's employees in order to find out how ready they would be to accept a different way of working, in order to provide feedback for the firm's senior managers before they decide whether to introduce such a system.

3.0 FINDINGS

3.1 Principles of the Flexible Working Hours System

The essence of a flexible working hours system consists of establishing two distinct bands of working hours within a weekly or monthly cycle and of ensuring that staff work an agreed total of hours in the cycle.

3.1.1 Core Time Band

During this period (say 10.15 am to 3.45 pm) all staff are present at work, allowing for lunchtime arrangements

3.1.2 Flexi-time Band

Periods at the beginning and end of the day (say 7.45 am to 10.15 am and 3.45 pm to 6.15 pm) are worked at the discretion of individual staff members in whole or part, allowing for essential departmental staffing requirements.

3.1.3 Credit/Debit Hour Banking

According to previously agreed limits and procedures,staff may take time off if a credit of hours has built up, or make time up, having created a debit to be made good. Most companies require that the agreed weekly hours total (in the case of head office staff, 37½ hours per week) is reached but not exceeded, though some firms adopt a more flexible approach, which permits some time to be credited/debited in a longer cycle.

3.1.4 Recording Hours Worked

In all systems, it is essential that logs or time-sheet records are kept and agreed by employee and supervisor for pay and staff administration reasons.

3.2 Discussions with Departmental Managers

Most departmental managers were in favour of introducing a flexible working hours system,anticipating an improvement in both productivity and staff morale. The sales manager saw advantages in his office being open longer during the day to deal with customer calls and visits. Reservations were expressed by both the office administration and accounts managers arising from the likelihood of increased workloads to administer the system.

3.3 Sounding of Staff Opinion

Discreet enquiries were made via senior staff regarding the likely response of staff at more junior levels.

3.3.1 Summary of Favourable Responses

Secretarial staff in particular would welcome the means of tailoring their work and attendance to fit in with their principals' presences and absences. Many staff would enjoy working when they felt at their personal 'peaks'. Over 35% of female staff are mothers with children of school age, and would welcome the opportunity to fit their work around family responsibilities and according to seasonal daylight hours. Weekday shopping opportunities would be improved and travelling in peak rush-hour times avoided.

3.3.2 Summary of Unfavourable Responses

Few staff at junior levels intimated an unfavourable response but more senior staff were concerned about key personnel not being available when needed for consultation, etc. Older staff seemed less enthusiastic and any introduction of flexible working hours would need to be carefully planned and full consultation carried out.

3.4 Cost of Introducing a Flexible Working Hours System

The increase in costs of heating, lighting and administration of the system would be offset to some degree by a decline in overtime worked and the cost of employing temporary staff to cover for staff absences, which may be expected to reduce. (Appendix 3 provides a detailed estimate of the cost of introducing and running a flexible hours system.)

Figure 4.4 (Reproduced from D W Evans, *Secretarial Procedures in the Electronic Office*, Addison Wesley Longman, 1989)

Using the report's schematic layout as an aid to extracting meaning

Earlier in Chapter 4, we saw how the technique of making notes took the writing process back a stage, to where the author's skeleton structure was rediscovered by stripping away material of minor importance. Schematic documents make this job much easier, since they follow much more closely a skeletal structure. For instance, if you look back through Figure 4.4, you will see that the *FINDINGS* section is made up of four main sub-sections, and that each one is helpfully numbered to enable us to identify it immediately. Notice, too, that the references 3.1, 3.2, 3.3 and 3.4 all occur in a vertical column down the page. As you will recall from your studies of Chapter 2, this is in fact telling the reader that these sub-sections are of equal importance. Therefore, it is reasonably obvious that each of these major sub-sections ought to include a main point.

For instance, 3.1 tells us that the flexible working hours system consists of two distinct bands of working hours. 3.2 explains the main outcomes of discussions with departmental managers, 3.3 does the same on the topic of how more junior staff are likely to react, while 3.4 introduces the subject of the costs of moving across to the new system.

KEY POINT

Use headings to locate main points

Whenever seeking to extract key meaning from schematically displayed documents, go for the main sub-sections first for the sequence of main points beneath a major section heading.

As you will have noticed, some of the *FINDINGs'* main sub-sections are broken down into a series of more minor sections, each of which is given a number reference. These minor sections each contain a point which serves to add meaning to the main point. For example, the major point 3.1 is extended by the points 3.1.1, 3.1.2, 3.1.3 and 3.1.4. These references are also shown in a vertical column.

Read the minor points bearing in mind that their role is to add meaning to the main point. For instance, in the 3.1 section, the identification of the two work bands is made clearer by explaining what is meant by core and flexi-time bands, and how the employee records the hours worked in each band over a weekly period.

Thus, when making notes of section 3, we might well set them out as follows, making use of the schematic lay-out:

3.1 **Flexible Working Hours System** = two working bands

3.1.1 Core Time Band: usually 10.15 am – 3.45 pm – *all* staff must work

3.1.2 Flexi-time Band: usually 7.45 – 10.15 am and 3.45 – 6.15 pm – staff can choose what hours to work in each period

3.1.3 Credit/Debit Hour Banking: staff can work more hours or fewer hours on any given day, but must have worked agreed total weekly hours by end of each week (or month), e.g. 37.5

3.1.4 Recording Hours Worked: all staff must record daily hours worked on time-sheets

KEY POINT

Use display techniques to make notes

Remember that making effective notes is made easier if you use the display techniques of capital letters, underlining and so on. Also, remember to use your own words to make notes whenever possible, rather than copying the originals word for word. In this way, you will be much more likely to note down the sense of the original document in a brief and simple way, for example:

all staff must record daily hours worked on time-sheets

Other documents display information in a mix of abbreviated entries, such as addresses, lists or numbers, which are often called **schedules**, and still others mix image, word and number information in charts or diagrams. Full sentences in prose sections are most likely to contain information which may be safely passed over, whereas that in lists or numbered sections is more likely to need including, unless the lists merely provide examples to add meaning to a previous main point.

INDIVIDUAL SKILLS-BUILDING ACTIVITIES

Extracting information from a variety of documents

Task 1 Read the schedule in Figure 4.5 on page 257 carefully, and then make a set of notes of its main points, beneath a suitable set of headings.

Task 2 Extract the key information from the chart in Figure 4.6 on page 258 and present it in a suitable set of points, set out clearly:

ACE COMMUNICATIONS SYSTEMS LIMITED

ORGANISATIONAL INFORMATION

HEAD OFFICE:	Ace House, Bridge Street, Southwich, Southshire SW15 2BS Telephone: 01777 223344 Fax: 01777 223355
FACTORIES:	Birmingham, Coventry, Oxford
RESEARCH AND DEVELOPMENT:	Ace Laboratories, Swindon
TRAINING HEADQUARTERS:	Greenwood Manor, Minchester, Southshire
PERSONNEL:	15,880; Head Office: 592
DEPARTMENTS:	Research and Development, Production, Marketing, Sales, Accounts, Office Administration, Personnel, Distribution and Transport, Training, Communication Services

CONDITIONS OF SERVICE (Head Office Staff):

A flexible working hours system is in operation at the company's head office; all jobs are graded in accordance with a job appraisal scheme; promotion and pay are based upon a regular assessment of performance.
Holiday entitlement: four weeks plus bank holidays.
A staff restaurant provides meals subsidised by the company. Sports and social club facilities are available at the company's own leisure centre close to the head office.
House mortgages are available from the company at preferential rates.

CAREER OPPORTUNITIES:

The company's employees are encouraged to develop a knowledge of company activities as a whole and a clear career structure exists in a number of departments. The company promotes from within whenever possible.

TRAINING:

The company's training centre at Greenwood Manor, Minchester, offers residential courses which are a central feature of management development. A standing review committee reviews all applications to attend day-release higher education courses.

SALARIES:

Management salaries are reviewed annually and paid monthly in arrears. Management posts are linked to an incremental scale and salary increases, which are performance related, are zoned within defined upper and lower limits, for example:

Trainee Manager Grade 5:
Starting salary: £13,000 p.a.
First increment: £600-1200 p.a.
Second increment: £800-1500 p.a.

All incremental scales are reviewed annually.

SALES INFORMATION:

Total sales turnover last year exceeded £370 million. The introduction of the Ace 2 system contributed substantially to the increased turnover and secured a number of important new customers for the company.

FUTURE DEVELOPMENTS:

An important development over the next year will be to expand the company's global markets. In the words of the Chairman, Richard Henderson, 'Ace has a substantial share of both the UK and the European market and is now in a position to compete further afield, particularly in the US and the Far East. Plans are well advanced and we will be making important announcements early next year.'

Figure 4.5

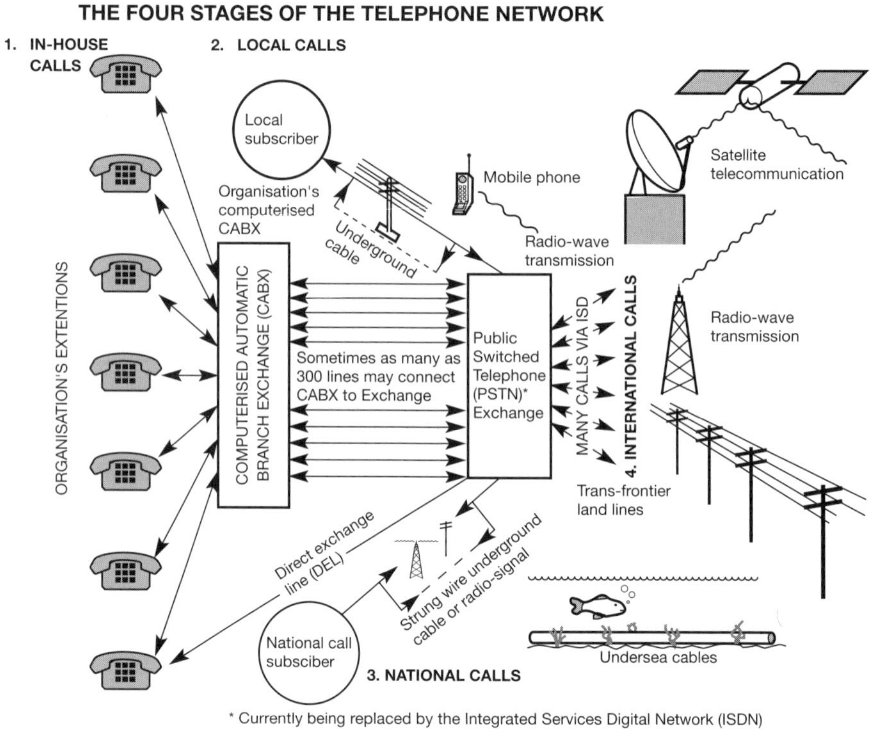

THE FOUR STAGES OF THE TELEPHONE NETWORK

* Currently being replaced by the Integrated Services Digital Network (ISDN)

Telephone calls are transmitted into an organisation by means of signals carried by telephone lines, undersea cables or radio signals beamed by satellite. In larger organisations all calls are routed first to a local telephone exchange (Public Switched Telephone Network – PSTN) and then to the receptionist in an organisation who manages an internal switchboard (CABX – Computerised Automatic Branch Exchange). Some switchboards are capable of handling up to 300 calls simultaneously and need several operators to handle them. The incoming calls are routed to individual telephone extension users spread throughout the organisation. Senior staff members may also be given a private telephone line which connects directly to the local telephone exchange in order to make calls completely confidential.

Figure 4.6 **Local and international telephone network** (Reproduced from D W Evans, *Secretarial Procedures in the Electronic Office*, Addison Wesley Longman, 1989)

How to pass on information extracted from reading material

This final section of Chapter 4 examines the techniques of passing on to other staff information extracted from written documents:

Basically, there are three ways of passing on extracted information:

- by word of mouth
- by means of an especially produced written document
- by means of an especially designed image (see Chapter 3)

Passing on information by word of mouth

If rather obvious, it is still true to say that no one in an organisation 'can know everything about anything'. Indeed, the more senior employees become, the less they know about the detailed nitty-gritty of the routine daily activities carried out by support staff and supervisors.

It occurs therefore quite often that more junior staff need to draw the attention of line managers and senior managers to a piece of information which they have read, but which management has had neither the time nor the opportunity to read. Such information may prove to be very important. For example, an employee in a sales department of a motor-cycle manufacturer may read an article – say in *Motor-cycle Weekly* – which details the launch of a bike with a revolutionary engine design. As its development was carried out under wraps, its launch has taken the industry by surprise. In such a circumstance, the sales employee may well decide to telephone his sales director and relay an oral message detailing the key points of the article (to save senior managers' time) in case he or she has missed such an important piece of news.

Again, a supervisor or manager may receive from head office a lengthy memorandum which sets out important changes on how the organisation is to be run in future. To save time and also to answer arising questions, the manager may decide to call a staff meeting in order to outline the memorandum's main points and answer questions.

In both examples, a similar process has to take place for the information to be passed on successfully:

1 The original documents have to be read carefully

2 Key points have to be identified and set down in a logical sequence

3 The set of notes made has to be relayed orally

Preparing to deliver the message

This section is concerned with the third of these stages. Relaying information effectively relies upon a two-stage process. Firstly, thought needs to be given as to how the oral message will be delivered:

- informally to the boss in his or her office
- formally to a group of staff in a meeting or discussion

Consideration should also be given to the degree to which the message needs to be supported by audio-visual aids (AVA). For example, a short, informal message can be readily relayed simply by delivering it in a logical order of points. However, a longer and more complex message delivered to a group more formally may require the support of an OHP foil and/or a diagram plus text hand-out.

Whatever the degree of formality, and however simple or complex the message, it helps to have a brief set of points (the notes made from reading the document) to refer to when delivering it. This helps to ensure that the key points are set down in a clear structure and that the message-giver does not lose the thread during the delivery. Remember to use a suitable structure for the points of the message, using the **Beginning** (the five Ws), **Middle and End** approach, and check back to Chapter 2, pages 110–115, on commonly used structures for written messages, since the principles involved are the same.

Using cue cards when delivering messages

A particularly helpful technique for storing the key points to make of material read is to transfer them on to a set of cue cards. In essence, a cue card acts as a very brief prompt by displaying on a small card first a key main point, and then two or three connected sub-points (see Figure 4.7). A short message might need only two cue cards, and an involved one five or six. These can be numbered and set in numerical sequence. They should fit into the palm of the hand and display printed text large enough to be read easily from a distance of 0.5–0.75cm.

Delivering the message

If you have ever had to listen to someone reading a speech – word for word from prose paragraphs on sheets of paper – instead of delivering it from bullet-point notes, you will know how irritating this can be. For most of the time such a speaker will have his head buried in his papers, thus losing all eye-contact with his audience. He will speak down into the floor instead of to the audience, and is likely to lose his place many times in trying to move his eyes from his papers to his audience.

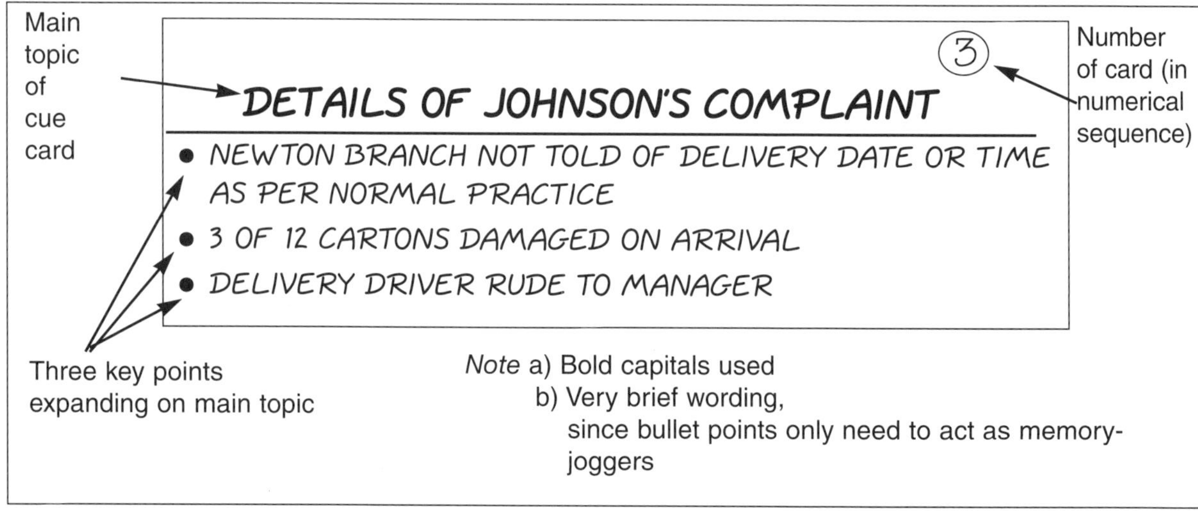

Figure 4.7 **Example of cue card**

This is where the time and trouble to produce delivery notes on a set of cue cards pays dividends. Because of their size and design, it is possible to maintain eye-contact with the message-receiver, and therefore to check whether the message is being taken in and understood. The following checklist also provides helpful guidelines to support your delivery of a spoken-word message using notes:

CHECKLIST

Eight steps for delivering a spoken word message

1 Devise a clear sequence of points from your notes.

2 Set out your points in sequence on a set of cue cards.

3 Catch your breath and organise your cards, etc.

4 Don't feel at all shy about *referring to your notes as you speak* to check out a name or exact quantity, etc.

5 As you are speaking, *keep an eye on your receiver* to check whether he or she is taking in what you are saying. *Make regular pauses at the end of delivering main points* in case your receiver needs to clarify a point or ask a follow-up question.

6 At the end of your message, *repeat what you consider the most important point or action needed:*

> So it became clear on speaking to Sandersons that, unless we can guarantee delivery by this Saturday, they'll definitely cancel the order!

7 All the time you are speaking, listen to yourself and *take pains to avoid irritating speech mannerisms* such as 'umming or erring', repeating phrases like 'sort of', 'you know', 'know what I mean?' etc.

By the same token, *take your time and do not gabble.* Many people change into fast gear when they are nervous or excited; but always remember that listeners take much more in if the pace is steady and the message is delivered clearly.

8 Whenever possible – and depending upon the importance of the oral message – *make a brief written summary, perhaps in memorandum form, to confirm your spoken report.* Such a memorandum may begin:

> Further to our conversation of this morning, I am writing to confirm the following: . . .

(Reproduced from D.W. Evans, *Effective Business Administration and Communication*, Addison Wesley Longman, 1992)

Passing on information in writing

There are two ways of passing on information which has been initially extracted from reading materials:

1 to set down a summary of it and to send it with a covering note (and sometimes with a copy of the original documents)

2 to send a polished version of your notes (plus covering memo and possibly copy of originals)

How to compose a summary

The following section provides a tried and tested technique for producing a summary of written material. Keep in mind that we have already covered in detail a number of the ten steps outlined in the sections on reading a document for a purpose and on how to extract information. Nevertheless, the following ten-step plan explains the whole process from A–Z, and a little revision never did anyone any harm!

The ten-step plan for producing a summary from textual source material

Follow this step-by-step plan carefully and you will produce summaries which are not only faithful to the original, but which also make sense to their readers!

1. Check to make sure you fully understand your brief – *what is it exactly you have been asked to produce in summary form?* Establish clearly in your own mind whether there is an imposed word limit (of say 300 words for a press release), or whether you are to use your own judgement in producing a summary or original material to about a third of its length.
2. Devise a working title for your summary – you can always modify it at the final drafting stage.
   Such a title should reflect accurately what the summary is about and what its main points should concentrate upon e.g.

How To Use Company Stationery Cost-Effectively

or

What To Do In Cases Of Emergency

3. Gather together all source documents – manuals, memos, letters, reports, photocopied articles etc relevant to the summary you wish to produce.

   Read through each carefully, say, three times to:

a catch the general drift of the meaning of the document's content;
b identify any difficult words or phrases to check out in the dictionary, as well as any key technical terms;
c obtain a clear understanding of how the piece is structured – e.g. how the main points appear to be sequenced and where examples and illustrations have been placed.

4. Make notes – *in your own words and in an abbreviated form* – of the points which, according to your devised title, are most relevant and essential. The point of writing them in your own words is that first, you will set them down more briefly, and that second, you will be better able to link such points together in a continuous paragraph.

However, there will almost certainly be some phrases or terms of the original which you will need to use. For example, it takes several words of our own to convey what is meant by specialist words such as:

recession   wow and flutter   contagious

Set out your notes in double spacing and with plenty of space between each one, so that you can later add a point or amend your wording etc.

5. When you have selected your main points, go back to the original and double check the following:

a You have not omitted a main point.
b Your wording clearly conveys the gist of the point – *even though, for the moment you have set it down in a form of note-taking abbreviation.*
c You have not included points which are repetitions or restatements of other points or which are examples or illustrations which can be omitted without losing some essential meaning. (Note: sometimes examples are important and do need to be included).
d Make a final check that the points you have chosen are all relevant to the title you devised.

6. Decide upon the most appropriate format in which to present your summary. In so doing consider:

a Who is the summary for?
b What is the nature of its content – would it be easily read as continuous prose, or better set out in a schematic layout?
c Do any graphic or visual items need to be included?

7. According to the layout decided upon, produce a first rough draft using double spacing. Seek to communicate the sense of the ideas of the original, rather than trying to produce a 'scissors and paste' cut-down version of sentences or phrases from the original – it is very difficult if you do this to link points together successfully.

When connecting your points together as a sequence of related ideas, remember to use 'cementing' words or phrases like: *Next, As a result, Moreover, This being so*, etc which help the reader to move from one point to the next.

8. If you are subject to a limit on the number of words, seek to produce a first draft which has about 10% more words than you are allowed. It is much easier to prune out 30 words from 300 than to cast around for some additional points to expand in a draft of 240 words where 270 is the limit.

9. Read through your first draft carefully. Check it against your list of abbreviated points to ensure that you have not overlooked any. Look for spelling or punctuation errors or omissions (especially apostrophes and full stops). Most of all check that your sequence of sentences makes sense as a connected piece of writing. The most common fault committed when summarising is to produce a series of points which appear to have no connection with each other!

   This is your last chance to change your wording, polish it or omit a point, so take pains and proof-read carefully.

10. Produce your final version using appropriate office equipment. Do any final transcription checks at this stage. Add items such as circulation details, details of sources etc.

The acid test

The acid test of all summaries is that they should be read by recipients as if originals in themselves. No one should need to read the original first to make sense of the summary, nor to feel that some material has somehow been left out.

Summarising: worked examples

Consider the following sentence:

> Although the journey from work was not particularly long, the train was crowded with commuters and other travellers and when the office manager eventually arrived home, he felt tired and drained.

This sentence contains some 31 words, the key ones are:

> journey from work, not long, train crowded, office manager arrived home, tired, drained

There are 13 key words. Other words like 'particularly', 'commuters and other travellers', and 'eventually' all help to make the sentence more interesting and to make its meaning more precise and detailed.

However, if we were required to reproduce the key ideas of the sentence, we could write:

> The office manager's journey from work was short, but his train was crowded and he arrived home feeling tired.

This shortened version contains 19 words, but a more polished and refined version is possible:

> Travelling on a crowded train, the manager was left exhausted by the short journey home from work.

Though the omission of the word 'office', and the substitution of 'exhausted' for 'drained and tired' may change the meaning of the original sentence somewhat, its sense remains the same, and its meaning has been broadly conveyed in less than half the words of the original.

When considering the summary of a collection of sentences in a paragraph, it will be necessary to identify the *key points* of the paragraph in much the same way as the key words of the sentence were located:

> The new young office assistant glanced nervously around the busy, open-plan office, and stood at the door, not certain where she should go. Almost at once, a smartly-dressed man wearing gold-rimmed glasses rose from his desk and walked over to her, with a welcoming smile on his face.
>
> 'Good morning,' he said, 'I'm Peter Harris, senior clerk, and you must be our new assistant. Miss Jenkins, isn't it? Do come with me, and I'll show you to your desk.'
>
> 'Oh, thank you, Mr Harris. I was wondering where I should go,' answered Penny gratefully. She was escorted to a pleasant position near a window, and on her desk someone had thoughtfully placed a small vase of fresh flowers.

117 words

Making notes

The paragraph contains six key ideas, which may be expressed briefly in note form:

1 Penny Jenkins – new assistant – stops at office door
2 Not sure where to go
3 Peter Harris (senior clerk) rises – greets her warmly
4 Escorts PJ to desk
5 Desk pleasantly located by window
6 Fresh flowers on desk – put there thoughtfully by someone

The rough notes contain some 39 words.

If we assume that the passage is to be summarised in about a third of the length of the original, then the rough notes are probably too generously written, since it usually takes as many words again to transform notes back into complete sentences. Since the target length of a summarised version is to be 40 words, it may be necessary to reduce the notes further, before attemping a first rough draft.

It may be necessary to re-phrase ideas like 'not sure where to do' and 'put there thoughtfully by someone' so that they are expressed more economically. Similarly, 'by the window' may be left out.

Notice that the rather lengthy wording of the direct speech exchange between Peter Harris and Penny Jenkins has been expressed much more simply by 'greets her warmly' and 'escorts PJ to desk'.

When summarising a passage, it is generally better to put over the sense of the original, than to try to use either the same words or sentence structures. Of course, it is necessary sometimes to make use of specialist words, where a great deal of meaning may be contained within a single word.

Writing a rough draft

A first rough draft of the summary may emerge as follows:

> Penny Jenkins, the new assistant, entered the office hesitantly, unsure of where to go. Immediately Peter Harris, the senior clerk, greeted her warmly and escorted her to her desk, which was pleasantly located. On her desk someone had thoughtfully placed a vase of fresh flowers.
>
> 45 words

A little careful pruning is needed to shorten the rough draft by some five words. Notice that the rough draft has been set out on alternate lines, so that any alterations may be made clearly:

> *hesitated at* *the office entrance*
>
> Penny Jenkins, the new assistant, ~~entered~~ the office ~~hesitantly~~, unsure of
>
> where to go. Immediately Peter Harris, the senior clerk, greeted her
>
> warmly and escorted her to her desk, which was pleasantly located.
>
> *, and on which*
>
> ~~On her desk~~ someone had thoughtfully placed a vase of fresh flowers.

The final version

The final version of the summary appears, then, as follows:

> Penny Jenkins, the new assistant, hesitated at the office entrance. Immediately, Peter Harris, senior clerk, greeted her warmly and escorted

her to her desk, which was pleasantly located, and on which someone had thoughtfully placed a vase of fresh flowers.

40 words

If the original paragraph had been part of a longer story or article, then it would need a title. A suitable one might be:

Penny's First Day at Work

If you compare the summarised version with its original, you will notice that certain parts have been omitted, since they were not considered absolutely essential. Ideas like 'busy, open-plan' have been left out as have the references to Peter Harris's smartness and glasses. Ideas like 'with a welcoming smile on his face' have been conveyed much more briefly by 'greeted her warmly'.

(Reproduced from D.W. Evans, *Effective Business Administration and Communication*, Addison Wesley Longman, 1992).

SUMMARY OF KEY POINTS

How to pass on information extracted from reading material

- Information which has been obtained from reading written documents can be passed on either as an oral message – informally or formally – or as a written outline or summary version of the original document(s).
- Before delivering a spoken word message, ensure that its main points have been organised in a clear sequence, and if the message is lengthy, use cue-cards to help you to deliver it confidently and effectively.
- Remember to deliver spoken word messages at a steady pace and not to gabble; maintain eye contact with the message receiver(s), and answer any questions clearly and simply. Above all, stick to the key points.
- When delivering a message by means of an outline or summary, remember to use the ten-step plan which puts into a simple sequence the steps of reading the document(s), identifying the main points, setting them down as notes and then writing out a final version in your own words. Remember that a summary is usually about 30–40% as long as the original document.

SELF-CHECK REVIEW TEST

Using reference sources, taking notes, and passing on information

1 List four different kinds of information which are supplied for each entry in a good English language dictionary.

Continues

2 What sort of information is contained in an English language thesaurus?

3 How does a spelling dictionary work?

4 List two other kinds of useful dictionaries.

5 Where would you expect to locate important points in a prose document?

6 Outline two ways of passing on information gained from written material.

7 What is a cue card? How is it used?

8 What is the advantage of reading a document three times before producing a summary of it?

When you have completed your answers to the above questions, check them against those provided on Page 308. Re-read the relevant section of Chapter 4 to revise any answer you got wrong.

INDIVIDUAL SKILLS-BUILDING ACTIVITY

Reading a document for a purpose, making notes on it and then summarising it

Read the following piece carefully, and use your reading and note-making skills to produce a summary of it in about a third of its length.

People who manage their work time effectively monitor what tasks they must personally undertake, what is properly the responsibility of colleagues, and what may be safely ignored...

TIME IS OF THE ESSENCE! HOW TO USE TIME EFFECTIVELY AT WORK

Have you ever heard a colleague say at 4.45 pm, 'Is that the time? And the report not half finished. I just don't know where the day's gone, I do not!'

Some people at work seem to be constantly under a heavy pressure of time. They never seem to have time for a proper coffee break, nor to eat a decent lunch and take a stroll for a breath of fresh air over their lunch hour. And yet the funny thing is, neither do they seem to get any more done than their co-workers, who do take their permitted rest-breaks. And the reason? The one kind of employee is better organised and makes better use of his time than the other.

Managing one's time at work is not a magic skill or a genetic feature that some people are born with and others not. It is, quite simply, a matter of self-discipline and self-organisation. For example, some employees plan their activities for the day and remain in control of them, while others simply let the day roll over them like a huge wave which all but washes them away.

There are a number of support tools which the effective time manager uses to help use time to best advantage:

- a diary which breaks the day down into half or quarter hour segments
- an appointments diary which is used to control the start and finish times of all visitors to the time manager, both from inside and outside the organisation
- an alarm bleeper to remind the time manager of appointments to keep, or outside visits to make; many of today's desk-top computers include such alarm bleepers
- a clock which is easily visible, and preferably located behind the chair in which a visitor sits during an interview or discussion
- a placard which can be hung on the office door, or open office partition, which states that the occupant is not to be disturbed, and is working during 'blocked out personal time'; some such signs also show the time at which the occupant is once again available
- an internal telephone extension which allows incoming calls to be transferred for a time.

All these tools help the time manager to use time more effectively. But in addition, it is important to adopt regular habits of reviewing – say late the previous afternoon – what the key tasks should be for the following day, when they should take place, and how long each one needs in terms of time. Then a priority jobs list can be made up to which the time manager will stick, barring emergencies or calls from the managing director!

The effective time manager also rations carefully but never rudely the time given to other people – colleagues, phone-callers or customers – so that the day does not get taken over by reacting solely to the needs of others.

Lastly, the effective time manager plans ahead for a week at a time, and plots in the diary sets of blocked out time to:

- read important in-house documents, trade magazines or newspaper articles
- work on writing up letters, reports or memos
- see other colleagues one-to-one or in meetings
- make visits to outside contacts or customers.

By using a mix of these techniques, the effective time manager gets his or her work done on time, through a mixture of planning, self-discipline and allocating time to set tasks which does not get poached by others.

PORTFOLIO-BUILDING ACTIVITIES

Reading and extracting information on straightforward subjects from at least two of the document types in the range

1 Read the following two letters, make suitable notes on the exact nature of the complaint Miss Julie Dawson made, and how it was put right by Mr Franklin, branch manager of Domestilectrix. Your notes should consist of about 75 words, clearly set out.

6 Norfolk Gardens
Newton
Midshire NT4 6TG

23 March 199-

The Branch Manager
Domestilectrix Limited
5 Hugh Street
Newton
Midshire NT2 3AJ

Dear Sir

On Thursday 21 March 199- I purchased a Johnson Glida electric iron from your branch, Model number HT456341, receipt number 094 for £27.42. The iron immediately proved defective when I tried to use it later that day.

Before using the iron, I followed the instructions carefully about filling it with water and setting the temperature control correctly in order to iron my linen skirt.

However, as soon as I placed the iron on my skirt, it immediately scorched it, burning a hole in it and consequently ruining it. A replacement will cost at least £60.00. Apart from the damage to my skirt, I am now without an iron and so put to considerable inconvenience, since my job requires that I am smartly dressed at all times.

I should therefore be grateful if you would arrange for both the iron and the skirt to be inspected without any delay and arrangements made to replace them as soon as possible.

Yours faithfully

Julie Dawson (Miss)

(Reproduced from D W Evans, *Effective Business Administration and Communication*, Addison Wesley Longman, 1992)

DOMESTILECTRIX LIMITED
5 Hugh Street Newton Midshire NT2 3AJ
Tel: Newtown 89764/6

Your ref:
Our ref: TF/AD

24 March 199-

Miss J Dawson
6 Norfolk Gardens
Newtown
Midshire NT4 6TC

Dear Miss Dawson

JOHNSON GLIDA IRON COMPLAINT

I was extremely sorry to learn from your letter of 23 March 199- of the trouble you have experienced with the Johnson Glida electric iron you recently purchased from this branch.

I have made arrangements for our service engineer to contact you as soon as possible, so that he may call to inspect the iron and the damage done to your skirt.

Once the iron has been inspected and proved to be defective, he will be pleased to supply and test a replacement for you, which he will bring with him. Also, if you would kindly inform him of the replacement cost of your skirt, I will make arrangements on his return for a cheque to be sent to you for the full amount.

May I once again offer my sincere apologies for the inconvenience which you have been caused and express the hope that the action outlined above will prove to be to your satisfaction. The Company values your custom and I hope this regrettable incident will not prevent you from using my branch in the future.

Yours sincerely

T Franklin

T.Franklin
Branch Manager

(Reproduced from DW Evans, *Effective Business Administration and Communication*, Addison Wesley Longman, 1992)

2 Read carefully the notice on page 272, and make suitable notes. Then devise a message to send to a fellow employee, Jackie Williams, who is off sick at present, but has heard about the performance of The Grisly Boys and would like to know how to make sure of a seat on 19 July. Your message should be about 25–30 words long.

ATTENTION ALL ROCK FANS!

WORLD TOUR PERFORMANCE: THE GRISLY BOYS
FESTIVAL THEATRE
8.00 P.M. FRIDAY 19 JULY 199–

An amazing group discount deal has been struck with the Festival Theatre management for the one night gig of The Grisly Boys on their World Tour. This tour is already famous for its special-effect lighting and sounds, not to mention the stupendous costumes and backdrops!

The performance starts at 8.00 p.m. prompt and is scheduled to finish at about 11.30 p.m. Afficionados will recall the splendid review this tour received in last month's 'Rock Review'.

Tickets cost £7 each and are available from:
Janet Williams
Production Department
Ext: 519

SUPPLIES ARE LIMITED SO DON'T MISS YOUR CHANCE TO ENJOY THIS MARVELLOUS EXPERIENCE

Carol Johnson, Social Club Secretary 23 June 199-

Authorised: Chris Peters,
Communications Officer

Display from: 3 June to 19 July

3 Examine carefully the charts and text opposite, and then make suitable notes which will explain clearly the nature of the problems of Fred, who starts off running a business selling fruit and vegetables single-handed; the business then expands over some five years into two large branches. Your notes should not exceed some 85 words.

4 Read carefully the newspaper report on page 274 and make notes on its key points. Then produce an outline set of revised and polished notes for your immediate line manger, Joe Bunker, who is the project manager for Reliable Roads Limited, and who is therefore very interested in the possibility of being able to tender for the contract to construct the bypass – if it is given planning permission.
Your finished version should consist of about 100 words.

1. Fred starts out on a stall at the weekly market

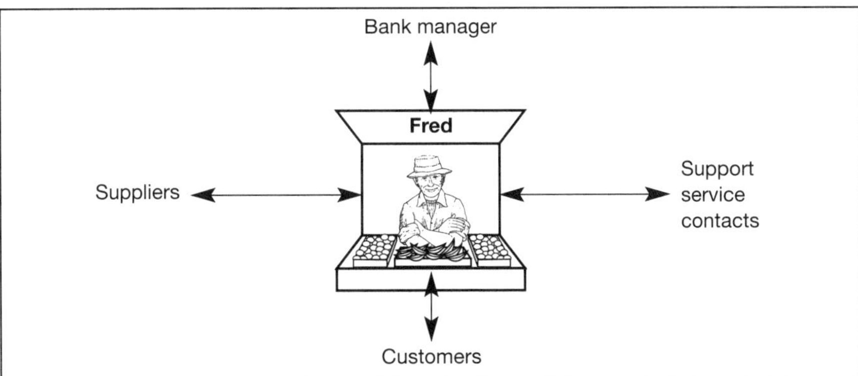

When Fred started up *Juicyfresh*, he rented a stall at the local, weekly Saturday market. Life was simple for Fred in those happy, start-up days. Not only did he run a one-man fruit and veg stall, he was also a one-man communication supremo! He handled all the sales, took all the money and dealt with all his suppliers, not to mention his friendly, neighbourhood bank manager. In fact, nothing happened that did happen that Fred did not do himself and therefore know all about.

2. Fred opens his first shop

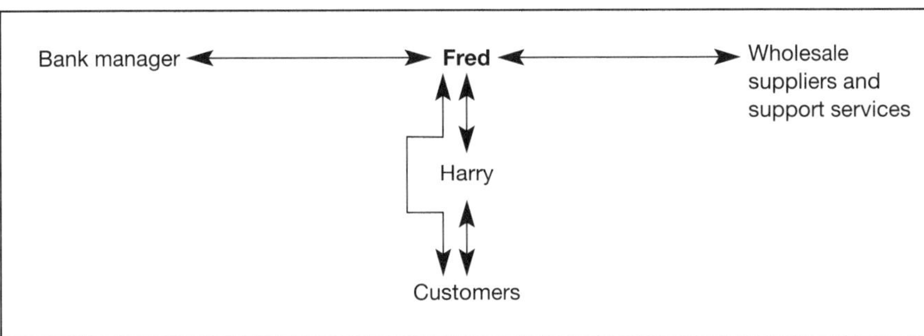

About two years after renting his market stall, Fred's business had prospered to such an extent that he was able to rent his first retail store, and to take on his first employee, Harry White. By now, Fred was so busy getting up early to buy his produce wholesale at the market, and generally coping with increased administration, that he had to rely on Harry to serve most of the customers. As a result, Fred inevitably lost some control of his business, and had to place quite a lot of trust in Harry's selling ability and honesty when taking cash.

3. Fred opens his second store

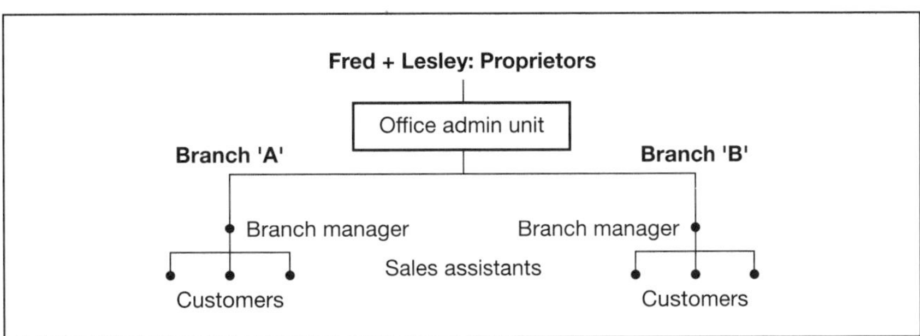

After a further two years, Fred was able to open his second store on the other side of town. By this time, he had enlarged his first shop and purchased a second as large. He also found it necessary to set up a small administration office, which he and his wife Lesley supervised, with tasks such as processing account purchases of produce, and credit sales to local hotels and restaurants. Such was the size of each store's turnover, that the staff of each one consisted of a manager and three sales assistants. By now, Fred had not served a customer for some eighteen months. He ran each shop through the branch managers, who saw to sales, advertising and staff matters. In fact, if Fred tried to tell a sales assistant how to do something, one or other of the branch managers would secretly get upset and complain to the other about Fred's 'interference'!

EST. A.D. 1778

The Midstead Chronicle

'Truth illumines the darkest corner.'

FRIDAY, MAY 3rd 19_ _

GARTHHOLME - SIR CHRISTOPHER CONDEMNS THE 'COSY CONSERVATIONISTS'

by Christine Jackson

The proposed industrial development project centred at Gartholme Meadows on the western approaches to Midstead last night had a noisy public airing.

As this newspaper last week forecast the Town Hall was packed to capacity for a public meeting chaired by Lord Forderdale. Over 450 local residents arrived anxious to listen to both sides of the argument over the proposed building of an industrial estate on Gartholme Meadows.

Green conservationists have been locked in combat with local business people during the last three months. The cause of the controversy – which has divided local families – centres upon the proposed demolition of Garth Cottage, which dates back to the 17th century, and the adjacent blacksmith's forge, last used in 1948.

Hard-hitting speech

Development plans also include the construction of a bypass running south and west of Midstead, passing through Denholme Park, a favourite Sunday strolling spot for local residents. Denholme Park was formerly the home of the dukes of Midshire.

One of the last night's principal speakers was Sir Christopher Crawshaw, local businessman and chairman of the Gartholme Development Consortium. He concluded a hard-hitting and controversial speech with these words:

'And so, ladies and gentlemen, I would put the following alternatives to you. The conservationists may win. A single period cottage may remain as a silent reminder of the do-nothing forces of stagnation. The six hundred unemployed people in this town may feel reassured, as they continue to search for non-existent jobs, that the honeysuckle still entwines Garth Cottage, and that the disused blacksmith's forge remains preserved for a nation of car-owners. It may be that the backward-looking forces of the cosy conservationists may triumph.'

'Alternatively, the proposed industrial estate at Gartholme Meadows may receive planning permission, in which case, Midstead will once again enjoy full employment and the exciting prospect of the return of the feel-good factor. The proposed tannery alone will employ at least fifty people. Moreover, the access route to the Estate, running off the bypass in Denholme Park, will relieve congestion around the Market Cross in the town centre, The entire construction of this much-needed bypass will only affect a very few old, decaying properties. The industrial estate and bypass will supply a very much needed 'shot in the arm' for Midstead, which every sensible resident will agree is at present suffering from a severe shortage of jobs and grid-lock on its roads!

Noisy heckling

'What Midstead needs, then, is not some form of 'mothballing' to preserve a few remarkable examples of a by-gone age, but the building of a new business park which will give local working people and their children the means of securing a happy and prosperous future!'

SIr Christopher's speech was punctuated with noisy heckling and has certainly added more fuel to the fire of controversy raging over Gartholme Meadows.

Next week's council elections will give Midstead voters a chance to have *their* say and to tell the Town Hall in no uncertain terms what *they* want!

Back page, Column Three

5 Read the following details about the Red Kite Garage, and then extract the information you believe is needed to answer the questions below.

The Red Kite Garage sells new and used cars, carries out car servicing and repairs and sells petrol and accessories. Last year sales were as follows: new cars: £754,550; used cars: £524,360; servicing and repairs: £196,200; petrol: £584,850; accessories: £62,600.

Sales of new cars last year were as follows: Jan: £74,340; Feb: £55,680; March: £62,530; April: £78,230; May: £82,240; June: £83,680; July: £68,400; Aug: £47,920; Sep: £54,240; Oct: £45,650; Nov: £51,400; Dec: £50,240.

Sales of used cars last year were as follows: Jan: £51,350; Feb: £36,240; March: £41,700; April: £52,760; May: £56,960; June: £44,300; July: £30,480; Aug: £34,100; Sep: £42,350; Oct: £41,910; Nov: £45,430; Dec: £46,780.

Sales of new cars last year exceeded the previous year's sales by £172,600; sales of used cars exceeded the previous year's sales by £75,350.

Last year the garage employed 28 staff, which was five more than the previous year (two additional car salespeople and three extra mechanics had been taken on). Last year's sales for servicing and repairs were 28% up on the previous year's sales.

The garage's net profit last year was 14% of total sales. In the previous year the net profit had been £197,300.

(a) What does the number information reveal about the seasonal trends in new and used car sales turnovers at the Red Kite Garage? You will need to draw a line graph using the figures supplied to enable you to answer this question.

(b) Consider the following table:

Net profit produced in each sales category

New car sales	12.5%
Second-hand car sales	20%
Servicing and repairs	18%

Given the levels of sales for last year in each of the three main sales categories, work out which sales product made most profit last year, and which least. On the basis of what you discover, advise the owner of the Red Kite Garage on which of the three main sales products he should concentrate his advertising and sale promotion efforts this year in order to have the best chance of increasing the firm's sales and net profits.

(c) Using all the information you have obtained from the above schedule, produce a set of bullet points which the owner can use when explaining to his staff how the business has performed over the past two years. Remember to make use of the line graph you produced for (a) above.

6 Read the following report on how to prevent the wasteful use of stationery and photocopying materials carefully. Then, compose a memorandum to these head of your department, Mr John Wilkins, Personnel Manager, which clearly outlines the main points and recommendations of the report. You should set out the points in your memorandum as two sets of bullet points, one for the main findings, and one for the recommendations. Your memo should not exceed one side of printed A4, and your information should be displayed so it can be easily read and absorbed.

CONFIDENTIAL

FOR: Mrs K Pearson, Office Manager
FROM: Christine Fellows, Personal Assistant
Ref: CF/A8
12 August 199-

REPORT ON THE PREVENTION OF WASTEFUL USE OF STATIONERY AND REPROGRAPHIC SERVICES

1.0 INTRODUCTION

On Tuesday 28 July, you asked me to investigate the current wasteful use of stationery in the department and to suggest ways in which it might be used more economically in future. My report was to be submitted to you by Friday 14 August 199-.

2.0 INFORMATION

2.1 Stationery Use Investigated

The range of departmental stationery investigated comprised: headed letter and memoranda notepaper, fanfold, tractor-fed printer paper, cut-sheet printer and photocopying paper, fax paper and the range of envelopes in use.

2.2 Stationery Associated with Correspondence/Internal Mail

The suspected increase in wasteful practices was confirmed upon investigation. I spoke to executive staff, who confirmed that, despite our extensive use of WP drafting, a significant proportion of ostensible final copies were being returned because of errors still present.

Observation and discussion with secretarial staff confirmed that clerical and executive staff in particular are using printed stationery and unused envelopes on occasion as message pads.

Regarding envelopes, white ones are being used where manilla would serve, and much non-confidential internal mail is being sent in sealed envelopes. No member of staff appears to be re-using envelopes. Also, despite the introduction of the LAN, staff are still distributing paper-based memoranda and attached copy files when multiple distribution could be achieved through the network with commensurate cost-saving on photocopying.

2.3 Photocopying Practices

The departmental copier is in need of servicing and staff are wasting extensive amounts of copy paper as a result of a fault which creases the paper. Furthermore, departmental staff continue to use our three single-sheet copiers for batch copying instead of the much cheaper departmental and company systems copiers, despite regular requests not to do so.

2.4 Increase in Stationery Costs

I analysed the cost of departmental stationery, comparing this year's second quarter with the first, and this year's consumption to date against last year's.

The stationery bill for the second quarter of this year is 29% higher than for the first quarter (Jan-March £1110.22, April-June £1432.18).

Allowing for increases in price, the department's stationery bill for this year to date against an equivalent period last year is some 18% higher - £4202.25 compared with £3561.23 last year. This increase does not appear to be justified by an equivalent increase in the output of the department. Moreover, the rate of increase is rising.

3.0 CONCLUSIONS

The investigations I have made do justify the concern expressed about excessive waste of office stationery and reprographic services and its impact on departmental running costs.

The increase in careless use of stationery is not confined to one section but is to be found, in different forms throughout the department. If action is not taken immediately the department is unlikely to keep within its administration budget.

I should therefore like to recommend the following measures for your consideration:

3.1 A meeting with senior secretarial staff should be called to discuss the gravity of the problem and to obtain their cooperation in improving both managerial and secretarial performance. A refresher course could be mounted by the training department.

3.2 Control of stationery issue should be tightened; sections should be required to account quarterly for stationery if this proves practicable in principle.

3.3 Consideration should be given to centralising all reprographics work carried out in the department so as to ensure that cost-effective approaches are optimised.

3.4 Departmental policy on LAN Emailing procedures and message routing should be revised and all staff notified.

(Reproduced from D W Evans, *Effective Business Administration and Communication*, Addison Wesley Longman, 1992)

7 Read the following advertisement carefully, make suitable notes on its key points, and then, in liaison with your teacher, deliver an oral report of its main features to someone familiar to you. Your report should take between 1 and 2 minutes to deliver.

THE SKY'S THE LIMIT!

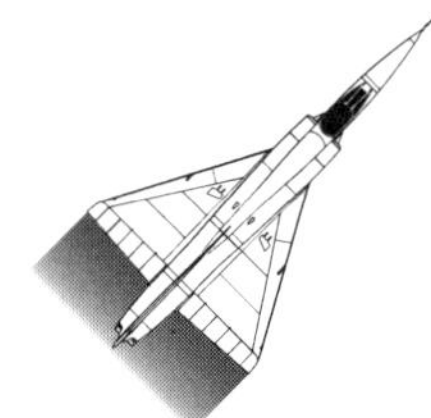

We are looking for a team of high-fliers to train as our managers of tomorrow!

Do you fit the bill? We are looking for:

- Go-ahead, dynamic people in the 17 – 23 age range
- Educated to GNVQ Intermediate/ Advanced standard in a people-friendly subject – no matter what!
- Developed English language, Communication, Number and Computer skills
- An appreciation of the needs of working in a large busy organisation
- People with a determination to work hard, and to get ahead – fast!

We are prepared to offer:

Excellent career opportunities in one of our production, marketing, sales, personnel, administration or accounts departments

First-class training and development delivered by our experts to leading-edge industry standards

A top-flight pay and conditions package according to age, qualifications and relevant experience

For further details and an application form, write now to:

Ms Caroline Starwood
Personnel Manager
Global Electronics plc
Global House
Euston Road
LONDON NW13GL

TEL: 0171-345-6789

FAX: 0171-396-1234

EMAIL: caroline starwood@gbe.co.uk

8 Read the report in **6** above carefully. Make suitable notes on its content, devise a set of cue cards and then, in liaison with your teacher, deliver an oral version of its main points to someone familiar to you (e.g. another teacher). Your delivery should take between 1 and 2 minutes.

9 Read the newspaper report in **4** above carefully. Make suitable notes and cue cards or another type of oral delivery support, then, in liaison with your teacher, provide someone familiar to you with a spoken word report of the public meeting's main points.

10 Read the newspaper article in **4** above carefully, and then make notes which will help you either to support or oppose the proposal to construct the bypass and to demolish Garth Cottage. Use your notes to support your contribution in a group discussion lasting some 10–15 minutes.

11 Read the material in **3** above and make suitable notes on it which will enable you to take part in a group discussion on the communication problems and challenges which face business proprietors as their businesses grow. This discussion should last between 10 and 15 minutes.

APPENDIX

Punctuation and spelling guidelines

Guide to correct punctuation practices

The purpose of punctuation in English writing

Basically, the purpose of punctuation is to make it easier for the reader to understand what the writer means, and to ensure that no message is ambiguous (capable of being understood in different ways). Effective punctuation, therefore, does not force the reader to lurch along (say when too many commas interrupt the flow of a sentence), but it does provide pauses and longer stops which make the meaning of the text clear and easy to follow.

The punctuation marks in use today

Today, there are eleven punctuation marks which are commonly in use:

. the full stop
, the comma
; the semi-colon
: the colon
' the apostrophe
( ) brackets
? the question mark
! the exclamation mark
- the hyphen
– the dash
“ ” ‘ ’ double or single inverted commas

Each of these punctuation marks is explained in turn, in terms of what its job is and how to use it correctly.

The full stop

Full stops have two main functions:

1 To signal that the end of a grammatically correct sentence has been reached.

This is the end.

2 To indicate that a text entry is an abbreviation:

e.g. i.e. p.a. etc.

Remember, however, the growing practice of omitting full stops to indicate abbreviations in letters and in some published writing.

The comma

Commas have several jobs to perform. Firstly, they are used to provide the reader with a breathing space or pause in a long sentence, so as to be able to digest what has been read so far:

> The last man in walked to the crease with a determined expression on his face and was promptly out first ball, which was a pity since we only needed one run to win!

Another use of the comma is to separate items in a list:

> The hotel's features include: three fully licensed bars, an indoor swimming-pool, a fitness room and a sauna.

Notice that a comma is not needed to connect the last two items in the list. This is always done by the words *and* or *or*.

Also, commas are used to work like a pair of brackets, to show that a phrase has been inserted into the normal structure of a sentence, usually to provide further information:

> The woman, who was strikingly beautiful, was also extremely un-selfconscious.

When, however, such an insertion defines or identifies the previous noun, then no commas are needed:

> The *dress you* were interested in *yesterday has* unfortunately been sold.

Sometimes commas are used to separate two parts of a sentence which are capable of standing on their own:

> She decided to carry on and to finish processing the report, even though it was now obvious that it would miss the afternoon post.

But not always:

> I shall arrive at the party for the launch of the new *snack when* I choose to and not before!

Much depends on the length of the sentence and whether the writer wishes it to run on in a fast way, or to pause for effect.

There are a number of words which are used to begin sentences which need a comma after them:

However, Moreover, Nevertheless, Furthermore, Even so, etc.

Also, some expressions require commas to bracket them when used in the middle of sentences:

This power tool can be used, say, to unscrew stubborn screws or to ...

The main effect can be, for example, to deter people from ...

The semi-colon

This particular punctuation mark seems to inspire fear and rejection in many modern writers, since it is not seen very often any more! And this is a shame, because it can be very helpful. Its use is rather like that of the full stop. However, instead of separating two different sentences, it is used to separate two ideas within a single sentence which are connected – usually by referring to the same idea or message:

The sales for the past six months have proved most disappointing; in fact, they have been appalling!

As the above example shows, the use of the semi-colon to force a pause gives a strong and dramatic emphasis to the sentence's second half.

Sometimes semi-colons are used to provide stops in longer checklists:

The detective went through the traveller's bag methodically and found: a fully-loaded Luger pistol; two thousand dollars in one hundred dollar bills; three passports all made out for the same person, the traveller, and two pounds of Semtex explosive.

Note here the use of the comma to separate the last two items in the list.

The colon

The colon today is most frequently seen as a stop which introduces items in a list, as has already been shown in some of the above examples:

The detective went through the traveller's bag methodically and found:
The hotel's features include: three fully licensed ...

The colon also was used some years ago as a stronger version of the semi-colon, but this use seems to have largely disappeared.

The apostrophe

Apostrophes in punctuation have two main jobs to do. Firstly, they are used to show that a letter has been left out of a word, which is thus printed in a shortened or contracted form:

don't wouldn't can't etc.

The second use is to show that something belongs to someone or something:

the fitter's tools the ladies' hats the agent's brochures
the report's binding the machines' maintenance

There are a few simple rules to learn in order to place the apostrophe which shows possession in the right place.

For all words in the singular the apostrophe comes **immediately before the final, added on *s***, which is separated from the previous letter in hand-writing:

the pool's temperature a day's work the lady's bag the fox's earth

For all words which simply add an *s* to form the plural: the apostrophe comes **immediately after** this final *s*:

the pools' temperatures the days' work (= of days) the girls' drinks

Some words (but very few compared with the ones which add an *s*) have different ways of showing plural possession, which you must learn:

(a) a few left-overs from Anglo-Saxon:

child (sing.)	children (pl.)	of children = children's
woman (sing.)	women (pl.)	of women = women's
man (sing.)	men (pl.)	of men = men's

(b) words ending in *-x, -ss* or *-zz* in the singular:

box	boxes (pl.)	of boxes = boxes'
buzz	buzzes (pl.)	of buzzes = buzzes'

pass passes (pl.) passes' winding paths
[same for all words ending in *-ss* in the singular]

the same goes for *fox*, *cox*, *pox* and *fuzz*

(c) other words which add -es to form a plural:

witch witches (pl.) witches' broomsticks

[same for all words ending in *-tch* in the singular]

(d) words ending in *-y* in the singular, changing to *-ies* in the plural:

lady ladies (pl.) ladies' places

country   countries (pl.)   countries' flags

Be on your guard to avoid inserting an apostrophe in *its* when it means *of it*; only when *it's* means *it is*, does it take an apostrophe.

KEY POINT

Apart from category (a) above, all the others – (b) – (d) – follow the same rule as for normal plurals – in effect, of placing the apostrophe after the final *s*.

Brackets

Brackets appear in print either as ( ) or [ ]. Sometimes they are referred to as parentheses. Their job is to separate additionally supplied information – often further details or an explanation – from the rest of the sentence:

> The weary salesman (who had already made twenty-three calls that day) shuffled from one foot to another, waiting to speak to the shopkeeper.

Used this way, brackets act very much like commas, which they replace.

They are also used in this way:

> The chairperson (Mrs Faith Downey) declared the meeting open.

Rule: use either commas or brackets, but not both together.

The question mark

Question marks are used for one reason only, to show that a direct question has been asked:

> 'Excuse me, can you please tell me the time?'

The above example shows a direct question being asked within the inverted commas of what is also called direct speech. Notice that the question mark comes before the final direct speech marks. However, a writer can also pose a direct question within a paragraph:

> The problem, then, is to solve this continuous level of high unemployment in western countries. For who would care to be seen as someone who is all for high unemployment and the misery it brings? Very few politicians, if any, I dare say.

Such direct questions are called rhetorical, since they do not expect an answer, and are used simply to create an effect.

Be on your guard if you ever write indirect questions like these:

I wonder whether my dream girl will be at the dance.

She did not know if she would be going to the dance.

He asked if he could have a second helping.

Such remarks are really statements, not questions, and so do not take question marks because they follow on from: *I wonder* (statement), *She did not know* (statement), etc.

The exclamation mark

As its name suggests, the exclamation mark is used to show that a point made or something said is dramatic, highly unusual, the result of excitement or danger and so on:

Look out! You cannot mean it! So this is the last one of its entire species!

Exclamation marks should be used very sparingly in writing, or they lose their effect. They should *never* appear in groups, but only singly – except in comics:

Take that, you bounder !!!

The hyphen

Hyphens act just like the couplings linking goods wagons. They connect two or more words which, between them, supply a single meaning:

jack-in-the-box sub-section side-saddle

In many ways, the use of the hyphen to connect words marks a half-way house in the process of two or more words becoming one. For example, the medieval *blakke berde* later became a *black-bird*, and is today a *blackbird*! For this reason, if you are at all unsure about using a hyphen, you must consult your dictionary for the current practice.

Another use of the hyphen is to separate syllables in words which are pronounced separately:

co-operation pre-empt de-activate

Again, the trend is for such syllables to be merged:

coordinate reinstate

So, here you must always check in the dictionary for the currently accepted use.

The dash

The dash is used in writing to introduce an added on piece, or afterthought:

> The semi-colon is becoming much less widely used – though I've always found it jolly helpful.
>
> 'Fetch me the staple-gun on the office table would you – oh, and while you're there, I could do with the scissors too.'

Direct speech marks

Direct speech marks are used to distinguish clearly between recording what someone actually said, and other ideas written in what is called narrative prose. These punctuation marks are always the first and last marks set around what is said, as if they were bracketing it off, which in effect is exactly what they are doing:

> 'I say,' asked the ramblers' leader, 'has anyone left a mac in the pub?'
>
> 'We shall simply never know exactly what happened to him,' concluded the professor, sucking in deeply upon his briar pipe, and looking around all the group's puzzled faces.

Notice in the above examples, that when the direct speech is interrupted by a narrative piece: *asked the ramblers' leader*, the speech marks close and open again, and the direct speech restarts with a lower case sentence (because what is being said is all one sentence). But notice too:

> 'That's Kate's mac,' shouted Maggie. 'She must have forgotten all about it.'

When the next direct speech utterance is a new sentence, a capital is needed, just as for connected prose sentences.

Most publishers set direct speech in single speech marks.

KEY POINT

Correct punctuation *matters*!

Above are the essentials of all the punctuation uses you will ever need to know about! Remember that correct punctuation really does matter in effective writing, so never be tempted to guess or to be lazy and fail to use punctuation marks properly – they mark the difference between an amateur and a professional writer.

Guide to correct spelling

At the very outset, it is important to remind you that the English language is truly a beast, when it comes to spelling it. There are almost no absolute rules, but always plenty of exceptions to the ones which hold true most of the time. So if you find spelling something of a pain, at least you can relax in the sense that you are not alone, but one of the vast majority of English speakers and writers.

However, the fact that English is not the easiest language to spell is no excuse for giving up the ghost on setting down words correctly. Despite what anyone else may have told you, correct spelling really does matter at work, and no manager in his or her right mind will allow a written document to leave the organisation knowing that it contains spelling errors.

So, determine that you can and will learn to spell what you write correctly! But also remember that today you have more support tools to help you than your parents or grandparents had.

What rules there are

Other than words imported from abroad, all words containing a *q* place a *u* after it: *queen, quickly, query,* etc.

There is no English word which ends in *-j*, nor any ending in *-v*, other than foreign or slang words: *Molotov cocktail*, *chicken Kiev*, *spiv*, *lav.*

Plurals

As has been explained in the apostrophe section, almost all English words add an *s* to the singular to form their plurals. But remember those which add *-es* after a double consonant at the end of the singular:

thrush thrushes   miss misses   pass passes   address addresses

and those ending in *-y* which change to *-ies* in the plural:

entry entries   sentry sentries   factory factories

There are, too, just a very few relics from Anglo-Saxon:

man men   woman women   child children

And there are those which add *-ves* after a singular word ending in *-f*:

scarf scarves leaf leaves loaf loaves dwarf dwarves knife knives

Lastly, there are those which follow their original language's plural form:

bureau bureaux formula formulae* stadium stadia*

*Today, many words stemming from Latin have moved over to adding the English *s* in the plural: *formulas, stadiums,* etc.

Prefixes and suffixes

A very useful guideline is that almost all core or base parts of words stay the same when a prefix (added on at the beginning) or suffix (added on at the end) is joined on to it:

regard disregard conscious consciousness different indifferent

However, there is something of a problem when suffixes like *-ing*, *-ible* and *-able* are added on to words ending in-*e*:

For the most part the *e* is omitted when adding *-ing*:

move moving love loving

But notice:

moveable loveable mileage reducible whining

Another helpful rule concerning the adding of the *-ing* suffix is that, if the core word ends in a single consonant, it is almost always doubled before the suffix is added to it:

fit fitting top topping flap flapping

But remember:

benefit benefiting suit suiting

Also, a large number of words exist which end in *-y*, which changes to i when the *-ing*, *-ness* or *-ful* are added:

lovely loveliness beauty beautiful empty emptiness

But remember:

countryside

Other useful guidelines

Words which end in *-ful* change to *-fully* to form an adverb:

hopeful hopefully

So do those ending in *-al*:

practical practically natural naturally

A long vowel in a syllable is usually followed by a single consonant, and a short one by a double consonant:

◡	—	◡	—	◡	—
jammed	tamed	bigger	tiger	bitter	biter

'Shuss' sounds at the ends of words are often spelled as *-cious*:

conscious precious delicious

Words which start with an *f* sound, but which are imported from Greek, often start with *ph-*:

photograph phonograph pharmacy philosophy

Words starting with an *n* sound and stemming from Anglo-Saxon or Old English often start with *kn*:

knack knead knuckle knave knife knee

The *j* sound in the middle of an English word is very likely to be spelled *-dge*:

gadget fidget hedge fudge midget

But beware:

major soldier wager

KEY POINT

There's no shame in checking a spelling!

Always remember that anyone who says that he or she has no trouble spelling either speaks or writes only in monosyllables, or is telling you porky-pies! Therefore, square your shoulders, buy a good English language dictionary and/ or spelling dictionary and use them – like everyone else does!

PUNCTUATION AND SPELLING PRACTICE ACTIVITIES

Rewrite the sentences in the following punctuation activities correctly

1 Rewrite the following in sentences:

(a) jenny arrived in the office at half-past nine she was out of breath and flustered normally she was very punctual however this morning the alarm-clock had rung as usual at seven o'clock it was not like jenny to sleep through it quietly she made her way to the manager's office to apologise for arriving late she was readily excused by Mr Jones who knew of her usual good time-keeping and valued her work

(b) don't stop i just wanted to borrow some disks if you don't mind i hope i'm not disturbing you i know how easy it is to lose the place when people interrupt since you have stopped i might as well ask for some letterhead paper as well as you probably know we're overdue for some stationery in the department i can't understand why there's been a delay thanks very much i'll return it later

2 Insert commas correctly in the following sentences:

(a) In his pocket the junior clerk had a penknife two postage stamps a piece of string four brown rubber bands and a keyring.

(b) 'Excuse me could you tell me if Mr Brown has left for Dover or if he is still in the office?'

(c) 'Ask Mr Jones the chief buyer and he will explain the procedure to you.'

(d) The secretary who had left a confidential memorandum on her desk for all to read was reprimanded by her principal.

(e) Collecting the mail opening it sorting it into piles for each section and delivering each pile were Jane's first task each morning.

(f) Anyway if he does come I shall make every effort to see him although I can't promise as I have a very busy morning in front of me.'

3 Rewrite the following, using the apostrophe *s*:

(a) the supply of the month

(b) the switchboard of the receptionist

(c) the lights of the disco

(d) the coats of the girls

(e) in the time of three months

(f) the news of the week

(g) the coats of the women

(h) the horses of the jockeys

(i) the hats of the ladies

(j) the pen of the clerk

4 Insert the apostrophe in the following to create their shortened forms:

(a) could not

(b) is not

(c) I am

(d) you are

(e) they are

(f) cannot

(g) I have

(h) we are

(i) will not

(j) who is

5 Rewrite the following passage, inserting the apostrophes in the places you think they should be:

'Its a fine day,' said John, 'Lets go to the river for a swim!'

'Im all for that – the suns so hot! But dont forget the dogs lead or hell be running off again.' 'Wheres my swimming costume? Whos borrowed it?'

'Its all right, its in its place, next to ours in the cupboard. Have you seen the childrens inflatable boat?' '

'Whose coat?'

'No, boat! Oh, it doesnt matter, Ill get it myself.'

'Wheres Ruth? In Peters car?' '

'Yes, theyve gone on ahead to see if the gates unlocked.'

'Well, off we go! Last one ins a cissy!'

6 Rewrite the following in their plural forms, using the apostrophe *s*:

(a) the room of the girl

(b) the rim of the glass

(c) the cart of the ox

(d) the toy of the child

(e) the halter of the donkey

(f) the basis of the formula

(g) the wool of the sheep

(h) the church of the pilgrims

(i) the style of the dress

(j) the handkerchief of the lady

7 Insert a question mark where you think necessary in the following sentences:

(a) 'Mary, have you seen the petty cash book.'

(b) 'What do you want it for' asked Jenny.

(c) She wondered whether she should telephone Mr Jones, or wait until he returned.

(d) The problem is simply stated. Why should anyone spend more time at work than is necessary. The answer is that some people are 'workaholics'!

(e) Jenny asked Mr Jones if there were any more letters to be word processed.

(f) 'If I do go,' asked Peter, will you come with me.'

(g) Managers do not give enough consideration to the problem of secretaries who are over-qualified for the work they do. Indeed, I ask myself frequently whether some managers really care. Is there, then, a need to improve the secretary's career structure if he or she is to find true job satisfaction.

(h) 'Whether I go or not will depend on whether Penny comes with me.'

(i) 'What we want is fair shares for all.'

(j) I doubt whether the key will fit.

8 Punctuate the following correctly, paying particular attention to the direct speech:

(a) have you spoken to miss harrison yet

(b) jack could not let the opportunity pass im anxious that we set a firm date for the exhibition he said otherwise this meeting will have proved a waste of time

(c) whatever you do called susan going out of the door dont forget to lock up before you go

(d) the main sales feature is the removable hood emphasised the sales manager indicating the chart it can be put on or taken off in thirty seconds

(e) the two secretaries were having lunch in the company restaurant on the third floor what sort of day are you having asked pauline helping herself to another biscuit oh not too bad answered jenny mr hawkins has been out all morning but hes due back at two thirty thats the trouble sighed pauline either there is little or nothing to do or the work comes in frantic bursts well time i was off

9 Insert hyphens appropriately in the following:

(a) This custom built car has hand made upholstery.

(b) The office intercom works on a two way switch.

(c) The boss's blue eyed boy is really a good for nothing.

(d) The firm's news letter is produced on a small printing press.

10 Insert dashes or brackets appropriately in the following sentences:

(a) The letter is fully blocked though I have nothing against that but I do object to the mistakes in punctuation and spelling.

(b) The method more fully explained in chapter six is quite straightforward.

(c) The chairman or chairperson if you prefer heads the committee structure.

11 Punctuate the following correctly, inserting semi-colons wherever you think it appropriate:

(a) the duplex computer displays edits stores and prints its programmed documentation and is instantly accessible yet it costs little more to rent per month than the average plain paper copier

(b) communicating entails selecting an appropriate language it requires consideration of the needs of the recipient it depends on the selection of the right medium or channel to transmit it correct choices have to be made in each of these areas if the communication is to be effective

(c) miss johnson is loyal discreet and conscientious i can thoroughly recommend her for the post

(d) the use of a wider range of electronic office equipment and the introduction of increasingly complex electronic filing and recording systems place heavy demands on todays office worker it is therefore particularly important that relevant and practical office studies courses are developed in schools and colleges

(e) a successful sales assistant needs to be enthusiastic tactful hardworking and loyal finding all these qualities in one person is no easy task

(Activities reproduced from D W Evans, *Communication at Work*, 2nd edition, Addison Wesley Longman, 1987)

Write correctly each item in the following spelling activities

1 Write out the plural form of each of the following words, then check whether your plural version is correct by consulting your dictionary:

soprano wharf belly chief dynamo turkey menu valley sheaf batch

2 Write down the single form of the following and check you version in your dictionary:

heroes bureaux messieur enemies sheaves

3 Complete each of the following so as to spell it correctly:

(a) b - - - - - purchased

(b) w - - - - - entirely, completely

(c) g - - - chew

(d) - - - r one who will inherit

(e) - - - - d use knuckles to make dough

(f) i - - e another word for island

(g) p - - - - - d go along

(h) fr - - z - decoration around a cake

4 Add the correct prefix or suffix to make up the word defined:

(a) - - - - osopher one who thinks about the meaning of life

(b) - - - - - - navigate to sail around the world

(c) - - - - - - dict to speak against what someone has just said

(d) - - - - natal before the birth of a child

(e) fish - - - - - - one who sells fish

(f) tele- - - - - - - written message sent speedily

(g) tire- - - - tedious, boring, irritating

(h) hill- - - a little hill

(i) athe - - - one who does not believe in God

5 Write down the word which meets the following definitions:

(a) a person who has bad morals is called …

(b) someone who relies on another is said to be … on him or her

(c) a person using the spoken word is said to be communicating …

(d) someone using too much of a substance is said to have used it to …

(e) if you are able to get at something, you are able to … it

(f) After leaving the summit, the … of the mountain proved very tiring.

(g) Having seen that they had all finished the main course, the waiter went over to ask them what they would like for …

6 Supply a list of words and their meanings which sound just like the ones printed below, but which are spelled differently:

affect complement holy they're principal dependent assent counsel freeze loose stationery might

7 Correct any spelling errors you spot in the following sentences:

(a) And I mean this most sincerley, folks!

(b) Thankyou one and all, your applaus means alot to me.

(c) Can I plees have a receet.

(d) Whe'd like to have our bills seperately, if thats alright with you.

(e) Their not two bad, when you get to know them proparly.

(f) I have to admitt, her work is extreemly through!

(g) Hes got a reelly good sense of humor, and his charm is absolutley irresistable!

(h) I'm really looking foreward to reknewing my freindship with Jim again. Last time we met, we drank about three liters of draft beir!

(i) She always enjoys her morning serials before proceding to travell to work.

(j) Owe, know, I just can't weight to ewes my spelchecker to put all these sentences rite for me. Then we can beet it strait down to the disko! Hew cares about corect speeling anywhey?

Answers to self-check review test

Page 12

1 Common types of organisation are public limited company, private limited company, county council, district council, government agency and charity. Select any four.

2 Private sector organisations aim to make profits, and public sector ones to provide an efficient and cost-effective service.

3 Employees are likely to be affected by the drive to get on at work, the status and role in the organisation of the other people involved, the need to work together to get a job done.

4 Customers are an organisation's whole royal family because without them, the organisation would soon close down.

5 The term *hierarchy* is used to describe the various levels or tiers which go to make up an organisation in the shape of a stepped pyramid. Generally, the higher the tier, the more authority it gives to employees placed upon it.

6 As an organisation grows, the number of its tiers and stages in its communications chain also grow, making fast and clear communications more difficult to exchange. Also, dispersing work locations in several different areas makes it more difficult for employees to communicate, and as an organisation grows, the channels of communication become more complicated, so employees tend to limit their interest to their small part of the organisation.

7 A junior employee's network is likely to include: senior managers, a line manager, a supervisor and co-workers, as well as customers.

Page 18

1 The spoken word at work is commonly used to instruct, explain or query, provide feedback, sell, aid decision-making and problem-solving, trouble-shoot and persuade.

2 The features of effective spoken word messages are clear speech, subject expertise, rapport, use of emphasis and intonation, logical structure of the message and the use of a suitable style.

3 Spoken word communication can break down when dialect or slang words are used which the listener does not understand, when words become slurred and clipped, when the message is delivered in a flat and monotonous way and when an inappropriate register is used.

4 The term *register* is used to describe a scale of, say, formality/informality, distance/friendliness, factual/persuasive language, etc. – in fact any scale along which various shades of strength or weakness may be expressed by the choice of different words and expressions.

5 *Emphasis* describes the strength of delivery placed on certain syllables of words, and *intonation* describes the raising and lowering of the voice in order to express word clusters in a certain way, say to ask a question or to signal the end of a sentence.

Page 36

1 Active vocabulary is a set of words both understood well and used regularly. A passive vocabulary is a set of words which are more or less recognised when met, but which are not used. An absent vocabulary is made up of those words which are completely unfamiliar and never used.

2 The steps involve using a notebook to set down words met when reading or listening, looking them up in a good dictionary and then using them as soon as possible, so as to shift them into one's active vocabulary.

3 A good English dictionary details in each entry: pronunciation, accepted plural spellings, part(s) of speech, examples of common use and origins.

4 An English language thesaurus provides sets of words and expressions which are similar in meaning. It also supplies cross-references to various different sets of words.

5 The key feature of a spelling dictionary which helps weak spellers is its phonetic way of listing words, such as *sikoloji* instead of *psychology*, etc.

6 A doer word is the subject of a sentence and an action word is the finite verb in a sentence.

7 A finite verb possesses a number (singular or plural) a person (I, you, he she it, we, you, they) and a tense (present, past, future).

8 To be grammatically correct, a sentence must possess a subject and a finite verb.

9 Choose any five from: and, but, yet, then, next, although, though, even though, if, whether, so that, in order that, when, where, why, that, which, as, since, because.

10 Supporting: moreover, furthermore, indeed, definitely, That's right. Countering: however, nevertheless, even so.

Page 45

1 Body language is a term used to describe the signals sent out by people by using their bodies to communicate attitudes and responses to what others say or do.

2 Body language is signalled through: facial expressions, gestures and posture.

3 Body language often sgnals what people are thinking unconsciously, since their bodies react sometimes automatically, without the conscious mind realising.

4 A speaker can use facial expressions such as smiles or serious looks to establish rapport or to signal a serious topic. Gestures such as pointing (to a flip-chart) help to focus attention, and an erect posture communicates confidence.

5 a) calm, relaxed and confident etc.
b) nervous, agitated, worried etc.

Page 51

1 Abbreviating the initials for the names of participants enables them to be used quickly when jotting down notes.

2 The notepad should be divided into three appropriately sized columns, the left-hand one for speaker's initials, the middle one for key points made, and the right-hand one for responses.

3 The outline notes should be used to provide prompts to aid a speaker while delivering a contribution.

4 ie = *id est*, Latin for *that is*; this abbreviation introduces an explanation or additional piece of information. pa = *per annum*, Latin for *per year* or *each year*. excl = *excluding*.

5 @ stands for approximately; ( ) in notes are set around a point of secondary or lesser importance; arrows are used to link points which have a connection, so as to guide the eye from one to the other.

6 Emphasising symbols include: asterisks against words, underlining (single, double or wavy) and setting words in capitals.

Page 59

1 Discussions are held at work to: enable decisions to be made, to consult with co-worker, to brainstorm, to motivate.

2 Meetings which require written records include: board meetings of company directors, meetings of committees, local council meetings, some departmental meetings in organisations (if so set up).

3 Brainstorming meetings are held to enable participants to come up with new and unusual ideas – for, say, a new product, or to solve a thorny problem. No-one is allowed to criticise negatively or to put down another's ideas; all may speak freely and equally; an observer who takes no part makes careful notes.

4 A chairperson's main role is to take charge of the conduct of meetings so as to ensure that they take place within established laws or procedures; to encourage all participants to take an active part, to 'referee' in cases of dispute and to ensure that decisions taken are carried out. A meeting secretary takes the minutes of the meeting, handles all the correspondence and administration, sends out the agendas for meetings and liaises with the chairperson. The treasurer administers the finances relating to the organisation, pays bills, monitors bank records, produces regular financial reports and gives an annual financial report and balance sheet etc.

5 Impromptu means without any prior arrangement, unexpectedly.

6 An agenda's purpose is to give a meeting's members a clear idea of what topics will be discussed at a forthcoming meeting, and also to allow them time to prepare for the discussions.

7 Resolution minutes only communicate the bare bones of a decision reached. Narrative minutes provide mini summaries of the debate which led up to a decision or outcome.

8 *Minutes of the last meeting* enables members to bring to the chairperson's attention any errors in fact or omissions or any inaccuracies in the wording of the minutes of the previous meeting. If it is agreed that an error has occurred, then a correct form of words is framed and put into the minutes of the current meeting as a correction – with which a majority of members must have agreed.

9 The chairperson signs and dates each set of minutes in order to show that they are officially approved by him or her and relate to the meeting dated and outlined on the signed document – which is then stored by the secretary for future reference and as an honest record of what took place.

10 Any other business is an agenda item included to enable any member to raise a topic of interest to the meeting. Usually the chairperson keeps this item short and sweet. If it seems important, it usually becomes an item for the next agenda and meeting.

Page 67

1 An effective participant seeks to be constructive and to build on the ideas of others, since only in this way are useful outcomes likely to be achieved.

2 A statement based on facts is supported by concrete evidence with a rational and logical basis. An assertion is merely a statement of views, beliefs or prejudices which may have no basis in reality or provable fact.

3 Sometimes it pays to hold back, so as to learn first what others are thinking and how they are responding to a situation. This can help a participant to angle his or her words accordingly.

4 Note-taking helps to give a speaker confidence as a ready prompt.

5 Body language signals sometimes supply information which a participant does not reveal in words spoken.

6 Never put someone down in a discussion so causing them to lose face, and never lose your temper.

7 Becoming distracted results in losing your place in a discussion, which can result in embarrassment if suddenly asked to make a contribution.

8 A passenger in a discussion is someone who takes no part at all in it, leaving all the work and effort to others.

9 Information hoarders are often the glue which gums up an organisation because they fail to share important information on developments, problems or management decisions. They are usually insecure people who are soon recognised and given their own medicine by the group they work with.

10 Actions which help are to take notes, watch speakers' body language, ask direct questions and make contributions.

Page 90

1 Documents are produced at work to act as a written record, to inform employees, to remind staff of spoken word promises made, to explain complex points, to persuade others.

2 Six main types of written documents are the business letter, the memorandum, the report, the advertisement, the factsheet, the invoice (part of the series of documents issued for credit sales).

3 Any four from: a senior manager, a line manager, a supervisor, a co-worker, a customer, an external contact.

4 The factors are the nature of the message, a need for confidentiality, how easy it is to see the recipient fact-to-face, the degree of urgency, the need for a group of people to receive the message simultaneously, the need for a written record, the amount of time and cost involved.

5 IT has simplified the production of documents by enabling them to be created, edited and stored electronically, where a single person can carry out very quickly all the steps from drafting to sending the document.

Page 109

1 Slang and colloquial expressions are out of place in most workplace documents, because they create an over-familiar tone unsuited to the relationship of either manager and support staff, or customer and employee.

2 'Head' words are those used to communicate a factual and logical message, while 'heart' words seek to appeal to a reader's emotions and prejudices.

3 Multisyllabic means possessing many syllables (e.g. ack/now/ledge/ment) monosyllabic means possessing just one syllable (e.g. sun/moon/stars/earth).

4 Multisyllabic words tend to stem from Latin, since this was a language with many words for abstract or 'brain-work' activities (e.g. studious, administer, governor, etc.); simpler words came from old European Germanic and Norse languages – all as a result of the waves of invaders of Britain.

5 a) subject b) finite verb c) conjunction

6 (a) A column of ants *was* … (b) a *lot* … *Thank you* (c) *I should* … *if you would* … (d) It wasn't the mountains, but the mountaineer who felt on top of the world: *The mountaineer felt on top of the world, seeing the mountains stretched out in front of her.* (e) with the doctor *whom* you … (f) if there were *fewer* …

Page 118

1 The five W's – who, why, what, when, where – are important to the beginning of a message because they remind its writer to set it into a clear context which provides all the introductory information needed.

2 Middle section structures: from most to least important, in a series of logical (or chronological steps); a pros and cons series of arguments.

3 Middle sections possess a series of short paragraphs or sections made up of points in order to help the reader to digest their information more easily.

4 The end part of a letter usually makes clear what actions are requested from its recipient and by when. It also ends with a courteous closing remark.

5 A report's conclusions tend to summarise key points, to indicate a decision reached, or to make recommendations based on the data researched.

Page 150

1 A fully blocked letter is one with all its text-processed entries starting from the same vertical, left-hand margin. The open punctuation system omits all punctuation (save for an apostrophe *s* in an address) outside the main body of the letter.

2 Dear Madam … Yours faithfully, Dear Mr Smith … Yours sincerely.

3 enc/encs, copy/copies to

4 *Our ref* and *Your ref* allow a letter writer to insert a unique reference for the outgoing letter and to record that of the letter being replied to. These references are used to identify specific letters in other documents and to find them quickly in a filing system.

5 A subject heading summarises a letter's contents, and helps a sorter or filer to route it and fetch it out.

6 TO, FROM, DATE, COPIES TO, SUBJECT

7 Wrong! They only include the body of the memorandum.

8 A schematic layout is one which sets out text in various positions on the page – either centred or indented, and which uses reference numbers and techniques for making text stand out, such as using bold and italic.

9 INTRODUCTION, INFORMATION, CONCLUSIONS

10 By using bold and italic, by underlining.

11 An email message is created on a networked computer and sent to other(s) on the network electronically (in a trice) through a cable connection (or by radio signal).

12 a) a main slogan or headline b) an image or images c) persuasive text in short word clusters

Page 163

1 a) the situation in which the document is written b) the person(s) to whom it is written c) the nature of the subject and the desired outcome.

2 His or her age, education, qualifications, experience, level of technical expertise and views/prejudices

3 Documents are proof-read in order to spot and correct errors in the use of English, spelling and punctuation.

4 A *typo* (short for typographical error) is a mistake caused when keying in the text of a document.

5 Main errors include omitting a word or section, errors in sentence construction, clipping final letters off words, errors of spelling and punctuation.

6 Questions may be asked about the accuracy of a title, the chosen running order of points, cutting out unneeded words and phrases, omitting repetitions, rephrasing awkwardly expressed sections, breaking long paragraphs or sections into two, making text stand out by using display techniques like bold, italic, etc.

Page 176

1 Organisations make use of images for these main reasons: to sell, to persuade, to record, to inform, to provide variety and a visual break, to emphasise and reinforce, to enrich a document. Choose any four.

2 Graphics software has enabled in-house documents to look more appealing by making available clip-art, photographs, sketches, etc., imported via a scanner, sets of symbols ready for importing into a document, drawing, etc.

3 The types of document are advertisements, posters, newspapers and magazines, bulletins, reports and briefing documents. They tend to include images to catch the eye and to communicate information quickly and easily.

4 An icon is an image which is used as a symbol or visual name for something, such as a print command or scissors for pasting in a software package; clip-art covers a wide variety of drawings which come as CD-ROM sets these days and which are used to illustrate documents.

5 *Signage* is a term used to describe the various directional signs used in large buildings and transport systems.

Page 187

1 The four images are table, line graph, pie chart and bar chart.

2 Tables are good at storing information, because they can display numbers up to several decimal places in long columns; however, the human eye finds it difficult to take in easily such a wealth of numbers.

3 Line graphs can communicate trends – up, static or down – over the period shown by the graph; they can also be used to estimate likely near future movements of the plotted items.

4 Normally, quantities, sizes or amounts are plotted vertically, and elapses of time horizontally.

5 Line graphs, pie charts and bar charts do not enable a reader to read off individual totals with any great accuracy (unlike those of the table).

6 The calculation is:

$$\frac{360 \times \%}{100} \quad \begin{array}{l}\text{amount of items}\\ \text{to be plotted}\end{array}$$

7 A bar chart is a set of pillars or columns set side by side which are equal in width but vary in height; they are used to compare quantities.

8 A stacked bar chart is basically the same as that described in **7** above, but with several different items of varying amounts, stacked on top of each other to make up each overall bar.

9 Title, author, date of publication, labels describing individual amounts, sub-totals and grand totals.

10 Colour enables a chart designer to make individually plotted lines, segments or bars stand out more distinctly; the dots and dashes used in black and white designs are not nearly so easy to distinguish between.

Page 196

1 An organisational chart shows who performs what job and where he or she stands compared with others in the organisation in terms of authority.

2 Diagrams which display processes include flow charts, decision trees and numbered step charts.

3 A collage is a set of items – menus, circus posters, pop-star faces, etc. which are set in an overlapping design on a sheet of paper, in order to achieve a particular overall effect.

4 Typical drawing aids include sets of arrows, framed boxes, circles, stars, visual effects – comets, rainbows, etc.

5 An effectively drawn map should include a title, author, date of production, scale and key.

Page 206

1 Photographs in organisations are used in advertisements and packaging to sell goods/services, to illustrate printed documents (annual reports, in-house newspapers), to obtain visual records, to enable staff to be recognised, to provide visual support in talks and presentations, to illustrate manual and instruction booklets.

2 The aperture setting in a camera is the term for the size of the opening created behind the lens to let light through on to the exposed piece of film; the shutter speed setting in a camera refers to the amount of time for which light is allowed to hit the film, usually measured in 1/00ths of a second.

3 Film speeds vary according to how well they will pick up an image in different light conditions, and are called 'fast' or 'slow' accordingly. Films with a high DIN setting work well in bright light and with fast-moving subjects.

4 Helpful tips include: use a tripod whenever possible, check that the subject is well within the boundaries of the viewfinder, don't ask people to pose for long periods before taking the photo – prepare beforehand; keep subject compositions simple; make effective use of light and shade.

5 Common pitfalls include: a failure to wind the film on; blurring caused by hand-shake; thumbs or leads obscuring lenses; subject too far away; pointing the camera directly into the sun; clipping off part of the subject.

6 Camera shake is a term used to describe the effect of blurred shots, resulting from not holding the camera still when the camera's button is pressed.

7 A point and click camera is one which possesses many automatic features which simplify the taking of a photograph, which is done simply by pointing it at the subject and clicking the button.

8 SLR stands for Single Lens Reflex.

Page 214

1 A drawing with a plan view is one in which the reader looks down from overhead on to the subject; side elevation (or front or rear) shows a drawing facing the viewer and displays only one side of a three-dimensional subject.

2 A sketch drawn with perspective is one which provides a three-dimensional effect on a flat, two-dimensional sheet, by making buildings, scenery, etc., appear to be placed in a foreground and a background.

3 The vanishing point in a sketch with perspective is an imaginary distant point at which lines moving from foreground to background appear to converge.

4 Essentially the effects of bright light and shade falling across people or things in the sketch; showing such light directions helps to bring a picture to life and lift it from a flat appearance.

5 Cartoons are used to get across sensitive or controversial messages without causing offence; to provide warnings and good practice messages, to illustrate long sections of text.

6 Effectively drawn cartoons are bold and simply drawn; they focus on expressions and gestures; background details are very bare, and they deliver their visual message instantly.

Page 235

1 Such documents tend to form part of an ongoing series or process; they frequently contain technical terms and internal references; and seek to keep information short.

2 Factual.

3 Prose paragraphs.

4 Delivery notes, invoices, statements, spreadsheet print-outs, specifications and financial documents.

5 As people grow up and gain experience of reading, they are able to take in word clusters which convey a block of meaning, instead of moving slowly from one individual word to the next, as they did when learning to read.

6 The ability to pick out subjects and their finite verbs enables a reader to go straight to those parts of a sentence which contain its key meaning.

7 Adjectives add descriptive meaning to nouns or pronouns, and adverbs do the same for verbs.

8 A fully complete and grammatically correct sentence contains a subject and a finite verb at the very least.

Page 267

1 A good English language dictionary provides for each entry information about: how it is pronounced, acceptable forms of its spelling, what part of speech it is, explanations of what it means and examples of its use, which languages it stems from.

2 An English language thesaurus provides sets of words and expressions which are similar in meaning and which are cross-referenced to other groups.

3 A spelling dictionary lists words according to how they sound and sets opposite them their correct English spelling.

4 A dictionary of abbreviations, a dictionary of technical terms, a dictionary of foreign words.

5 a) in its title, in its very first and last sentences, at the beginning and end of each section or paragraph.

6 a) orally b) as a written outline or summary.

7 A cue card is a small, hand-held card which lists boldly a few main points about a topic; it is used as a support tool when relaying messages orally.

8 By reading a document three times, a person gains an impression of its general theme, checks in detail the meaning of individual words, and identifies its skeletal structure.

Index